Genreflecting

Genreflecting
A Guide to Reading Interests in Genre Fiction

Betty Rosenberg
Senior Lecturer, Emeritus
Graduate School of Library and Information Science
University of California, Los Angeles

1982
LIBRARIES UNLIMITED, INC.
Littleton, Colorado

LIBRARIES UNLIMITED, INC.
P.O. Box 263
Littleton, Colorado 80160-0263

Library of Congress Cataloging in Publication Data

Rosenberg, Betty.
    Genreflecting : a guide to reading interests in
genre fiction.

    Includes index.
    1. American fiction--Stories, plots, etc.
2. English fiction--Stories, plots, etc.
3. Popular literature--United States. 4. Books
and reading. 5. Fiction--Bibliography. 6. Fiction
--Handbooks, manuals, etc. 7. Book selection.
I. Title.
PS374.P63R67   1982   016.813'009   82-14067
ISBN 0-87287-333-1

Libraries Unlimited books are bound with Type II nonwoven material that meets and exceeds National Association of State Textbook Administrators' Type II nonwoven material specifications Class A through E.

Rosenberg's First Law of Reading:

Never apologize for your reading tastes.

Table of Contents

Acknowledgments

Grateful acknowledgment is made for permission to reprint the following copyrighted material:

To Sean O'Faolain for "Texas," *Holiday*, October 1958 [page 38].

To Dorothy Salisbury Davis for her *A Death in the Life*, New York, Scribner's, c1976 [page 87].

To *Times Literary Supplement* for Eric Korn's "So Many Notions to the Page" (a review of six science fiction novels), July 8, 1977 [page 172]; and A. N. Wilson's review of Elizabeth McAndrew's *The Gothic Tradition in Fiction*, March 14, 1980 [page 137].

To Georges Borchardt, Inc. for George Steiner's review of Thomas Keneally's *Gossip from the Forest*, *The New Yorker*, August 23, 1976 [page 141].

To the Putnam Publishing Group for Georgette Heyer's *The Quiet Gentleman*, c1951 [page 151].

To Xerox Corporation for the advertisement [page 164].

To Delacorte Press/Seymour Lawrence for Kurt Vonnegut, Jr.'s *God Bless You, Mr. Rosewater*, c1965 [page 172].

Introduction

"I hope you have my weekly supply ready: a mystery, a romance, and a cat book."
— Overheard in a public library in rural England

Distrust a course in reading. People who really care for books read all of them.
— Andrew Lang

"Sir," he said, "I would put a child into a library and let him read at his choice."
— Dr. Johnson to Boswell

GENERAL REMARKS

This book is the fruit of a blissfully squandered reading life — except for the exigencies of a formal education, I read only what I enjoyed. Granted, I enjoyed, and enjoy, some extremely odd reading matter: these pleasures are impertinent to my also enjoying a considerable body of genre fiction.

The reading of genre fiction is an escape into fantasizing. The reader identifies with the hero or heroine, vicariously, in a daydream, sharing adventures — physical, romantic, intellectual — quite beyond the grasp of reality but not beyond the imagination. The reader may then live in different countries, historical times, or even other worlds, entering into a society and meeting persons impossible to know or see otherwise. Or it may be fantasy of a familiar world, but still one providing experiences dreamed of but outside the realm of possibility or probability for the reader. (The common reader is interested, obsessively at times, in the lives of other people. In all fiction, the reader identifies with the characters. In genre fiction, however, the characters are elemental heroes and heroines — heroic or romantic — and the exact image of the reader's fantasy self. Readers who do not read fiction are often persistent readers of biography and autobiography, next to fiction the most popular reading matter. Here the reader chooses the type of person admired, one whose life provides the same fantasy world given the fiction reader but with the substance of reality.) All genre fiction readers are Walter Mittys, their rich fantasy lives coexisting cosily with humdrum daily living — the parallel worlds of fantasy are their natural habitat. They are not like poor Miniver Cheevy who "loved the days of old" and "mourned Romance," knew he was "born too late," and, sadly "kept on drinking." There is no despondency for the genre readers who know they are fantasizing and welcome fantasy's leavening of the necessary monotony within their lives. Each reader may choose the desirable worlds or characters, the type of genre, to identify with.

"Why certain fictional characters inhabit a reader's imagination can only be explained subjectively," states Jessica Mann in the book *Deadlier Than the Male* (London: David & Charles, 1981).

Genre fiction is for entertainment — its intent is to divert and amuse, to hold the mind in enjoyment. Reading for pleasure is carefree; purposeful reading to improve the mind is not within its province. Not for genre fiction is the evasion used by early writers for children: to edify *and* amuse, the amusement a tool to ensure edification. Like all sweeping generalizations, this one is, of course, in error. There's science fiction: all is not edifying but much is instructive. It is still read largely for entertainment.

Intellectuals are uneasy when confronted with genre fiction and popular taste. " 'The reading of detective novels,' wrote Edmund Wilson, 'is a kind of vice.' He equated it with the drug habit — addictive, wasteful of time and degrading to the intellect. He thus demonstrated the scorn for popular taste which is characteristic of those who take it upon themselves to judge the recreations of others" (Mann, 1981). Literary critics and academics view Literature with respect, often tinged with awe. Genre fiction is not to be taken seriously and analyzed to death. It should be written about by those who enjoy it.

The academic world has taken upon itself the study of genre fiction. Courses in the western, the detective and the mystery story, science fiction, and fantasy are found at the secondary and college levels. Approaches to these courses vary — as literary history, the genre's roots are traced through writings of all times and types; as sociology, genre fiction reflects and interprets the society that nurtures it; as psychology, genre fiction may be used to analyze the nature of reading interests, why they differ, and how fiction is used for communication.

Such studies afford innocent pastimes for critics and scholars and provide considerable pleasant reading for certain fans of the several genres, fans who find every aspect and detail concerning a particular genre of consuming interest. This delving in depth is, in effect, a hobby. The common reader, contentedly patronizing the public library or buying paperbacks off the stands, continues to read in simple unawareness of the abundant scholarly and critical exegeses constantly appearing.

We have, therefore, the reader of genre fiction who studies it, the fan who not only reads the genre but reads all about it, and the common reader who simply reads the genre to enjoy it. Fortunately, the scholarly critic may enjoy the genre as well as study it — the resulting commentaries are then graced both by light wit and the amateur's understanding. If enjoyment is lacking, however, the criticism often suffers from the kiss of dullness. Genre authors have resented the intrusion of academe, considering the scholars' attitudes snobbish and their comments condescending (i.e., all genre fiction should be taken out of the classroom and be put back in the street or gutter with the common reader where it belongs).

Genre fiction as an aspect of popular culture is one of the subjects included in *The Journal of Popular Culture*, a quarterly publication of the Popular Culture Association and the Modern Language Association of America. That there is adequate academic writing on genre fiction available is obvious; just recently the Bowling Green University Popular Press started *Clues: A Journal of Detection*. The program for the eleventh annual convention of the Popular Culture Association held in 1981 had 37 sessions on or related to genre fiction, including presentations on "Female Perpetrators: Female Pursuers — Killers, Sleuths, Writers"; "Image and Irony in Science Fiction"; "American Women:

Readers, Writers, Subjects"; "Archetypal Patterns in Science Fiction and Fantasy"; "British Mystery/Detective Fiction"; "Popular Horror Fiction"; "The Western and American Values." Many of the papers presented will appear in *The Journal of Popular Culture*.

NATURE OF GENRE FICTION

Genre fiction is a patterned fiction. Each genre follows rules governing plot and characters — and abides by some taboos — that are acknowledged by the authors and required by the publishers. This is not to say that a maverick author may not flout the rules and still be published; this is, however, the exception. The pattern is usually established by one or more successful novels that become the prototypes imitated or emulated by later authors, any of whom may achieve the status of prototype by a single novel. Manuals for apprentice authors are explicit on the formulas wanted by the publishers, as in the following one:

Koontz, Dean R. *Writing Popular Fiction.*
Writer's Digest, 1972.
Has chapters on science fiction and fantasy; suspense; mysteries; Gothic-romance; westerns. Gives the formulas and rules for characters, plot, techniques, and notes verboten ploys.

(Separate manuals for mystery, detective stories and science fiction are listed later in this book with the secondary works on these genres.)

The authors of genre fiction, with few exceptions, are notable for being prolific. They have to be to survive economically in so competitive a field of publishing. Also, genre readers are not only devoted to a genre, they become devoted to an author and are despondent unless there is a new book forthcoming each year. Once this following is established, it ensures the success of every book the author writes, however unequal in quality. One book a year is considered "respectable"; too many written and published each year suggests a factory-like hack writer. Hence, many genre authors use pseudonyms. They may write in the same genre under several pseudonyms or may use a different pseudonym for each of several genres, the name being identified with a genre. For example, Victoria Holt writes historical romances as do Jean Plaidy and Philippa Carr — all these names are pseudonyms for Eleanor Hibbert and appear on over 100 romances. Georges Simenon and Barbara Cartland readily turn out one a month and, being assured of their readership, have published several hundred titles under their own names with no diminution of respect. John Creasey could also turn out one a month but used a large number of pseudonyms. Creasey and Simenon capitalized on an important characteristic of genre fiction: the popularity of series. Each pseudonym used by Creasey was dedicated to the adventures of a series character.

The series appears in all types of genre fiction, providing a dual appeal to readership: the author and the series character. Readers become attached to the series books in their youth. Many of the indomitable series heroes, and a heroine as well, are found in Arthur Praeger's *Rascals at Large; Or, The Clue in the Old Nostalgia* (Doubleday, 1971). In this book can be found Tarzan, the Hardy Boys, Tom Swift, and many others, all evoking the absorption the author describes here:

> A few karmas ago, circumstance compelled me to raise a small
> daughter, without benefit of wife and mother, in the insecure
> atmosphere of a large hotel. Emily was ten, and because of my busy
> schedule, she had to spend a great deal of time alone, inventing her
> own amusements. One evening I observed her curled up in a ball on
> the sofa, shoes off, face unusually serious and preoccupied.
> Interrogated, she answered in a manner so vague, so ruminative, that
> if I had been a husband of ten years instead of a father I would have
> been certain she had taken a lover. She had discovered Nancy Drew.
> —From *Rascals at Large; Or, The Clue*
> *in the Old Nostalgia*

The straight love story is the only genre that seemingly discourages the
series—there is something so final in that closing clinch "and they lived happily
ever after" (unless, of course, one is writing a family saga where, given a
sufficiency of offspring, there can be linked romances until the original heroine is
a great-grandmother!). The series detective dominates the detective-story genre,
and the spy series character is becoming increasingly important in that genre. The
recent proliferation of paperback series in the western and in adventure stories
is noted in discussing these genres.

The most amazing characteristic of much genre fiction is its immortality. It is
obviously not classic literature—the classic revered though seldom read—but
examples from all periods continue to be read, with pleasure, by successive
generations of readers. The style of writing of these "classics" in the several genres
may seem quaintly mannered and the background and characters of a world long
vanished. The patterned story still has the appeal—whatever magic is inherent in
the genre—that keeps the fan enchanted. (Libraries, both public and academic,
are now building historical collections of genre fiction, many based on the
libraries of private collectors. Several contain collections of pulp magazines,
which will, like the early paperbacks, have to be replicated in some way before
they disintegrate into dust.)

REVIEWS OF GENRE FICTION

The reader of genre fiction is more interested in being made aware that genre
of the desired type exists than in finding extended critical appraisal. Satisfactory,
then, is the usual reviewing allotted to genre fiction: annotation or inclusion in an
omnibus review. The unsatisfactory aspect is that too few reviewers can write that
most demanding of reviews: an annotation providing story-line synopsis without
revealing too much, but enough to ensure interest, and succinct critical appraisal
(the latter preferably no more than a phrase or brief sentence). A 500-word review
is child's play compared to framing 50 words or less of apt and decisive
evaluation.

Lacking in many annotations is what I consider *the* most necessary
information: To what genre or subgenre does the book belong? It is not adequate
to say "thriller" or "crime" or "suspense" or "adventure" or
"romance"—particularly misleading is to say "science fiction" when it is really
"fantasy." The reader wants to know the specific type of a genre: police
procedural, Victorian period romance, sword-and-sorcery, demonic possession,
and the like. The publisher's jacket description can be misleading. For example,
The Court of Silver Shadows, by Beatrice Brandon (Doubleday, 1980), is labeled

on the jacket "A Novel of Romantic Suspense." It is that, indeed, but it is also a pure modern Gothic romance, including the classic Gothic illustration on the jacket.

The best examples of annotations for genre fiction were written by Henri C. Veit, a librarian at the Brooklyn Public Library. From 1972 to 1980, he wrote the column "Mystery ... Detective ... Suspense" for *Library Journal*, and confessed candidly to the "development of a deplorable literary taste: an enchantment with the riveting rubbish of the thriller." His annotations were succinct, witty, and often devastatingly critical, but the enchantment sparkled in every word. You knew exactly what the book offered, whether you wanted to read it, and, frequently, the caustic annotations would entice you to read the book. Anyone desirous of writing successful annotations would do well to read and emulate Veit.

Reviews of individual genre are generally found in their fanzines, and some of these are listed in this book among the secondary works on each genre. The journals discussed in this section on reviews are those readily available to librarians and the common reader. Background books on genre fiction are reviewed in these, in the fanzines, and in *The Journal of Popular Culture*. The *Book Review Digest* is indexed for some genres, fiction and secondary works, but is quite selective of titles included.

The "Forecasts" in *Publishers Weekly* provide annotation for genre fiction, both hardcover and paperback, in advance of publication date. There is necessarily selectivity in titles annotated, however, and westerns and paperback romance series get short shrift. Under fiction there are separate groupings for mystery and suspense (including Gothic, spy/espionage) and science fiction (including fantasy). Occasionally there has been a separate grouping under romance, usually included among the general novels. Being aware that these annotations are for the use of booksellers to alert them to potential good sellers, the reader not in the trade can use them with discrimination. They are critical—the reviewer knows the book will sell but does criticize its quality.

The *Virginia Kirkus* annotations are rarely accessible to the common reader. They are often quoted in publishers' advertisements. Public libraries and bookstores rely on the critical and often caustic evaluations. This weekly looseleaf service provides advance of publication coverage of a large amount of genre fiction, particularly in hardcover.

The *New York Times Book Review* often discusses thrillers in a review grouping three or four titles by currently best-selling authors. The column "Crime, by Newgate Callander" appears weekly and includes detective stories, spy/espionage, adventure, and other thrillers; the comment is critical and obviously by a canny and devoted reader of these genres. An excellent column on science fiction by Gerald Jonas appears sporadically, but he often reviews both science fiction and fantasy individually. The column "Paperback Talk" frequently discusses new trends in the publishing of genre fiction.

Of all the review media that have been mentioned, the *West Coast Review of Books* is the one dedicated to the common reader. Now distributed nationally, it is a bimonthly with articles and lengthy critical annotations. While covering almost all of the books found in the other U.S. review sources listed in this section, this journal does provide serious annotation for genre fiction, whatever the format, largely ignored elsewhere. In addition, it often publishes survey articles on a single genre, e.g., Gothic romance, romance, western, science fiction, detection.

TLS, the *Times Literary Supplement*, should be mentioned because of its general availability and the fact that it has extensive review and annotation for thrillers, science fiction, and fantasy. Some of the British titles will eventually appear in U.S. editions, but the British edition can be readily ordered. As many of the reviews are of U.S. titles now in British editions, the British reviews often provide an interesting contrast to the evaluations in U.S. reviews.

The professional journals for librarians provide good, though uneven, coverage for genre fiction. *Booklist* has annotations of fiction inclusive of all genre, both hardcover and paperback, and is the only journal consistently annotating westerns. The annotations are brief and critical. *Library Journal*'s general fiction annotations include romance, historical romance, adventure, and an occasional western. The column on thrillers alternates with one on science fiction and fantasy, both providing brief critical annotations. *Wilson Library Bulletin* runs a bimonthly column by Jon Breen, "Murder in Print," critical notes on thrillers and some science fiction, including excellent coverage of secondary works and publishing news.

The most rewarding way to keep aware of genre fiction is the simplest and the most fun — just read the advertisements in *Publishers Weekly*, particularly the seasonal announcement numbers, and, if obtainable, see those in the British *Bookseller*. The *Bookseller* seasonal announcement numbers, in addition to the bulk of advertisements, contain sections under historical, adventure and crime, and science fiction; within each is a running text under publishers describing forthcoming books. Most rewarding is to scan the publishers' catalogues — not the dull listings in the *Publishers' Trade List Annual* but the illustrated and annotated publicity catalogues sent to bookstores and libraries. Those from the paperback houses are issued frequently; many are monthly and are treasure troves of news. (Ask a bookstore clerk to show you the *Bantam News*, an exemplary publication.)

OVERVIEW OF THIS GUIDE

Organization

This guide derives from the syllabus for a class on reading interests I teach in the Graduate School of Library and Information Science, University of California, Los Angeles. The manner in which the class is organized derives from an article I read many years ago, written jointly by several recent library school graduates who became public librarians. They lamented that during their years in college they became unfamiliar with what the public library patron, the common reader, was reading. Nothing in library school had prepared them for understanding popular reading tastes, and they were dismayed on encountering their patrons.

In the class I teach, students read only genre fiction. We discuss secondary books, publishing, bookstores, best-sellers, and the role of the librarian in selecting genre fiction and acting as reader advisor. It is interesting to note that many of the students report happily treasuring their youthful reading of genre fiction before a college education interfered, and some confess to continued escape reading despite being harried students. But few have read more than one genre to fandom depth, and some are innocent of all. By the end of each quarter's class, the results of the students' reading are interesting. All know what genre fiction is. A few, while satisfied to have gained this familiarity, find genre fiction not to their taste and intend to do no further reading. Others have to be reassured the books will still be there after graduation and reminded to tend to their classes. Detective stories usually gain the most fans. Science fiction generally does not enlist new fans, but many of the students claim to have been fans in their teens. Although only a few had read westerns, most report enjoying those read for class but rarely intend to read more. Romance reading was a teenage addiction for some students; some continued to read them; and there are always a few who discover Georgette Heyer with plans to read all her books.

Materials in this guide, as in the class syllabus, are organized to define each genre and its subgenres. As detailed in the table of contents, the authors in each genre are grouped either by types within the genre or by subgenres, generally followed by a discussion of topics, such as best-selling authors, anthologies, history and criticism, book clubs, and publishers. The inclusion of these topics varies according to the genre being discussed. This type grouping is relevant to readers' tastes — they tend, often, to be selective within the genre. Indeed, many are specific, to the point of indignation, about the types of books they will not read. A wary bookstore clerk or library reader advisor would do well to discuss what types the patron likes before suggesting a new author to the reader. New types or subgenres continue to emerge as one best-selling book spawns many imitators, e.g., the adult western or the disaster thriller. The types of books included in this work are not exhaustive: readers are referred to the guides to individual genres listed in several chapters.

Selection of Authors

This book is not intended as a bibliography or as a history of the genre through a historical sequence of author listings. Authors listed are almost all prolific, popular, considered to be important in the history of the genre, significant for a certain type of the genre, and available either in hardcover or paperback editions. Those selected are used to illustrate an aspect of the genre. Many additional authors could be used but would not necessarily substitute for those listed.

Genre authors are notably prolific, many publishing a book each year. The number of books issued by any author under pseudonyms is limited only by the author's facility at writing and willing publishers. That some writers complete a book within six weeks is openly stated, e.g., John Creasey and Max Brand (both publishing under many pseudonyms) and Georges Simenon and Barbara Cartland (publishing under their own names). Thus, one criterion for inclusion in this guide is sheer quantity, not necessarily linked to quality. Prolific may be defined as producing from 20 to 100 titles, with 40 or 50 not uncommon. (Georges Simenon published over 200, and Barbara Cartland has written almost 300 books. *The Guinness Book of Records* once listed romance writer Ursula Bloom as the author with the greatest number of published books, at 420.)

Mere literary profusion, however, is not enough for an author to be included in this book — the writer must also be available. With few exceptions, the authors listed here have one or more works in print either in hardback or paperback, older authors being available in reprint editions in both formats. The few prolific authors listed who did *not* remain in print are usually readily available in many libraries. For some prolific older authors, only one or a few titles have survived the winnowing of time and are reprinted, but one title may ensure genre immortality. Vagaries of publishing and taste govern the in-print status of genre authors, inexplicably it often seems. Grace Livingston Hill wrote her first romance in 1882 and her eightieth in 1947 — they are still being reprinted regularly in paperback. Mary Roberts Rinehart, mistress of the Had-I-But-Known school, wrote her first mystery in 1908 and her last in 1953; many were on the best-seller lists and, after being reprinted in paperback from the forties through the sixties, are now uncommon. The thrillers of Dorothy B. Hughes, paperback reprint best-sellers in the forties, vanished from the stands to be reprinted again with acclaim at the end of the seventies. Publishers' reprint programs, both hardbound and paperback, may suddenly rejuvenate an author by reprinting one title or a substantial number.

Although most genre authors are prolific, several of the most renowned attained their secure fame through only a few genre titles: Owen Wister with *The Virginian*, having only one other western, *Lin McLean*, among his works; Dorothy L. Sayers, Dashiell Hammett, and Raymond Chandler remain acknowledged classic detective authors with only 12, 5, and 7 titles published in the genre; Margaret Mitchell wrote only *Gone with the Wind*.

Most of the authors listed in this guide are established — publishers are confident their books will sell; readers are impatient for each new title; and libraries stock them knowing patron demand. I have been reluctant to list new authors whose first, and sometimes second, book indicated that here was an important new author in the genre. There is always the chance that with only one or two books an author may become a recognized key author in the genre. However, the few new authors included are those I consider will continue writing in the genre, usually with a series character. A book title (or titles) is usually listed with these authors.

No attempt has been made to list the myriad authors, many writing under several pseudonyms, currently writing for the paperback romance series. Publishers of the romance series support a "stable" of authors, all writing to formula and many producing a large volume of indistinguishable titles. For example, several Harlequin authors have published 50 or more titles, but their names are unknown except to the devoted readers of Harlequins. (Many of these authors are British, deriving from the merger of Harlequin and the older British firm of Mills and Boon.) Harlequin has published over 50 genteel Janet Dailey romances, but she later became "America's Queen of Romance" with lusty romances issued by Pocket Books. Many of the romance series are quite new; and over continued years of publication, the names of key romance authors should become defined.

In this work, authors are listed as published without pseudonym labels. Thus, some prolific authors may be listed under one or more pseudonyms without reference to being a single identity. Special note is made of the pseudonyms of certain authors: e.g., Max Brand and John Creasey, who both wrote under a great many pseudonyms and whose currently reprinted works are usually issued under the one best-known name.

I have conscientiously (fairly?) avoided evaluating authors; yet complete impartiality is impossible. (See the later discussion on annotations.) The criterion of authors being prolific for inclusion suggests the non-critical equation of quantity with quality but, in fact, reflects the wide diversity of reader tastes. Prolific authors, though similar in quantity, are not necessarily of like type or quality. My own preferences naturally favored certain inclusions, and my lack of acquaintance with certain other authors may have caused them to be slighted. To ameliorate this personal bias, some lists of "best" authors, compiled from various sources, have been included for the western, detective story, and science fiction. The secondary works listed for each genre often provide "best" reading lists.

Selection of Titles

There is no intent in this book to provide title lists for any author. When the author is listed without title, it may be assumed that most of the author's works fall into the category in which the author is found. That a title is listed does not indicate the author has not written other books of a similar type; the one noted may be of notable importance or popularity, perhaps the first work that established the author's name. Some authors are listed more than once under different types of a genre or different genres; a title given distinguishes among these. (The Author Index links these.) In a few instances, the title is given for a first and, to date, only book by an author when I considered it of special quality or interest.

Publication Dates

Genre fiction is timeless, if not immortal. The reader eager for a particular kind of fiction cares not when it was written or published. A pristine paperback may be an original genre novel in its first appearance or a reprint of a novel published 135 years ago. (There is seemingly a new edition of Charlotte Brontë's *Jane Eyre*, 1847, issued every year.)

Were this a study in the history of reader tastes in genre fiction, the sequence of editions, their dates and formats, would be essential. How long did the original edition and printings remain available? What were the periods when no edition was in print? Did some of the author's titles, or a title, remain perennially popular while the others were forgotten except by literary historians? Did a particular genre fluctuate in popularity, causing an author's works to be erratically kept available? A chronological listing of titles in any genre would illustrate changes in style, akin to changing fashions, but not in basic genre patterns nor readers' tastes.

Publication or reprint dates are generally not given in this guide as, first, it is not a history of genre fiction, and, second, the reader of genre fiction will read a genre title whatever the publication date. Occasionally, however, an original publication date is noted to emphasize the perennial nature of genre fiction. For one subgenre, spy/espionage, the original date of each prototype novel is given to illustrate the extended period during which prototypes in a genre may emerge, each distinctively defining important and much-imitated aspects of that genre. Similar chronologies of prototypes could be cited for other genres and subgenres — a critical exercise beyond the scope of this guide, however desirable.

Annotations

The ideal guide would annotate each author to identify quality and individual genre characteristics so that the reader might discover those authors whose styles are conformable to the reader's tastes. This assistance is provided, unevenly (there is, alas, no single ideal guide to any of the genres), in the guides and bibliographies listed for each genre. The annotations in this guide (excepting for romance discussed below) are used to distinguish prototype, classic, or perhaps exceptionally popular authors.

The extensive annotation for the romance genre is a deliberate (and perhaps desperate) stratagem. Almost all genre novels are, despite their patterned plot and characters, indistinguishable from the standard novel in narration and style. Some hover, uneasily, between status as a genre novel and a mainstream novel. Critics and reviewers, intrigued by an author's intelligence and stylistic artistry, will insist that this genre novel must be evaluated amongst the mainstream novels. Almost all genres are so considered, with the notable exception of the romance genre, although a few classic prototype romances are given the status of standard novel.

The romance genre is *sui generis*, a polite way of saying peculiar. There is no mistaking the romance despite the distinctive types within the genre, soap opera to historical. Were I to attempt description of narrative style, dialogue, characterization, and feminine tone in this most enduring of genres, I might be thought to be denigratory or ridiculing. I have skirted the issue by allowing critics, authors, and publishers to define the genre. The annotations and quotations will, I hope, make clear the diversity of types within the genre and their divergent quality. As in any genre, the quality of narrative style does much to ameliorate the defects inherent in the genre's patterned form (characteristics of plot, character development, dialogue, etc.). The romance, the most circumscribed of the genres in its pattern, may provide a narrative of delightful charm if the author has wit, humor, and a true writer's gift for language. There are a few such authors among the multitude of hacks.

Secondary Sources

The lists of bibliography, history and criticism, guides and background books are selective and only suggest the wealth of material available. Only the original edition is listed, and some are available in paperback reprint.

Publishers

Publishers listed in this book are those regularly issuing genre fiction, either hardback or paperback, original titles or reprints, in substantial numbers. Many publishers issue their genre fiction in distinctively labeled series, knowing that fans faithfully select by "brand" name. Series are listed and described, but these descriptions are subject to change as new types within the genre become popular or older types lapse in appeal.

Purpose and Use

The primary purpose of this book is to provide a textbook for library school students to familiarize them with the common reader interests in genre fiction that they will encounter in libraries, particularly in public libraries. The secondary purpose is to provide a guide for persons selecting genre fiction for libraries and bookstores or expected to assist patrons in identifying genre authors and titles of desired types. The paragon who is equally well read in all genres would be a freakish anomaly; however, anyone serving in a library or bookstore is presumed by the patrons to know everything about all books. *Genreflecting* may help advisors who are not readers in genre fiction to become knowledgeable about this fiction.

As the book's emphasis is on authors currently available, its users will need access to the retrospective bibliography for each genre, and such bibliographies are found listed in the sections for secondary works. The bibliographies, guides, histories, and criticism provided list and describe a large proportion of the authors included in this book; for, as has been noted, genre authors seem immortal, and many now available and popular were first published in the early part of this century and a few in the prior century. The annotations for the secondary works indicate their provision of lists of "best" books and prize-winners in the genre. All of these titles are not in print but should, largely, be available in libraries. Lists of "best" or classic authors and titles are given for several genres and are meant to be illustrative, not exhaustive.

The author listings for several categories in this book include the name of the series character or characters with whom the author is particularly identified. Indeed, so important is the series character to the reader that the books are commonly referred to by the series character's name: for example, Sherlock Holmes, James Bond, Conan, Hornblower, Hopalong Cassidy, and many others. The reader advisor needs this recognition: patrons may request books by series character rather than by author. Lists of series are included in some secondary works listed, and such lists are sometimes compiled in libraries as reader-advising aides. Series characters are dominant in detective fiction, and the secondary works frequently include biographical lists of the detectives or a name index. (So alive are the detective characters to the readers that several compilations of biographies of series detectives have appeared and are annotated among this book's secondary works.)

A cautionary note is necessary for the user of this book. It should be used as an introduction in need of continual supplementation. New authors, new series, and new subgenres proliferate, although not all survive to assured popularity. Regular scanning of reviews and book trade news, along with attention to the new secondary works on the genres, is essential. If you are a constant reader of a genre, or several genres, you are one-up.

Postscript

A polymath of genre fiction would be needed to do equal justice to all the genres. I am indebted to my students, many of whom have been enthusiastic readers of certain genres, for they augmented and revised the author lists with their critical estimation. I would appreciate comment from users of this book on categorization of authors and titles and interpretation of the several genres. Have I slighted or omitted a favorite author? Should a second edition be needed, your criticisms would generate the revisions.

1 The Common Reader, Libraries, and Publishing

> I rejoice to concur with the common reader....
> — Samuel Johnson

> I simply read books because someone had printed them.
> — Walter Kerr

> ...Impossibility of finding another amusement equally cheap or constant, equally independent on the hour or the weather. He that wants money to follow the chase of pleasure ... will be forced to seek in books a refuge from himself.
> — Samuel Johnson

> What is not found in life — success, prestige, pleasure — is sought in reading material.
> — Richard Bamberger ("Promoting the Reading Habit," Unesco Reports and Papers on Mass Communication, 72, 1975)

THE COMMON READER AND GENRE FICTION

Critics, and often librarians, look somewhat askance at the types of literature enjoyed wholeheartedly by the common reader. Some will, albeit shamefacedly, admit to indulging in a favorite genre in those late hours when the stress of life must be relieved. They take the literature of storytelling too seriously, forgetting their own enjoyment, as children, in reading everything.

Impelled by omnivorous curiosity, ignoring selectivity, and innocent of critical taste, children read whatever is enjoyed. Isaac Bashevis Singer, in accepting the Nobel Prize for literature in 1978, explained why he began to write for children: "They still believe in God, the family, angels, devils, witches, goblins, logic, clarity, punctuation and other obsolete stuff.... They love interesting stories, not commentaries.... They don't expect their beloved author to redeem humanity." Asking only for a strong story line, lots of dialogue, and a happy ending with all loose ends tied, the child happily devours beloved "trash"[1]

---

[1]Arthur Praeger's *Rascals at Large* (Doubleday, 1971) delightfully dissects this beloved "trash" and provides story synopses and abundant quotations for those benighted adults whose "golden age" was bereft of such reading.

(rejected by many teachers and librarians as totally lacking in literary value): the Wizard of Oz books, Tarzan, Nancy Drew, Tom Swift, and others of their ilk. This golden age of leisure reading introduces children to almost all types of genre fiction.

Genre fiction no doubt developed out of that childhood capacity for innocent enjoyment. It has its roots in the time when books were unavailable and grandfather told tales, or minstrels and bards sang songs, around the fire. Literary history records that these narrations were full of miraculous adventures, wondrous beings, gods and goddesses, and fabulous beasts, with ordinary mortals as the heroes or the heroines who played out their stories in a world full of magic and the supernatural. These tales provided an escape from the drab reality of everyday life into a world of adventure, mystery, and romance—wars, sea voyages, quests in search of excitement and treasure. And so the stage was set for the common reader, avid for action-filled narratives, the chase plot, and gory, revenge-filled tales. For a time, ballads and chapbooks catered to the tastes of the common reader by providing a gallery of picaresque heroes in highwaymen pirates, and outlaws. The ballads lamented the cruel fates of star-crossed lovers; necromancy and ghosts were commonplace in many types of stories and dramas. Through the centuries, the forms of popular fiction varied, but the subject matter remained the same. It wasn't until the nineteenth century, however, that genre fiction was really able to "take root."

A new and large reading public emerged in the nineteenth century as a result of increased urbanization and industrialization, accompanied by extended education and literacy. New technology provided fast and cheap means of printing. Some of the earliest mass-produced books were the "yellowback thrillers"—lurid accounts of adventure, mystery, crime, and detection—sold at the railroad station stands in nineteenth-century England. And it was at the railway stations in Europe that the first paperback line for the common reader, the Tauchnitz Editions,[2] was marketed. The "dime novel" and pulp magazines followed. By the 1940s, the common reader could choose from a variety of genre fiction as the paperback lines proliferated.

A history of popular reading tastes is beyond the scope of this book, but the following books provide essential background:

Altick, Richard. *The English Common Reader: A Social History of the Mass Reading Public, 1800-1900.* University of Chicago Press, 1970.

Goldstone, Tony, ed. and comp. *The Pulps: Fifty Years of American Popular Culture.* Chelsea, 1970.

Goulart, Ron. *Cheap Thrills: An Informal History of the Pulp Magazines.* Arlington House, 1972.

---

[2]The final defeat of Napoleon allowed the English to travel on the continent again, and travel they did in large numbers, especially the increasingly large and prosperous middle class who went on travel agent Thomas Cook's tours. The Tauchnitz Editions, published in Germany, were begun in 1837 and provided these tourists with the works of popular English and American authors.

Griest, Guinevere L. *Mudie's Circulating Library and the Victorian Novel.* Indiana University Press, 1970.[3]

Johannsen, Albert. *The House of Beadle and Adams and the Dime and Nickel Novels.* University of Oklahoma Press, 1950-1962. 2 vols.

O'Brien, Geoffrey. *Hardboiled America: The Lurid Years of Paperbacks.* Van Nostrand Reinhold, 1981.

Schreuders, Piet. *Paperbacks U.S.A.: A Graphic History, 1939-1959.* Translated from the Dutch by Josh Pachter. Blue Dolphin Enterprises, 1981.

The best studies of the common reader can currently be found within the broad field of popular culture. A scanning of the *Journal of Popular Culture* (published by the Popular Press, Bowling Green State University, Bowling Green, OH) shows articles on the common reader's genre interests as a component of the popular arts called mass culture. These studies of what constitutes popular entertainment cover all media—theater, music, motion pictures, radio, television, comic strips—in addition to books, the circus, and sports.[4] Viewed in this perspective, the common reader's interests in genre fiction correspond to the nonreader's devotion to radio and television soap operas, television series in several genres, and motion pictures in which the genres from western to horror have always been standard productions.[5] To fully understand the nature of the common reader's interests, one must see these interests in relation to the popular culture of society as a whole. A delightful introduction is provided by Russel Nye's *The Unembarrassed Muse: The Popular Arts in America* (Dial, 1970), covering the arts, very broadly defined, and reading interests from colonial times to the present. Among the chapters in *The Unembarrassed Muse* are: "The Dime Novel Tradition"; "Novels in the Marketplace," discussing best-sellers and popular tastes; "Murders and Detection"; "The Future Is History: Science Fiction"; and "Sixshooter Country." A more specialized approach to the popular arts is found in J. G. Cawelti's *Adventure, Mystery, and Romance: Formula Stories as Art and Popular Culture* (University of Chicago Press, 1976). Anthologies on the popular arts provide a synthesis of the broad purview in the *Journal of Popular Culture*, an example being *Mass Culture: The Popular Arts in America*, edited by Bernard Rosenberg and David M. White (Free Press, 1957). The *Handbook of American Culture*, edited by Thomas M. Inge (Greenwood Press, 1978-81; 3 vols.), is an attempt to

---

[3]From the 1840s to the 1890s in England, the commercial circulating libraries largely determined the nature of the English novel. They catered to popular tastes at the higher economic levels, and the history of the dominant one is found in this book.

[4]The scope of what constitutes popular culture is, of course, much more extensive than the media noted here and includes many aspects of folklore, hobbies, and, indeed, any activity in which the mass of people in a society participate.

[5]In the following chapters, there is a section for several genres that lists books on the genre in film. *The Movies*, by Richard Griffith and Arthur Mayo (Revised edition, Simon & Schuster, 1970), lavishly illustrated, covers the history through the sixties, and all the genres are represented.

define with academic precision the fields of study in popular culture. The *Handbook* contains chapters on the detective and mystery novel, Gothics, the pulps, science fiction, the western, historical fiction, romance, and best-sellers.

A discussion of the common reader and popular reading tastes would not be complete without mention of best-sellers. The controversies that have raged—and that continue to arouse critics—on the perniciousness versus the innocuousness of popular reading tastes tend to center around best-sellers, many of which fall into the several genre categories. Romance novels were the target of acrimonious debate in 1981. "These books are trash, antifeminist and pornographic," charged Ann Douglas, a professor of English, in a televised debate with romance novelist Janet Dailey. When *Publishers Weekly* ran a parody short story in a special section on romance in November 1981, an indignant author wrote: "The story was not only insulting to me as a writer, but to the ladies who buy and read my books! The message was plain: you consider romance writers morons, and the ladies who enjoy the books simpletons." Intellectuals become uneasy when confronted with popular taste. It seems that few have the assurance to recognize simply that "to judge this part [readers of light fiction] of the book reading world by the highest standards of literary criticism is an error, to despise it for its simplicity is arrogance."[6]

The persistence of this disturbance over the common reader's preference for best-sellers and light literature is tellingly shown in the books of two British critics, writing 50 years apart. Q. D. Leavis in *Fiction and the Reading Public* (London: Chatto, 1932) uses two approaches in her analysis of the reading tastes of the thirties: a questionnaire to 50 authors of best-sellers and a historical survey of publishing and reading tastes in England. Her conclusion is the "public has acquired the reading habit while somehow failing to exercise any critical intelligence about its reading." Her book, still in print, is frequently quoted and states the classic intellectuals' disdain for popular reading that they consider false in values, misleading in interpretation of society, and meretricious as literature. John Sutherland in *Bestsellers: Popular Fiction of the 1970s* (London: Routledge, 1981) discusses in detail and as types most of the best-sellers of the decade. His conclusions are as negative as Leavis', but he insists on the importance of best-sellers in studying British and American publishing history and culture. "They are anodynes. They soothe. No one could guide their lives by the codes, awareness and information which bestsellers furnish. But they clearly make lives more livable for millions of British and American consumers.... These pre-eminently successful novels provide much in the way of thrills and excitement, but nothing in the way of serious intellectual, moral or social disturbance of received stupidity."

---

[6]Mann, Peter H. *Books: Buyers and Borrowers* (London: Deutsch, 1971), page 174. In the chapter, "Light Fiction and the Romantic Novel," in this book, Dr. Mann, a British sociologist, synthesizes history and social attitudes as a background to readers' tastes. His article in *Journal of Popular Culture* (Summer 1981), "The Romantic Novel and Its Readers," reports on a survey made for the British romance publisher Mills and Boon and contrasts the publishing pattern (serious novels in less than 5,000 copies and light novels in printings up to the millions) and readership of serious fiction and mass-culture novels (light, popular, and read wholly for pleasure). The readers of light fiction wanted, if women, romances first, then historical novels; men preferred thrillers and mysteries, followed by war and adventure stories. Mann concludes that light fiction readers want escape and relaxation in a story that conforms to their mores and values. "Real life is often incredibly boring" to these readers, just as is the realistic novel.

Critics and librarians might find it helpful to peruse best-seller lists as they appear weekly and to read analyses of the popular books in *80 Years of Best Sellers, 1895-1975*, by Alice Payne Hackett and James Henry Burke (Bowker, 1977). The running commentary in the Hackett and Burke volume indicates fashions in popularity. The author and title listings show the continued popularity of types of books while reflecting changes in society's attitudes and mores. That the complete 1895-1975 list now appears in three forms (hardcover titles, paperback titles, and a combined list of both formats) reflects dramatically the affect the paperback revolution has had on both sales figures and the types of books appearing on the lists. Paperback titles have, of recent years, displaced the long-standing hardback leaders, replacing total sales in the thousands with sales in the millions. Many of these new leaders are genre fiction titles.

All types of genre fiction appeared on the best-seller lists from the beginning, and their history will be found in two now old but still informative and interesting books: James Hart's *The Popular Book: A History of America's Literary Taste* (Oxford University Press, 1950), and F. L. Mott's *Golden Multitudes: The Story of Best Sellers in the United States* (Macmillan, 1947).

Two recent collections of essays on individual best-sellers highlight that genre titles are memorable and long-lived. It is interesting that a genre title is the only title duplicated: P. C. Wren's *Beau Geste*. Geoffrey Bocca's *Best Seller: A Nostalgic Celebration of the Less-Than-Great Books You Have Always Been Afraid to Admit You Loved* (London: Wyndham, 1981) has essays on 15 books. The genre titles in addition to Wren's are: H. Rider Haggard's *King Solomon's Mines*, Kathleen Winsor's *Forever Amber*, E. Phillip Oppenheim's *The Great Impersonation*, Ouida's *Under Two Flags*, Edgar Rice Burroughs' *Tarzan of the Apes*, Elinor Glyn's *Three Weeks*, E. C. Bentley's *Trent's Last Case*, George Barr McCutcheon's *Graustark*, R. C. Sherriff's *The Hopkins Manuscript*, Owen Wister's *The Virginian*, and Baroness Orczy's *The Scarlet Pimpernel*. Claude Cockburn's *Bestseller: The Books That Everyone Read, 1900-1939* (London: Sidgwick, 1972) also discusses 15 books, and, while some possibly fall in the romance genre, his obvious genre choices, including the Wren title, are: Erskine Childers' *The Riddle of the Sands*, Jeffery Farnol's *The Broad Highway*, and E. M. Hull's *The Sheik*.

LIBRARIES AND GENRE FICTION

As might be expected, the controversy over genre fiction also rages in library circles. Disdain for the tastes of the common reader is apparent in some librarians. One of this author's students, interning in a public library branch, checked out a western to read for the class on genre fiction, and the branch librarian said disdainfully, "Of course, you know westerns are trash!" Fortunately, there are some public librarians who read and enjoy "trash." Unfortunately, the public library has always been defensive about stocking popular fiction: its educational and informational services are lauded, but there has too often been a suggestion that providing readers with entertaining books was pandering. Not all libraries are so blessed as is the Little Rock, Arkansas, Public Library: a local trust company set up a trust fund so that the librarian could, in clear conscience, buy "not so good books" — defined as westerns, detective stories, science fiction, romances, and the like. A former British librarian writing "Of 'Luv's and Lights' " (K. F. Kister in *Wilson Library Bulletin*, January 1967) cites disparaging remarks about such fiction, e.g., that it "subverts the public's perspective of society." (Nothing changes: In 1877 in the United States, a librarian, William Kite, wanted to exclude all fiction from public libraries as novels gave persons in "lowly but honest" occupations "false ideas about life." In 1966, *Library Journal* headlined a news note: "Oz Comes to D.C. Libraries after 66 Years." Fond aunts still steadily gave the Oz books as gifts during the banned period.)

Librarians are also castigated for providing books of poor literary quality. There is pressure on them to be concerned with improving patrons' tastes. The professional library journals worry about this sporadically, the problem becoming complicated with implications of censorship. Librarians *do* get upset. In 1960, *Library Journal* ran an article criticizing the selection of books for the *Fiction Catalog*, used by librarians to identify authors and titles deemed necessary in a public library's permanent stock of fiction. The article was so controversial that the editor solicited comment to accompany it, and also published a later group of comments and letters to the editor of an irate nature (Dorothy Broderick, "Libraries and Literature," August and October 15, 1960). One passage gives the tenor of the article: "We know that librarians read mysteries. We know this because ten per cent of the total entries in the 1950 edition [*Fiction Catalog*] are mysteries. Does anyone actually believe that these approximately 340 mysteries are worth the space they take up? It has been my experience that the most useful mystery is the newest one and once read it can be forgotten. Obviously one would retain a few of the 'classics' in the field and this would mean the entries in the *Catalog* would be truly selective." Other types of genre fiction were also to be ruthlessly weeded out, allowing for an increase in the number of worthwhile fiction titles. Among the comments: "I see little virtue in stocking a library with books that will not be read, simply because the librarian has a fixed idea of what her borrowers *should* read" (Margaret E. Cooley, book editor, *Library Journal*). A library school professor, Howard W. Winger, objected to some of the deletions: "I don't want to be accused of defending *all* the trivial books in libraries—just those I liked!"

An academic librarian entered the fray, stating flatly, "The function of libraries is to get people reading and to keep them coming back" (Ellsworth Mason, "The Sobering Seventies: Prospects for Change," *Library Journal*, October 1, 1972). Citing his own youthful devouring of pulp magazines and Hopalong Cassidy before writing a doctoral thesis on James Joyce, he queries, "Who in the world can tell at what age, or by what book, anyone is going to get an interest in anything under the sun?" The thinking of librarians disturbed him: "There is a deprecation of reading for pleasure, and much pride in the great increase in serious books in their collections for serious readers."

"Trash in the Library" is the forthright title of an article written by a branch librarian in New York's Queensborough Public Library, Rudolph Bold (*Library Journal*, May 15, 1980). He spoke out against the elitist librarians who would not stock Harlequin romances, though conceding, "It's the human heart, not the mind, that Harlequins touch." Firmly on the side of the common reader, he concluded, "It is questionable practice to limit any public library's collection to material of a certain quality if a large percentage of the community does not find what it wishes to read in that collection." *Library Journal* received a lively spate of letters, supporting his thesis but objecting to his tone of "humanistic tolerance" as contemptuous of the genre readers.

The puritan ethic maintains all books must be useful. The hedonist holds if the books entertain, their justification lies therein. The poor librarian who wants to satisfy all the library's patrons may wish a plague on both philosophies, being, indeed, too poor to quiet both. What now bothers librarians is economics, not ethics — how to stretch increasingly inadequate budgets to cover both the useful and the entertaining. To the comment, "Let 'em buy paperbacks," the conscientious public librarian replies that the library should supply what the patrons want, knowing, sadly, that economics will frustrate desire.

Dissension among public librarians is by no means quiescent. Richard Hoggart, reviewing in the *TLS* (December 30, 1977) three books on the public library in Great Britain, noted that foes of the nineteenth-century Public Libraries Act said, "That the public libraries would be in the main ways of providing cheap fiction at public expense ... [and] to establish them would encourage laziness among the working class (especially through the reading of cheap fiction)." The apologists for buying cheap fiction in the public libraries could not call such fiction improving nor valuable but insisted libraries must be catholic in their buying: "Librarians must therefore cater for people's 'recreational' needs. They should not be highbrow, snooty, elitist in their attitudes to popular fiction. A further turn of the screw resurrects the old and highly dubious 'ascending ever upwards' model, by which readers are assumed to move naturally from virtually pulp-fiction to George Eliot." Hoggart's conclusion is against "cheap fiction": "Librarians do not have to be what is fashionably called 'narrowly moralistic'; but they cannot escape the need to make judgments of quality. Their first duty is still to the idea of 'self-improvement,' with that phrase very imaginatively interpreted. To do less is a form of false democracy, which the whole history of the library service itself should call into question." When Hoggart addressed the Centenary Conference of the United Kingdom Library Association on the "Uses of Literacy," he stated bluntly, "The public's self-improvement, not its recreation, is the librarian's first concern." *Wilson Library Bulletin* (February 1978) reported, "The conferees were aghast at this 'imposition of middle-class values' and the moral superiority involved in 'censoring' the meretricious."

Assuming the attainment of that Elysium in which educate and recreate coexist tranquilly, the librarian still faces problems both in maintaining a satisfactory stock of genre fiction and in displaying it to assure optimum use by patrons. That a goodly part of genre fiction is now in original edition in paperback, or available for replacement largely in paperback reprint, complicates the problem.[7]

---

[7]One solution was reported in the *Publishers Weekly* (September 13, 1979): "The Selling of the Library: Baltimore County System Challenges Assumptions about Library's Role," by Kenneth C. Davis. Mini-libraries, blending bookstore and library atmosphere, were established in shopping centers. They stock genre fiction (80% in paperback, mostly romance) and best-sellers, reflecting the library's policy—what people want, not what librarians think they should read. Circulation jumped, and the library benefited as paperbacks allowed many more circulations per dollar expended. Overall (in the mini and the standard libraries), the system claimed 92% satisfaction in supplying books requested.

The common practice for display in public libraries is to segregate genre fiction, grouping by type on labeled shelves. (Bookstores, also, tend to group genre fiction, particularly paperbacks.) Those books usually labeled are westerns, mysteries, or thrillers, and science fiction in hardcover and paperback. Paperback romances are also separately shelved. Some libraries color-code labels on the books, color-code the catalog cards, or maintain card files by subject or type of genre. Many libraries dislike labeling and segregation, as some patrons will look only at labeled shelves, while others never use them. Books, then, that might be of interest to both patrons will never be seen by them. Few libraries can afford, or find manageable, to have copies on both the genre shelves and within the general fiction collection. An additional hazard is that it is often tricky to label a novel within the correct genre. Shelving all fiction, including genre, in one alphabet makes it difficult for the fan to find desired genre titles without knowing the author. Labeling by genre *and* interfiling within the general fiction collection is disliked by the genre fan, who wants the easy access of a separate shelving, and may offend the fiction reader who objects to labeling as denigratory.

No solution will please everyone. David R. Slavitt, writing in *American Libraries* (November 1973), takes a realistic view of what is published and readers' tastes in "Trash: Most Novels Are Trash. Most Books Are Trash. But There Is a Delight in Trash Heaps." However, in responding to a letter in the January 1974 issue, he said that segregating genre fiction on library shelves "represents a judgment on the books—and not a flattering one." Pyke Johnson, Jr., a publisher, had an illuminating stay at the Orange, New Jersey, Public Library, observing how a public library functions. The story appeared in *Publishers Weekly* (March 28, 1977) under the heading "What Publishers Should Know about the Public Library ... A Book Editor's Firsthand Report." The librarian wanted the publishers to do the labeling: "He would like to see categories printed on the spine. And at Orange he has solved the problem for himself by having small stickers reading " 'A Man's Book,' 'Gothic,' a 'Regency' placed on the spines of appropriate titles."

Unless genre fiction in paperback is cataloged, with or without binding, expediency leads to display of the books in a somewhat haphazard and uncontrolled manner. The stock proves transitory, and no basic collection is formed. That a good basic collection is desirable is determined by the library's degree of commitment to serving the genre fiction reader: a reader who discovers an author and wants *all* the author's titles, or a reader of omnivorous tastes who seeks everything ever published in the genre.

Selection of genre fiction for public libraries is fairly uncritical. One public library in England reported buying them "by the yard" from a dealer who specialized in review copies, expending 8% of his book fund for these books and providing over 20% of the books on the shelves. The number of genre titles in hardcover published each year is not beyond the means of most libraries. Paperback genre titles are becoming an increasing part of the collections. A survey reported in *Publishers Weekly* (October 9, 1981) said up to 30% of public library budgets were spent on paperbacks. Libraries have found that circulation increases with the paperback stock (readers evidently like the small size and light weight) and, on a per title basis, they have higher circulation than hardbacks. Librarians also "complained that the quality of hardcover books has deteriorated so much over the years that some paperbacks are now as durable as hardcover. Thus, paperbacks often give them more use per dollar." These relatively inexpensive paperbacks, then, are purchased with minimal selectivity, processed with minimal records, shelved with little order, and allowed to wear out or be lost without lamentation.

There is still the problem of which, if any, of these paperbacks should be bound, cataloged, and made part of the permanent stock—some of the titles are, after all, original works, however awkward the format for libraries. Replacement copies, if the library wishes to maintain a good collection, are often available only in paperback. The publishing trend toward trade (i.e., large) format paperbacks for some mass-market paperbacks is helpful. Also, many genre titles are being reprinted in hardcover large-print editions.

Reader advisory service is one of the most interesting and demanding functions in a library, drawing on the librarian's background of reading and awareness of current publishing. In its issue of November 15, 1977, *Library Journal* published "Day-One Basics for M[aster of] L[ibrary] S[cience]"; of the 36 basics, two pertained to reader advising—"... to utilize knowledge of books and authors in order to assist and advise patrons in selection of appropriate reading material in a variety of genres and subject areas" and "to write clear, concise reviews and abstracts of library materials in order to provide guidance in their use."

To provide guidance in genre fiction, librarians should, ideally, be readers of the genres. Few libraries, however, will have a staff of genre fiction addicts, indeed being blessed if one staff member is addicted to one genre. Therefore, the fan asking for assistance in selecting books in a genre too often knows more than the librarian being queried. As patrons have a touching faith in the omniscience of librarians—they have read everything!—subterfuge is necessary.

Book lists in the form of bookmarks, broadsides, or pamphlets are provided by many libraries. These may be lists of authors by genre or subject, or authors and titles, with or without annotation. A well-annotated book list is a delight, and a librarian adept at writing annotations is a treasure. Other devices are to retain the book jacket with its blurb or tip annotations from review journals (*Booklist, Library Journal, Virginia Kirkus, Book Review Digest, West Coast Review of Books*) or any available source into the book.

Special index files are made by librarians, granted staff enough and time. The ingenuity and interest of the compilers are suggested by a few examples: annotated list of series and sequels; detective genre file by name of detective; place name or locale file; professional background or subject file; permanent file of reviews, indicating genre or subject assigned to the book; "Women Will Like" or "Men Will Like" files of authors and titles.

A ploy too seldom used in libraries is to conjoin borderline or background books for genre fiction. Historical novels and historical or period romances, the historical novel of the West and the western, adventure novels and nonfiction adventure could be combined on lists or on the shelves. Displays of popular background books may catch the fancy of a genre reader—history and social customs; illustrated histories; books on the genre in motion pictures or television; biographies of characters often appearing in historical romances; science and space exploration; books on dragons, unicorns, fairies, magic, and the like.

There is, however, nothing so gratefully received by the patron as an interested common reader librarian. Readers love to talk about their reading. A librarian who can enthusiastically exclaim, "But haven't you read ..." is the desired advisor. Publishers have long known that the popularity of books is made by word of mouth. By listening when patrons pour out their interests, a librarian may learn more than is wanted but will be able to amaze the next patron with the same interests. No one likes to be told what to read but will listen with interest when the discussion is on the enjoyment of reading a certain book. The librarian "is a missionary. He wants to communicate to others the enormous pleasure he has had from personal discovery" (Frank M. Gardner, "To Fill the Empty Mind," *Library Journal*, October 1, 1964).

PUBLISHING GENRE FICTION

That publishing is a gamble as well as an art is trenchantly manifested by scanning *Publishers Weekly* for a few years. Book buyers' tastes are akin to the vagaries of fashion in their scurry after the current fad; and the publishers, particularly in paperback lines, imitate monkey see, monkey do. The amazing proliferation of romance series by paperback publishers (and one by a hardback publisher) in 1981 merely emphasized a well-established genre but also diversified the types of romance available, including several new series on teenage love. Additional new series continue to be announced. Three new commercial newsletters on romance are noted in the romance chapter. Pocket Books started *The Dailey Newsletter* for fans of "Janet Dailey, America's Bestselling Romance Novelist," and *Richard Gallen Books Newsletter* was started in 1981 to publicize his romance series. New series appeared for other genres in 1981, but they were nothing like those for the spectacularly publicized romances.

Genre fiction and best-sellers remain a solid core for paperback publishers. A delightful parody of mass-market paperback genre fiction was published in 1981 by Jove: "No Frills Books." With starkly white covers labeled simply western, science fiction, romance or mystery, each volume is simply marketed as a type. There is neither author nor title, and each consists of 60 pages. "After you've read one," maintains the Jove blurb, "you won't mind the others." However, several trends in publishing have emerged that will undoubtedly change the patterns for genre fiction publishing in both paperback and hardcover.

The distribution of mass-market paperbacks has been predominantly through nonbookstore display. Bookstores now, however, may display up to 70% of paperback stock, consisting of trade paperbacks from mass and hardcover publishers and mass-market format genre fiction. More books of all types, including genre fiction, are coming out in original paperback edition from both types of publishers. Hardcover publishers are reprinting more of their backlist titles in trade paperback rather than selling rights to mass-market paperback publishers, and many have their own paperback subsidiaries. Several paperback publishers have started publishing in hardcover as well. Top-selling authors in mass-market paperback have had the same title published in mass *and* trade paperback format, by the same publisher, and both formats sold well despite the price difference. Although the mass-market fiction price in 1981 topped at $3.95 (the "No Frills Books" were $1.50), two titles were announced for 1982 at $4.95 and $5.95 (James Michener's *Covenant*, 1,088 pages, and James Clavell's *Noble House*, 1,376 pages). A new romance series, Serenade Romances, published by Simon & Schuster, is in trade paperback format, with full-page illustrations, priced at $2.95.

Category or genre fiction is becoming more diverse in format and is an increasingly important seller in bookstores, particularly the many chain stores in shopping centers. These stores are making bookstore patrons of the approximately 50% of the population that had never previously entered such a store. The trade paperback format will make paperbacks more satisfactory to libraries.

A perennial problem is keeping titles in print. That paperback books in both mass and trade format have become a staple in bookstores should extend their in-print status beyond the few weeks on the paperback stands. Backlist reprinting by hardcover publishers in paperback format should also secure availability. Several specialist large-print publishers for the library market provide a substantial amount of genre fiction, largely in hardcover. Talking books (cassettes) are a recent type of reprinting, provide a large number of genre fiction titles, and are sold in many bookstores. (A recent catalogue included Dick Francis, Alistair MacLean, Frederick Forsyth, Jack Schaefer, Jack Higgins, Nevil Shute, Dennis Wheatley, Sir Arthur Conan Doyle, C. S. Forester, Charlotte and Emily Brontë, and John Le Carré.)

The supply of new genre fiction titles is augmented by "created" books, frowned on by the critics but selling merrily to the common readers. The most prominent "creator" is Lyle Kenyon Engel with his Book Creations Inc., formed in 1973: "When better books are built Book Creations Inc. will build them!" To date the firm has "built" 234 books in 29 series for 19 publishers and claims 61 million copies of these titles in print, with translations into 15 languages. "Constructed" in 1982 were to be 125 paperback novels, under the pseudonyms of 80 authors, for 10 publishers. These would include 31 series, with 19 of those being new, mostly historical sagas for both sexes. (For the firm's most famous historical saga, the Kent Family Chronicles in eight volumes, the sales figure was 35 million copies.) The firm's operating pattern is simple: Engel thinks up the plot, engages the writers, the staff does the editing, and the profits are split 50/50 with the author. Another "creator" is Richard Gallen & Co.: "Editing and promotion of books." The firm's largest line is "Richard Gallen Originals," romances marketed by Pocket Books. Two other lines are distributed by Dell and Pinnacle, with two new lines announced for 1982 for Dell and Ballantine.

Mention should be made of the popularity of specialist bookstores devoted to types of genre fiction, for they attest to the sufficient number of fans eager to buy the books to satisfy their passion. Many of these started in the seventies and have prospered: Murder Ink and The Mysterious Bookshop in New York; Scene of the Crime in Los Angeles, specializing in the thriller; Dark They Were and Golden Eyed, London; A Change of Hobbit and Fantasy Castle, Los Angeles, specializing in science fiction and fantasy. Other stores could be noted, both for new and antiquarian books, and advertisements may be found in fanzines for the genres.

L'Envoi

Should this introductory chapter seem portentous, remember that genre reading *is* for entertainment. Dorothy L. Sayers said it best (with an assist from Hamlet) in her "Author's Note" to *Gaudy Night*: "the novelist's only native country is Cloud-Cuckooland, where they do but jest, poison in jest: no offense in the world."

2 Western

They went thataway ....

Meanwhile, back at the ranch ....

Action, action is the thing. So long as you keep your hero jumping through fiery hoops on every page you're all right. The basic formula: good man turns bad, bad man turns good. Naturally, there is considerable variation on this theme.... There has to be a woman, but not much of a one. A good horse is much more important.

— Max Brand

The frontier, the rancher, the prairies, the dusty trails, the wide spaces under the lofty stars, the unending struggle between man and nature have bred a stubborn individualism, an admiration for every kind of personal skill, self-reliance, independence and unconventionality, bred their own tempo, their own humor, their own heroism. They have bred a real culture in T. S. Eliot's definition of the word — i.e., a complete life mode; not something to be hung on the wall like a picture or an antique, but life as it is lived, fully and skillfully.

Within that old frontier way of life men could enjoy the luxury of being persons; they could be different; they did not have to be buttons out of a button mold. They were sometimes interesting, sometimes what we call colorful, sometimes gaudy, and on special occasions they could perform gestures splendid enough for an old saga.

— Sean O'Faolain
(*Holiday*, October 1958)

The East is settled, it is orderly, it is governed by women's ideas. This is still a man's country. Make no mistake about that.

— Ernest Haycox
Free Grass

The Great American Novel probably would have to be a Western: the Old West has provided us with our national mythology.

— Brian Garfield

THEMES AND TYPES

The western is essentially an adventure novel but is too large and diverse a kind to subsume under the adventure genre. Although action and adventure usually dominate the plot, they are secondary to the setting, a compound of scenery and history. Nor is the western defined by its plot, although the standard pulp and paperback westerns and the motion picture and television horse operas seem to limit the genre to a few stereotypes. The plot sources are not confined to the cowboy of the 1865 to 1890 ranch lands. The story line derives from the entire westward movement in North America, beginning in the early nineteenth century with the traders, trappers, and explorers, and from the distinctive type of life continuing in the Far West in the United States in the twentieth century.

The western is defined by an attitude toward life, the "complete life mode" not dependent on the West within historical limits. Zane Grey has a cattle drive in Australia in *Wilderness Trek*. A classic Australian motion picture, *The Overlanders*, is a heroic saga of a cattle drive in Australia during World War II when, fearing invasion, the ranchers undertook a trek, lasting months, over deserts and mountains more daunting than the American West (only lacking the Indians).

The appeal of this genre is worldwide, based in a dream of freedom in a world of unspoiled nature, independent of the trammels of restraining society. The hero dominates the western: competent, self-reliant, and self-sufficient whether in conflict with nature or with man or himself. This most enduring of genres appeals to readers of all cultures, far removed geographically from the West and alien to their history and life modes. The nineteenth-century Wild West shows and the twentieth-century motion pictures were instant favorites in Europe as in Asia. Not content with translations of U.S. westerns, the Germans (Karl May in the nineteenth century), Scandinavians, and Britons write their own. Why this universal appeal?

The simplest reason may be that it is just a good story, strong on adventure and thrilling action, having readily defined characters, supplying a satisfying resolution of conflicts in terms of simple blacks and whites (good and evil, right and wrong—the black and white Stetson hats of hero and villain), and even supplying a minor romance. To this are added the characters and setting of the West but, still, without defining the western's appeal. (For example, the motion picture *Star Wars* has been labeled a horse opera in space. The saloon scene is immediately recognized as the classic western movie saloon. The Japanese motion picture *The Seven Samurai* appealed to fans of the western, not just because of the horses, and was later adapted by Hollywood as a western.)

Basic to the appeal is the lure of the frontier, offering an escape from towns, schools, churches, and women in a freedom that can't exist in communities of organized society. The western frontier showed the "savage" Indian living in adventurous freedom as a beckoning symbol. Allied is a nostalgia for a simpler way of life and simpler values—modern life is too complex, too technological, too oppressive toward conformity. The history of the westward-moving frontier in the United States is *the* great adventure story in U.S. history. The liveliest field of book collecting in the world is probably Western Americana. The Westerners Corrals, organizations of collectors, writers, and historians both academic and amateur, exist in many countries, and individual Corrals flourish in cities from West to East in the United States. Whether interest in this history spurs reading of the western novel for many readers is open to question, but the fact that the reader of westerns absorbs a good deal of history is not. The shoot-em-up standard western is long on action, but the history is lacking or negligible. Frequently, even the locale and time are undefined. What is capitalized on is the background of wild, open country and an often legendary way of life. Serious writers of westerns know both the country and the history—Zane Grey, however melodramatic, describes a West that old-timers could identify by specific place and time. Both types of westerns continue to be published.

The historical novel of the West, contrasted invidiously with the western, has been always published as a hardcover book (although this may change if the present trend toward trade paperback originals becomes general) and is usually longer than the novels labeled westerns. That many westerns are also historical novels of the West is obvious, but the denigratory label (or the original publication in paperback format) may deter the fan of Western Americana from reading westerns. Librarians and booksellers should be aware that the fan of the western might be interested in Western Americana (note the popularity of the several Time/Life volumes on the Indians, cowboys, gunfighters), and the reader of Western Americana might enjoy the many westerns with good historical background. That the genre western and the historical novel of the West may be differentiated by quality of writing is not a problem to be discussed here. Literary quality within the western varies as widely as within examples of the standard novel. Many westerns do suffer from stereotyped plots and characters, stiff or overly romantic dialogue (witness Zane Grey's which is often embarrassing to read), misuse of dialect, and other defects. The reader of westerns will develop personal standards of evaluation.

The popular stereotype of a genre is unfortunately too often accepted as defining the genre. The stereotypic western can be recognized on the first page: a lone rider is crossing the valley or desert and a shot knocks off his hat or hits a rock, startling his horse, and the range war begins. There is so much variety in themes in the western that the stereotype can be easily ignored. The following groupings by theme and type of western are not exhaustive nor do they include all authors who have used the themes. Also, many of the novels have multiple themes. The order of listing is to relate both history and themes.

Mountain Men

The trappers of the early nineteenth century often lived with Indians and became squaw men. They became the prototype loner who escaped society's restrictions and lived a free life. James Fenimore Cooper's Natty Bumpo in *The Leatherstocking Tales* (*The Pioneers, The Last of the Mohicans, The Prairie, The Pathfinder, The Deerslayer*) is the natural man free of a corrupting society and the prototype for the mountain man in the western. He frequently appears as a guide for the wagon trains. Guthrie's trilogy, among the following examples, provides the prototype:

Fergusson, Harvey. *Wolf Song.*

Fisher, Vardis. *Mountain Man.* Source for the motion picture *Jeremiah Johnson.*

Guthrie, A. B. *The Big Sky. The Way West. These Thousand Hills.*

Wagons West and Early Settlement

Wagon trains took settlers to the prairie country, the Rocky Mountains, and the Pacific Northwest and miners to the Dakotas and California. This type of novel may present the greatest diversity of characters in the western, including women. There is scope for varied adventures—the hazards of terrain and natural disasters as well as Indian attacks. At the end of the journey is the homesteading. Most of the aspects of this type of western appear in the following books, with Hough's being the early prototype.

Cook, Will. *The Drifter.*

Gulick, Bill. *They Came to a Valley.*

Haycox, Ernest. *The Earthbreakers. The Adventurers.*

Hough, Emerson. *The Covered Wagon.*

Merriman, Chad. *Mighty Big River.*

Taylor, Robert Lewis. *The Travels of Jaimie McPheeters.* Pulitzer Prize winner; a long, picaresque adventure.

Texas and Mexico

The settling of Texas and the war with Mexico are topics for many westerns. Here are a few books on the special character of the border country and the battles with Mexico:

Kelton, Elmer. *Massacre at Goliad. After the Bugles.*

Lea, Tom. *The Brave Bulls. The Wonderful Country.*

LeMay, Alan. *The Unforgiven.*

Taylor, Ross McLaury. *Brazos.*

Thomason, John W., Jr. *Gone to Texas.*

Land Rush

The opening of Oklahoma's Indian Territory to settlers appears as a part in many westerns, but it dominates Edna Ferber's *Cimarron*, which is also a classic motion picture.

Mormons

The Mormons are the focus of many westerns, with the Mormon's heroic journey to Zion (Utah) being a popular theme, and the Mormons as a group distrusted and hated by the Gentiles being a common plot. These books provide the basic story:

Bailey, Paul. *For Time and All Eternity.* One of the few novels written from the Mormon view.

Grey, Zane. *Riders of the Purple Sage.*

Ingram, Hunter. *The Trespassers.*

Wormser, Richard. *Battalion of Saints.* The Mormon Battalion marching to the Texas-Mexican War.

Merchants, Mule Trains, Stage Lines

Before the settlers arrived in the West, there were trading posts, largely for the fur trade and the military. With the coming of ranchers, farmers, and miners, the economy needed merchants and means of transportation. These examples show how vital trade and transportation were in building the West:

Culp, John H. *Whistle in the Wind.* The Comanchero traders in the Spanish Southwest. Trade along the Santa Fe Trail was active in the nineteenth century.

Giles, Janice Holt. *Six-Horse Hitch.* In effect, a dramatic and long history of the stagecoach lines in the West and the Pony Express.

Haycox, Ernest. *Canyon Passage.* Mule-train freight line in the Pacific Northwest.

MacLeod, Robert. *The Muleskinner.* Freighting in Arizona.

Reese, John. *Sure Shot Shapiro.* A Jewish traveling salesman in California's Mohave Desert.

Railroads

The building of the railroads is usually treated in the western in terms of the troubles encountered in the brawling construction camp towns, with Indians, robber gangs, and the like, and there is often a troubleshooter hero or railroad detective. (That Buffalo Bill was a hunter supplying meat to the crews is an aspect for a good story.) These prototype examples are full of adventurous action centering on the building of the railroad. That the railroad changed the character of the Far West is shown in many westerns, with the depot a vital center of town.

Grey, Zane. *U.P. Trail.*

Haycox, Ernest. *Trouble Shooter.*

Spearman, Frank. *Whispering Smith.*

Mining

The mining towns were undoubtedly the toughest in the West whether in the Dakotas, Rocky Mountain country, Arizona Territory, or California. The characters were equally tough, with claim jumping, lynchings, robbery of stagecoach shipments, and political and labor troubles to keep them busy. These examples include a ghost town setting in the picaresque *Dead Warrior*:

Ballard, Todhunter. *Gold in California.*

Cushman, Dan. *Silver Mountain. The Old Copper Collar.*

Hunter, John. *Death in the Mountain.*

L'Amour, Louis. *The Empty Land.*

Myers, John Myers. *Dead Warrior.*

Short, Luke. *Debt of Honor.*

Lost Mines

Among the most romantic legends of the Southwest are those of lost Indian and Mexican mines of fabulous treasure. These novels about fictional mines are remarkably realistic:

Henry, Will. *McKenna's Gold.*

Nye, Nelson. *A Lost Mine Named Salvation.*

Shirreffs, Gordon D. *Southwest Drifter. The Manhunter.*

The Army in the West

The Indian wars and the campaigns to control the tribes provide the background for an exceedingly large number of westerns. The cavalry and Indian story is usually told from the cavalry side. (The Indian version will be found in the next section.) Officers and scouts are the heroes. Here is the classic description of the life for men and horses: "Forty miles a day on beans and hay." Stories both realistic and romantic are among the novels listed here:

Bellah, James Warner. *Rear Guard.*

Brown, Dee. *Action at Beecher Island. The Girl from Fort Wicked.*

Chamberlain, William. *Forced March to Loon Creek. Trumpets of Company K.*

Cook, Will. *The Apache Fighter.*

Everett, Wade. *The Warrior. Cavalry Recruit.*

Grove, Fred. *Comanche Captives.*

Halleran, E. E. *Indian Fighter.*

Haycox, Ernest. *Border Trumpet. Bugles in the Afternoon.*

Jones, X. X. *Broken Lance.*

O'Brian, Frank. *Bugle and Spur.*

Olsen, Theodore V. *Arrow in the Sun.*

Prebble, John. *The Buffalo Soldiers.* There were several black regiments, with white officers. The Indians called them buffalo soldiers as their kinky hair was like the buffalo's.

Shelley, John. *Stallion Soldier.*

Short, Luke. *Ambush.*

Steelman, Robert. *Ambush at Three Rivers.*

Straight, Michael. *Carrington.*

Warren, Charles Marquis. *Only the Valiant.*

Whitman, S. E. *Change of Command.*

The Indian

The story as told by the Indian is usually a distressing one. It provides a telling contrast to the attitudes toward the Indian common in many westerns. Most of the novels are rich in detail on customs and legends. The story of squaw men, noted previously in the mountain men books, and of the half-breed appears here and in the novels in the following section. (See the later section on the Indian today.) Several of the following novels are narrated by an Indian character. All explore the troubled relations between Indians and Anglos.

Arnold, Elliott. *Blood Brother*. Source of the motion picture *Broken Arrow*.

Capps, Benjamin. *The White Man's Road*.

Comfort, Will L. *Apache*.

Fast, Howard. *The Last Frontier*.

Fisher, Clay. *Niño*.

Henry, Will. *From Where the Sun Now Stands*.

Ingram, Hunter. *Forked Tongue*.

La Farge, Oliver. *Laughing Boy*.

L'Amour, Louis. *Hondo*.

Lutz, Giles A. *The Magnificent Failure*.

Oliver, Chad. *The Wolf Is My Brother*.

Patten, Lewis B. *Bones of the Buffalo*.

Snyder, Cecil. *Big with Vengeance*.

Vernam, Glenn R. *Indian Hater*.

Indian Captivities

Popular since colonial times, captivity stories, factual and fictional, provide a narrative that is both sad and romantic. Captured as children or as adults, the captives may be rescued or may remain with the tribe to marry and become, in effect, Indians. If rescued, the women, who may have become squaws and borne children, may be unwilling to leave their Indian families. The following novels concern both the captivity story and the search for the captives:

Berger, Thomas. *Little Big Man*.

Capps, Benjamin. *A Woman of the People*. *White Apache*.

Cook, Will. *Two Rode Together*.

Culp, John H. *Whistle in the Wind*.

Johnson, Dorothy M. *Indian Country*. Source of the motion picture *A Man Called Horse*.

LeMay, Alan. *The Searchers*. *The Unforgiven*.

Buffalo Runners

The buffalo runners (hunters) left a sad litter of whitening bones, destroyed the economy of the Plains Indians, and almost reduced buffalo herds of millions to extinction. While many westerns have scenes of buffalo hunting, Fred Grove's *The Buffalo Runners* and *Buffalo Spring* are totally concerned with the topic.

Cattle Kingdoms

Cattle ranching, large and small scale, dominates the story of many westerns, with varying amounts of attention paid to ranching as such. The immense spreads provide the background for wealthy and powerful families. Ranching, of course, dominates the story of the cowboy, with its most dramatic aspect being the cattle drive to be noted later. These two examples illustrate the immensity of ranching operations:

Fergusson, Harvey. *Grant of Kingdom.*
Guthrie, A. B. *These Thousand Hills.*

"The Hired Man on Horseback"

The cowboy is *the* great folk hero of the West. He appears in legendary guise in too many westerns. He appears as a "working cowboy" in too few. The nonfiction books on the cowboy, noted later, treat both legend and reality. For example, although many cowboys may have been illiterate, many became inveterate readers in their lonely lives. That they were inveterate smokers abetted their literacy. (See the long passage, pages 63-65, in Eugene Manlove Rhodes's novel *Bransford in Arcadia* on the 303 books the cowboys obtained through the yellow coupons in each Bull Durham pouch!) The early prototypes listed here are by Adams and Wister, and the recent prototype is by Decker.

Adams, Andy. *The Log of a Cowboy.*
Borland, Hal. *The Seventh Winter.*
Bowers, B. M. *Chip of the Flying U.*
Decker, William. *To Be a Man.*
Gries, Tom. *Will Penny.*
James, Will. *Cow Country. Sand.*
Mulford, Clarence E. *Hopalong Cassidy.*
Schaefer, Jack. *Monte Walsh.*
Wister, Owen. *The Virginian.*

Black Cowboy

From the early westerns and the majority of popular westerns, the reader would never know that black cowboys existed. *The Negro Cowboy*, by Philip Durham and Everett L. Jones (Dodd, 1965), gives their history. Several recent westerns have a black cowboy as the hero. (The reader must still wait for the Mexican or Indian cowboy to receive similar fictional status.) These examples are realistic portrayals:

Everett, Wade. *The Horse Trader. Top Hand.*

Gaulden, Ray. *A Time to Ride.*

Henry, Will. *One More River to Cross.*

Range War

The troubles in the typical popular western frequently stem from range wars—conflict over water rights or with encroaching nesters, the marauding rustler gangs, barbed wire, and the end of the free range. Many books have the plot device of the hired gunman brought in to start or stop trouble. These few examples merely suggest the great number of westerns with this theme:

Grey, Zane. *To the Last Man.*

Haycox, Ernest. *Free Grass.*

Hoffman, Lee. *West of Cheyenne.*

LeMay, Alan. *The Smoky Years.*

Sheepmen

The sheepmen were always resented by cattlemen as spoilers of the range. Grey's novel deals with the historic Graham-Twekesbury feud, still a sore subject in the Tonto Basin area of Arizona. Readers of the western would enjoy *Sweet Promised Land*, by Robert Laxalt (Harper, 1957), the story of his father, a Basque sheepherder in Nevada. It is a moving story with a novel's structure and captures the loneliness and danger of the sheepherder's life. Grey's novel is the early prototype for the range war:

Grey, Zane. *To the Last Man.*

Cattle Drive

The drive to rail's head is the epic saga of the western. Hazards of nature and stampedes were compounded by problems with rustlers and Indians. The following examples cover many aspects of the topic, including ingenious instances in Australia and Siberia:

Adams, Andy. *The Log of a Cowboy.* The classic story, first published in 1903.

Barry, Jane. *A Shadow of Eagles.*

Capps, Benjamin. *The Trail to Ogallala.*

Flynn, Robert. *North to Yesterday.*

Grey, Zane. *Trail Driver. Wilderness Trek.* The second story takes place in Australia.

Bad Men and Good

The flawed hero is a popular figure in westerns. In the rough frontier world, a good man found it hard to remain good, at least if he wanted to stay alive. Whether treated as a romantic or a realistic figure, the hero in this type of western is always a dramatic one and, as in these examples, not always a stereotyped one.

Brand, Max. *Destry Rides Again.* *Not* like the classic motion picture that took the title.

Doctorow, E. L. *Welcome to Hard Times.*

Grey, Zane. *Lone Star Ranger.*

Haycox, Ernest. "Stage to Lordsburg." *The* classic short-story western, source for *the* classic motion picture *Stagecoach.* To be found in Haycox's *By Rope and Lead* and in the anthology by Durham and Jones, *The Western Story*, listed later.

Henry, Will. *Death of a Legend.*

Hoffman, Lee. *Bred to Kill.*

Rhodes, Eugene Manlove. *Pasó por Aquí.*

Law and Lawmen

The West was wide and lonesome and lawmen few. "An honest man is all the law you could find" (*The Virginian*). The western is full of men taking law into their own hands of necessity — lynch law, the kangaroo courts of the mining towns, the shoot-out at sunset. The U.S. Marshal in the territories was a powerful figure as were the Texas Rangers. ("Only one Ranger?" "There's only one war, ain't there?") Oklahoma's Indian Territory was a haunt of outlaws, and the name Robber's Roost appeared throughout the West in isolated areas. Commonly asserted in the western was that there was "No law West of the Pecos." These examples show the law in action in an often lawless society:

Bonner, Michael. *The Iron Noose.*

Ballard, Todhunter. *The Sheriff of Tombstone.*

Burnett, W. R. *Bitter Ground.*

Clark, Walter Van Tilburg. *The Oxbow Incident.*

Conquest, Ned. *The Gun and Glory of Granite Hendley.*

Everett, Wade. *The Whiskey Traders.*

Hawk, Alex. *Mex.*

Haycox, Ernest. *Trail Town.*

Leonard, Elmore. *Valdez Is Coming.*

Locke, Charles O. *The Hell Bent Kid.*

Poole, Richard. *Gun Vote at Valdoro.*

Portis, Charles. *True Grit.*

Sheers, J. C. *Fire in His Hand.*

Town Marshal

The frontier town—cattle, mining, or railroad—was a troublesome place, its saloons full of gamblers and dance hall girls. There was always a foot-loose stranger wandering through (as though the more stable residents couldn't cause enough trouble). The man with the star was the bulwark against anarchy and possibly the most romantic figure in western legend. In many westerns the marshal is the secondary figure, but in the following books, he is the dominant character:

Adams, Clifton. *The Hottest Fourth of July in the History of Hangtree County.*

Bennett, Dwight. *Legend in the Dust.*

Burnett, W. R. *Bitter Ground.*

Everett, Wade. *Shotgun Marshal.*

Haycox, Ernest. *Trail Town.*

Leonard, Elmore. *Valdez Is Coming.* Mexican town constable.

Patten, Lewis B. *Death of a Gunfighter. No God in Saquaro.*

Boy into Man

The frontier was demanding country, and the boys had to prove competence at an early age. Most of the western's heroes are young, but in these examples, they range from children to teenagers:

Bass, Milton. *Jory.*

Hoffman, Lee. *The Valdez Horses.*

Knibbs, H. H. *The Ridin' Kid from Powder River.*

L'Amour, Louis. *Chancy. Down the Long Hills.*

Leighton, Lee. *Killer Guns.*

McMurtry, Larry. *Horseman Pass By.* Source of the motion picture *Hud.*

Santee, Ross. *Cowboy.*

Mysterious Rider

Jack Schaefer describes him: "The man with the gun using it to right wrongs, in a sense the American version of a knight on horseback." Frequently he is the hero with a shady past who rides out as lonely as he came in. He is a highly romantic figure, often a secondary character in westerns, and in Schaefer's *Shane*, he became the legendary prototype.

The Singular Woman

The heroine in the western, less important than the horse, is rarely *the* leading character. However, the few dominant heroines are varied and notable. These examples combine the romantic and the realistic:

Bickham, Jack M. *The War on Charity Ross. Target: Charity Ross.*

Frazee, Steve. *A Gun for Bragg's Woman.*

Kent, Simon. *Charlie Gallagher, My Love.* First published 1961; the Signet reprint, 1976, is under the name Max Catto.

Locke, Charles O. *Amelia Rankin.*

Olson, Theodore V. *Arrow in the Sun.*

Overholser, Wayne D. *The Cattle Queen.*

Portis, Charles. *True Grit.*

Walsh, M. M. B. *Dolly Purdo.*

Doctor and Preacher

The hero in most westerns, even the unheroic hero of parody, falls into easily recognized types—cowboy, soldier, miner, lawman—making the doctor and the preacher unusual. These examples are such satisfactory westerns that one wishes for more non-typical heroes:

Everett, Wade. *Bullets for the Doctor.*

Reese, John. *My Brother John. Jesus on Horseback.*

Wild Horse Hunt

The horse is important in the western (although, in fact, the canny rider swore by the smart and surefooted mule) and often proves one of the most interesting characters. It is the wild horse, symbolically free and untamed, that provides the romantic story. Although a subsidiary theme in many westerns, the wild horse hunt dominates in the following books:

Grey, Zane. *Forlorn River.*

O'Rourke, Frank. *The Last Ride.*

Romance

There is romance, or a romance, in most westerns, often subordinate to the adventure interest but occasionally providing an important love story. A few books are unabashedly romances, for example:

Carroll, Shana. *Paxton Pride.*

Durham, Marilyn. *The Man Who Loved Cat Dancing.*

Grey, Zane. *The Light of Western Stars.*

Picaresque

The rogue hero is a staple in adventure fiction. He usually has some saving graces and often reforms, at least partially. Frequently an antihero or unheroic character, he is still cunning and competent: he survives and even wins out. His adventures are frequently comic, and he will often be found as the hero in the westerns in the following section on comedy and parody. The heroes in the following westerns are eccentric and often of quite a different pattern than the typical western hero:

Berger, Thomas. *Little Big Man.*

Culp, John H. *The Bright Feathers.*

Foreman, L. L. *Spanish Grant.*

McCague, Robert. *The Fortune Road.*

McCaig, Robert. *The Shadow Maker.*

Nye, Nelson. *Trail of Lost Skulls.*

O'Rourke, Frank. *The Swift Runner.*

Shelley, John, and David Shelley. *Hell-for-Leather Jones. The Relentless Rider.*

Shrake, Edwin. *Blessed McGill.*

Taylor, Robert Lewis. *Two Roads to Guadelupe.*

Comedy and Parody

Folk humor and vernacular humor are common in the western, both in characters and language. The western as a comic novel, having fun with the standard patterns of the genre and often inverting its values, sometimes becomes true parody. The reader is advised to know the standard western before taking on the parodies. These examples illustrate all periods of the western story:

Adams, Clifton. *Shorty.*

Bickham, Jack. *The Apple Dumpling Gang.*

Condon, Richard. *A Talent for Loving: Or, The Great Cowboy Race.*

Evans, Max. *The Rounders.*

Greenberg, Alvin. *The Invention of the West.*

Gulick, Bill. *The Hallelulia Trail. Liveliest Town in the West.*

LeMay, Alan. *Useless Cowboy. The* perfect parody. The motion picture based on it, *Along Came Jones*, is a classic.

Markson, David. *The Ballad of Dingus Magee.* For the sophisticated reader of westerns, being vulgar and bawdy.

Myers, John Myers. *Dead Warrior.*

Nye, Nelson. *Wolf Trap.*

O'Rourke, Frank. *The Bride Stealer.*

Purdom, Herbert R. *A Hero for Henry.*

Reed, Ishmael. *Yellow Back Radio Broke Down.* Included as a curiosity.

Reese, John. *Horses, Honor and Women. Singalee. Sure Shot Shapiro.*

Rhodes, Eugene Manlove.

Shelley, John. *Hell-for-Leather Jones.*

Turner, William O. *Destination Doubtful.*

Series

The popularity of the series character in the western has boomed with original paperback publishing. There are several of these series originally in hardback (Bowers, Foreman, McCarthy, Mulford). Many of the heroes are lawmen and are often in the picaresque tradition. (For other series, see the later section on the adult western.) The following listing is by series character:

Benteen, John.	Neal Fargo.
Bowers, B. M.	Chip of the Flying U.
Braun, Matthew.	Luke Starback.
Christian, Frederick H.	Justice.
Clinton, Jeff.	Wildcat O'Shea.
Cody, Al.	Montana Abbott.
Foreman, L. L.	Rogue Bishop and Don Ricardo de Risa.
Gilman, George.	Edge. Adam Steele.
James, William M.	Cuchillo Oro. Apache.
Knott, Will C.	Wolf Caulder.
L'Amour, Louis.	The Sacketts.
McCarthy, Gary.	Derby Buckingham. A New York writer of Wild West yarns goes West and is a marvelous tough-guy hero.
McCoy, Marshal.	Larry and Streak. Nevada Jim.
McCurtin, Peter.	Carmody.
Mulford, Clarence E.	Hopalong Cassidy.
Newton, D. B.	Jim Bannister.
Randall, Clay.	Sheriff Amos Flagg.
Slade, Jack.	Lassiter. Sundance.
Striker, Frank.	The Lone Ranger.
Tippette, Giles.	Wilson Young.
Ward, Jonas.	Buchanan.
Wynne, Brian.	Jeremy Six, Marshal of Spanish Flat.

Publishers' Series

Several historical series have appeared as paperback originals following the success of The Kent Family Chronicles. These are akin to the family chronicle or saga noted later in the chapter on romance. These are finite series. Except for *The Kent Family Chronicle*, each volume may have a different author. These examples show, in successive volumes, the usual pattern of following the westward movement.

Jakes, John. The Kent Family Chronicles. (Jove)

The Colonization of America Series. (Bantam)

The Making of America Series. (Dell)
The publisher labeled these eight volumes "romantic historical novels." Here the contents scope is briefly described in a listing of the titles: Lou Cameron. *The Wilderness Seekers.* Kentucky in the late 1700s; Aaron Fletcher. *The Mountain Breed.* The mountain men in the early 1800s; Jeanne Sommers. *The Conestoga People.* Westward migration in the mid-1800s; John Tombs. *The Forty Niners*; Paula Moore. *Hearts Divided.* The Civil War in the West; Jeanne Sommers. *The Builders.* The UP railroad; Elizabeth Zachery. *The Land Rushers.* The Oklahoma land rush in the 1880s; Georgia Granger. *The Wild and the Wayward.* The last days of the Wild West.

Wagons West series. (Bantam)

The West Still Lives—The Modern Scene

The western with a twentieth-century setting attests that the special mode of life distinctive in the western, particularly in ranching and with the cowboy and horse still dominant, continues in the wide open Far West. Many regional novelists could be included here: Wallace Stegner, Walter Van Tilburg Clark, Conrad Richter, Frank Waters, and others. The vitality of the western and its appeal as a genre emerge strongly in these examples with a modern setting:

Abbey, Edward. *The Brave Cowboy. Fire on the Mountain. The Monkey Wrench Gang.* The motion picture *Lonely Are the Brave* is taken from *The Brave Cowboy.*

Bradford, Richard. *Red Sky at Morning. So Far from Heaven.*

Brown, J. P. S. *Jim Kane. The Outfit: A Cowboy's Primer.*

Davis, H. L. *Winds of Morning.*

Evans, Max. *The Hi Lo Country. The One-Eyed Sky. The Rounders.*

Lutz, Giles A. *Wild Runs the River.*

MacLeod, Robert. *The Californio.*

McMurtry, Larry. *Horseman Pass By. Leaving Cheyenne.*

Miller, Arthur. *The Misfits.*

The Indian Today

The story of the Indian in the West after the wars, on the reservation or dispersed within the West, is still of a people belonging to a distinctive and cherished culture. There is conflict with Anglo society and its government as well as the more subtle and psychological distresses of adapting to or adjusting within an essentially incompatible culture. Folklore and poetry are found in several of these examples, and all are tinged with sadness.

Borland, Hal. *When the Legends Die.*

Eastlake, William. *The Bronc People. Portrait of an Artist with 26 Horses. Go in Beauty.*

Grey, Zane. *The Vanishing American.*

Heifetz, Harold. *Jeremiah Thunder.*

Hillerman, Tony. *The Blessing Way. Dancehall of the Dead.* Detective stories featuring a Navaho reservation policeman. (Also listed in the chapter on thrillers.)

Huffaker, Clair. *Nobody Loves a Drunken Indian.*

Momaday, N. Scott. *House Made of Dawn.*

Stuart, Colin. *Shoot an Arrow to Stop the Wind.*

Eccentric Variations

The combination of the western with other genres has not been tried too often, but here are a few examples:

Gothic Western

MacDonald, Elizabeth. *The House at Grey Eagle.*

Rowan, Deirdre. *Shadow of the Volcano. Time of the Burning Mask.*

Winston, Daoma. *The Golden Valley.*

Sweet-and-Savage Western

Matthews, Patricia. *Love, Forever More.*

Sakol, Jeannie. *Flora Sweet.*

Private Eye Western

Wren, M. K. *Oh, Bury Me Not.*

British Western

This is also called the "coyote in the sky" western because of the ludicrous error made by John Creasey, a prolific thriller writer who also wrote a few westerns under pseudonyms—meaning to note the vultures circling in the sky, he carelessly called them coyotes. There are several prolific British writers of westerns, but few of their books appear in the United States.

Edson, J. T. Floating Outfit series.
Reprinted in paperback by Berkley Books, the 26th in the series appearing in 1980.

Pike, Charles R. Jubal Cade series.
Chelsea House published 13 titles in 1981.

"Adult" Western

These are "hot" paperback originals, strong on sexual adventures by the tough series heroes. Playboy Press started this type in 1975 with the Jake Logan series, and the imitators quickly followed, with Playboy starting a second series in 1979, the J. D. Hardin series. Some critics consider them simply pornography, although the pornography is sometimes leavened by comedy. Several books in each series are published yearly and seem to be kept in supply by reprintings. The authors of most are "house names," several authors writing to fit the house's prescribed guidelines. Adult westerns may be considered the male adventure fantasy counterpart to the female sweet-and-savage romance. The tone of the following examples distinguishes these series from those listed in the previous "Series" section:

Evans, Tabor. Longarm series, featuring Deputy U.S. Marshal Long.
"Longarm is a lot more than sagebrush and shoot-'em-up. It's the Wild West with emphasis on the Wild! Beautiful Women, Barroom Brawling, Bits of Fascinating History, Lots of Humor, and—Plenty of Sex! All the elements that appeal to men and women—Alike!"
—Publisher's advertisement

Hardin, J. D. Series featuring Pinkerton agents Doc and Raider.
" 'The most exciting writer since Louis L'Amour.' Jake Logan." From the cover of several titles. Jake Logan is a Playboy Press "house name," as is J. D. Hardin.

Logan, Jake. Series featuring John Slocum.
"A little sadism, a little sex popularly blended and set in a West never known by the likes of Grey or Brand." 28th title in 1981.

Masters, Zeke. Faro Blake series.

Sharpe, Jon. The Trailsman series, featuring Skye Fargo.

Thorne, Ramsey. Renegade series, featuring Captain Gringo.

TOPICS

Classic Authors: Early

Most of the classic authors remain in print, largely in paperback. (See the section on reprint publishers.) Many of these authors are listed as examples in the previous subject groupings. The following authors have endured, either for one or a few titles or, as with Brand and Grey, for all their titles:

Adams, Andy.
His *The Log of a Cowboy* (1903) is the classic and authentic story of a trail drive from the Mexican border to Montana.

Brand, Max.
Pseudonym of Frederick Faust. Used 13 (or more) pseudonyms and wrote 215 westerns, publishing the first in 1919. His three top sellers (over two million copies) are: *Destry Rides Again, Fightin' Fool, Singing Guns*. Twenty-seven of his novels were made into motion pictures. (He also

wrote the Dr. Kildare series for MGM.) A great many of his titles are currently in print in paperback, with all of the pseudonyms now appearing as Max Brand.

Easton, Robert. *Max Brand: The Big "Westerner."* University of Oklahoma Press, 1970.

Burroughs, Edgar Rice.
Better known for his Tarzan series and science fiction adventures. Two of his westerns were reprinted in the Gregg Press Western Fiction series: *The War Chief* and *Apache Devil* (both serialized in 1927 and 1928 before publication in book form).

Grey, Zane.
From 1903 to his death in 1939, he wrote 89 books, including nonfiction. Westerns have been issued since 1939 "from the estate of Zane Grey," by Harpers, but the earlier titles are the classic ones. He appeared on the best-seller list in 1915, *The Lone Star Ranger*, and again each year from 1917 to 1924. Over 40 novels became motion pictures.

Gruber, Frank. *Zane Grey, a Biography.* World, 1970.

Harte, Bret.
Immortalized the miners, gamblers, and good-hearted fancy ladies of the West of the 1860s in "The Luck of Roaring Camp" and "The Outcasts of Poker Flat."

Hough, Emerson.
The Covered Wagon (1922) set a pattern for the Oregon Trail western.

Knibbs, H. H.
The Ridin' Kid from Powder River (1919) is a classic boy-into-man western.

Mulford, Clarence E.
Hopalong Cassidy (1910) became immortal in a long series on the Bar-20 Ranch, appearing in novel, motion picture, and television.

Raine, William MacLeod.
He wrote about 85 westerns, his first published in 1908, and they are still being reprinted in paperback.

Rhodes, Eugene Manlove.
"The Hired Man on Horseback" whose romantic western heroes, frequently at odds with the law, were, as his first book affirmed, *Good Men and True* (1910). Most remembered for *Pasó por Aquí* (1926), with its tag line, " 'We are all decent people.' " His typical humor is evoked by the compiler, W. H. Hutchinson of *The Rhodes Reader: Stories of Virgins, Villains and Varmints* (University of Oklahoma Press, 1957).

Twain, Mark.
Twain brought welcome humor to the western scene in "The Celebrated Jumping Frog of Calaveras County" (1867) and *Roughing It* (1872).

White, Stewart Edward.
A prolific writer on the western scene, White is chiefly remembered for *Arizona Nights* (1904), stories of the range, and a trilogy (1913-1915) gathered as *The Story of California*.

Wister, Owen.
The Virginian, on the best-seller list in 1902 and 1903 and never out of print, set the pattern for the popular cowboy western in hero, heroine (the schoolmarm), rustlers, shoot-out at sundown, and other incidents. It gave the genre its classic line: "When you call me that, *smile!*"

Classic Authors: Recent

This list of classic authors could be extended as certain authors are reprinted more fully or as new authors become established. Most of them are, or were, prolific and write westerns with a variety of themes.

Burnett, W. R.

Capps, Benjamin.

Garfield, Brian.

Gulick, Bill.

Guthrie, A. B.
Big Sky is one of the top-selling westerns.

Haycox, Ernest.
Rawhide Range and *Bugles in the Afternoon* are among the top-selling westerns. Haycox is important as a touchstone in the criticism of the western: his writings, in style and characterization, set standards for the genre that have influenced others writing in the genre.

Henry, Will.
Also publishes as Clay Fisher.

Johnson, Dorothy M.

Kelton, Elmer.

L'Amour, Louis.
His publisher claims L'Amour's sales now surpass Zane Grey's, 110 million copies worldwide (1980). His 78th western was published in 1981 in simultaneous trade paperback and hardcover by Bantam Books. "The Homer of the oaters." — *Time*.

LeMay, Alan.

Olson, T. V.

O'Rourke, Frank.

Patten, Louis B.
About 80 titles.

Schaefer, Jack.
Shane is one of the top-selling westerns and became a classic motion picture.

Short, Luke.
In some 57 novels, he covered most of the themes in the genre.

"Best" Westerns

Polls to determine the best westerns are idiosyncratic. A list in *The Roundup* (monthly journal of the Western Writers of America) in 1956 included A. B. Guthrie's *The Big Sky* and *The Way West*; Ernest Haycox's *Bugles in the Afternoon*; Owen Wister's *The Virginian*; Andy Adams's *The Log of a Cowboy*; Walter Van Tilburg Clark's *The Ox-Bow Incident*; and Conrad Richter's *The Sea of Grass*. A similar list in 1969 duplicated only *The Log of a Cowboy*; the others were Will Henry's *From Where the Sun Now Stands*; Benjamin Capps's *The Trail to Ogallala*; Tom Lea's *The Wonderful Country*; Oakley Hall's *Warlock*; Milton Lott's *Back Track*; Alan LeMay's *The Searchers*; Frederick Manfred's *Conquering Horse*; and Max Evans's *The Rounders*.

A list of the 10 best westerns in the London *Daily Telegraph* in 1976 is notable in that all were made into motion pictures: Zane Grey's *Riders of the Purple Sage*; Walter Van Tilburg Clark's *The Ox-Bow Incident*; A. B. Guthrie's *The Big Sky*; W. R. Burnett's *Adobe Walls*; Ernest Haycox's *Man in the Saddle*; Luke Short's *Ride the Man Down*; Alan LeMay's *The Searchers*; Jack Schaefer's *Shane*; Dorothy M. Johnson's "The Man Who Shot Liberty Valance"; Max Brand's *Destry Rides Again*.

Some of the winners of awards from the Cowboy Hall of Fame and the Spur award from the Western Writers of America (some are not listed elsewhere) should be noted: Leigh Brackett, Matthew Braun, Will C. Browne, Leslie Ernenwein, L. P. Holmes, Noel M. Loomis, Giles Lutz (over 50 titles), Stephen Overholser, Wayne D. Overholser (about 70 titles), and Glendon Swarthout.

Writers in this genre tend to be prolific: Tom Curry (125); J. T. Edson (British author, over 100); Cliff Farrell (about 30); Ray Hogan (about 90); Louis Masterman (the pseudonym of Norwegian author Kjell Hallbing, who has written over 100 westerns; some have been translated and published in England); Nelson Nye (about 90); T. V. Olson (over 30); Frank C. Robertson (116); Gordon D. Shirreffs (about 70); Tom West (over 50). But Peter Field, with a seemingly unending number, is a publisher's house name.

New authors emerge regularly, and as they continue to turn out new titles steadily, they become the familiar names as candidates for the best of genre lists, e.g., Kelly P. Gast and Frank Roderus, each now turning out about one book a year.

Anthologies

Into the 1940s, authors of westerns wrote steadily for the pulp magazines that published both short stories and serials, and also had a ready market in many of the slick magazines, notably *The Saturday Evening Post*. These magazines were a rich source for anthology stories. A partial list of these late and lamented pulp magazines in this genre makes obvious the popularity of the genre:

Ace-High Magazine: Real Western Stories

Big-Book Western

Cowboy Stories

Dime Western Magazine

Double Action Western

Famous Western

Pioneer Western

Ranch Romances

Rangeland Romances

Real Western Romances

Star Western

Texas Rangers

West

Western Story Magazine

Wild West Stories

Wild West Weekly

Since 1953 the Western Writers of America has edited an annual anthology, each on a theme of the western story. All stories are by members, and each volume is a good introduction to the writers in the genre. A few of the anthology titles reveal the use of themes: *Badmen and Good*; *The Fall Roundup*; *Holsters and Heroes*; *Branded West*; *The Wild Horse Roundup*; *Wild Streets*; *Trails of Adventure*; *Rawhide Men*; *They Opened the West*; *Iron Men and Silver Stars*; *Hoof Trails and Wagon Tracks*; *Rivers to Cross*. Most of the following anthologies are several years old, but the stories are ageless:

Collier, Ned., ed. *Great Stories of the West*. Doubleday, 1971.

Durham, Philip, and Everett L. Jones, eds. *The Western Story: Fact, Fiction, and Myth*. Harcourt, 1975.
    The fiction section has stories by Bret Harte, Jack London, Owen Wister, Stephen Crane, Clarence Mulford, Zane Grey, Vardis Fisher, Ernest Haycox, Max Brand, John M. Cunningham, Clay Fisher, Luke Short, Allan Bosworth, Thomas Thompson, Donald Hamilton, and Walter Van Tilburg Clark.

Knight, Damon, ed. *Westerns of the 40's: Classics from the Great Pulps*. Bobbs-Merrill, 1977.

Lenniger, August, ed. *Western Writers of America: Silver Anniversary Anthology*. Ace, 1977.

Maule, Harry E. *Pocket Book of Western Stories*. Pocket Books, 1945.
    Reprinted as *Great Tales of the American West*. Modern Library, 1945.

The Saturday Evening Post Reader of Western Stories. Doubleday, 1960.

Schaefer, Jack, ed. *Out West: An Anthology of Stories*. Houghton, 1955.

Short, Luke, ed. *Cattle, Guns and Men*. Bantam, 1955.

Targ, William, ed. *Western Story Omnibus*. World, 1945.
    Reprinted by Penguin as *Great Western Stories*.

Taylor, J. G., ed. *Great Short Stories of the West*. Ballantine, 1971. 2v.

Ward, Don, ed. *Pioneers West*. Dell, 1966.

Wollheim, D. A., ed. *A Quintet of Sixes.* Ace, 1969.

History and Criticism

Discussion of the western genre novel sometimes encompasses the regional novel of the West as well. While the two types may merge, the regional novel has a quite different plot structure and its authors rarely also write the western genre novel. The following books deal with the western as a genre; the books by Folsom and Milton extend their treatment to the regional novel:

Durham, Philip, and Everett L. Jones, eds. *The Western Story: Fact, Fiction, and Myth.* Harcourt, 1975.
Designed as a textbook. Classes on the western are now offered at the high school and college level. This is an anthology with critical introductions.

Etulain, Richard W., and Michael T. Marsden, eds. *The Popular Western.*
This anthology includes essays on B. M. Bower, Zane Grey, Clay Fisher/Will Henry, Luke Short, Jack Schaefer, and general critical essays.

Etulain, Richard W. "The Western." In Inge, M. Thomas, ed. *Handbook of American Popular Culture.* 1978. Vol. 1, pp. 355-76.

Folsom, J. K. *The American Western Novel.* College and University Press, 1966.
Begins with James Fenimore Cooper; the discussion is critical but selective of authors.

Gruber, Frank. "The Basic Western Novel Plots." In *Writer's Year Book,* 1955: 49-53, 160.

Milton, John R. *The Novel of the American West.* University of Nebraska Press, 1980.
The first chapter is on "The Popular or Formula Western," and the author then discusses those novels on the West that are "a higher form of literature, not a genre."

Sonnichsen, C. L. *From Hopalong to Hud: Thoughts on Western Fiction.* Texas A&M University Press, 1978.
The author's collected essays on the West of fact and "The West That Wasn't" include essays on the unheroic hero, sex, and violence in the western, fictional treatment of the Indian, and the influence of motion picture interpretations.

Tuska, Jon. "The Westerner Returns." *West Coast Review of Books* 4 (#6, 1978), pp. 73-79.
A discussion of Sonnichsen's *From Hopalong to Hud* and the Gregg Press Western Fiction series (listed below under reprint publishers) is a critical evaluation of the western genre.

Background on the West

Books on the American West in all its aspects are myriad. Many are specialized, e.g., on the history of barbed wire in the West. University presses in the western states, particularly the University of Oklahoma Press, publish Western Americana regularly. Both university and commercial press publications are often full of illustrations. The few listed here are intended to suggest the diversity offered:

Adams, Ramon F. *Western Words: A Dictionary of the American West.* New Edition, Revised and Enlarged. University of Oklahoma Press, 1968.
 The definitions reveal the way of life with humor and anecdotes. "Wish book. A cowboy's term for a mail order catalog...." "Montgomery Ward woman sent west on approval. A homely woman...."

Bergon, Frank, and Zeese Papanikolas, eds. *Looking Far West: The Search for the American West in History, Myth, and Literature.* NAL, 1978.
 An imaginatively selected anthology, with sections on the mountain man, "The Wild West," and western films suggesting its diversity.

Brown, Dee. *The Gentle Tamers: Women of the Old West.* University of Nebraska Press, 1968.
 First edition, 1958. They came as settlers, army wives, shady ladies, schoolmarms, mail order brides and were always in short supply. There is lively quotation from journals and letters.

Horan, James D. *The Authentic Wild West.* Crown, 1976-1980. 3v.
 The volumes are subtitled: *The Gunfighters, The Outlaws, The Lawmen.*

Myers, John Myers. *Print in a Wild Land.* Doubleday, 1967.
 They were hungry for news, and the tramp printers were seemingly always on hand in cow town or mining town. Bret Harte and Mark Twain wrote for the frontier newspapers. The editors, notably eccentric and often drunken, enliven the history. There are many selections, hilarious and poetical, from the multitude of newspapers.

Steckmesser, K. L. *The Western Hero in History and Legend.* University of Oklahoma Press, 1965.
 Four types are discussed: "The Mountain Man: Kit Carson"; "The Outlaw: Billy the Kid"; "The Gunfighter: Wild Bill Hickok"; "The Soldier: George Armstrong Custer."

The Cowboy

The great American folk hero—his image in fact, myth, picture, music, and motion picture provides the matter of an awesome bibliography. Many of the following books contain reference to the cowboy as represented in the western genre novel:

Branch, Douglas. *The Cowboy and His Interpreters.* Cooper Square, 1961.
 First published in 1926 and still possibly the most interesting analysis of fact, legend, and the novel. Illustrated by Will James, Joe de Yong, and Charles M. Russell.

Frantz, Joe B., and Julian Ernest Choate, Jr. *The American Cowboy: The Myth and Reality.* University of Oklahoma Press, 1955.
 Illustrated with photographs by Erwin E. Smith from the Library of Congress collection. Footnotes and bibliography.

Harris, Charles W., and Buck Rainey, eds. *The Cowboy: Six-Shooters, Songs, and Sex.* University of Oklahoma Press, 1976.

A lively and irreverent anthology with illustrations to match. A few of the essay titles give the flavor: "The 'Reel' Cowboy," "The Pistol Packin' Cowboy," "The Cowboy's Bawdy Music."

Hudson, Wilson M., and Allen Maxwell, eds. *The Sunny Slopes of Long Ago.* Southern Methodist University Press, 1966.

Texas Folklore Society Publication Number 33. Includes: "Cowboy Lingo," by J. A. Lomax; "The Cowboy: His Cause and Cure," by E. M. Rhodes; "The Cowboy's Code," by Paul Patterson; "The American Cowboy," by Andy Adams; "The Cowboy Enters the Movies," by M. C. Boatright.

Life on the Texas Range. Photographs by Erwin E. Smith. Text by J. Evetts Haley. University of Texas Press, 1952.

Photographs of ranch life and the working cowboy at the turn of the century that tell the whole story with artistry.

McCracken, Harold. *The American Cowboy.* Doubleday, 1973.

Art illustrations and photographs illustrate the history of the cowboy and the cattle country from Spanish times.

Meigs, John, ed. *The Cowboy in American Prints.* Sage Books, Swallow Press, 1972.

Seventy-five full page plates, 39 illustrations within the introduction, and 13 on the end papers give a glowing interpretation of the cowboy by nineteenth- and twentieth-century artists.

The Old West: The Cowboys. By the editors of Time-Life Books. With Text by William H. Forbis. Time-Life Books, 1973.

Extensively illustrated with drawings, maps, and photographs. The text is excellent.

Rounds, Glen. *The Cowboy Trade.* Holiday House, 1972.

Delightfully illustrated by the author to show the cowboy at work. For children, but why deny adults the pleasure of a charming and informative text — "... Western story magazines of all kinds were popular in the bunkhouses. The cowboys on paper led vastly more exciting lives than the readers, and such disagreeable subjects as barbed wire stretching and pigpen repairing were seldom mentioned."

Savage, William W., Jr., ed. *Cowboy Life: Reconstructing an American Myth.* University of Oklahoma Press, 1975.

This anthology of contemporary accounts of cowboy life from the 1870s to the turn of the century is fascinating in its variety. The 43 photographs and the narratives are from the Western History Collections of the University of Oklahoma Library.

Savage, William W., Jr. *The Cowboy Hero: His Image in American History and Culture.* University of Oklahoma Press, 1979.

The image is pervasive, drawn not from the working cowboy but from the folk hero embodied in the rodeo performer or the star of horse opera in motion picture and television series. The hero emerges in works of art, comic strips, or cigarette advertising. His garb becomes transmogrified into bizarre fashions.

Cowboy Songs

Cowboy songs are part of American folklore, many deriving from ballads and songs carried from the eastern states. Their popularity is shown in their many versions and in an extensive discography, surely attesting to the enduring interest in the western way of life and its story. The three works listed here are only examples of a large literature:

Ohrlin, Glenn. *The Hell-Bound Train: A Cowboy Songbook*. With a Biblio-Discography by Harlan Daniel. University of Illinois Press, 1973.
    The words and tunes for 100 songs have introductory notes by Ohrlin on the sources of the songs and the old-timers who sang them. Ohrlin, a working cowboy and rodeo rider, is also a folksinger.

Thorp, N. Howard ("Jack"). *Songs of the Cowboys*. Variants, commentary, notes and lexicon, by Austin E. and Alta S. Fife. Music Editor: Naunie Gardner. Clarkson N. Potter, 1966.
    Twenty-three songs and music. Included is a facsimile of Thorp's *Songs of the Cowboys*, printed in Estancia, New Mexico, in 1908.

White, John I. *Git along Little Dogies: Songs and Songmakers of the American West*. With a Foreword by Austin E. Fife. University of Illinois Press, 1975.
    White, the singing "Lonesome Cowboy" on radio's "Death Valley Days," collected material on western songs as well as singing and recording them. These essays present the history of many songs and their often questionable authorship, publishing history, and anecdotes about cowboy singers. Verses and often music are given. There are many illustrations of singers and from the songbooks.

Film—"Horse Opera"

The western motion picture created its own myth of western history that increased the popularity of the western genre worldwide. Many of the motion pictures derived, however loosely, from the genre westerns, and these works on the film contain frequent reference to the western novel. Discussion ranges from consideration of the western film as an art form to sociological analysis.

Brauer, Ralph, and Donna Brauer. *The Horse, the Gun and the Piece of Property: Changing Images of the TV Western*. Bowling Green University Popular Press, 1975.

Calder, Jenni. *There Must Be a Lone Ranger*. London: H. Hamilton, 1974.
    Aspects and periods of western history as depicted in films are discussed, with mention also of the novel.

Cawelti, John G. *The Six-Gun Mystique*. Bowling Green University Popular Press, 1975.

Eyles, Allen. *The Western*. A. S. Barnes, 1975.

Fenin, George N., and William K. Everson. *The Western from Silents to the Seventies*. Rev. ed. Penguin Books, 1977.
    This is a large-format paperback with extensive illustration and excellent critical text.

French, Philip. *Westerns: Aspects of a Movie Genre.* London: Secker & Warburg in association with British Film Institute, 1973. Cinema One, number 25. Illustrated.

Horowitz, James. *They Went Thataway.* Dutton, 1976.
A devoted fan of the horse opera from boyhood, the author seeks out and interviews his boyhood heroes. A delightful book. Illustrated.

Miller, Don. *Hollywood Corral.* Popular Library, 1976.
This large-format paperback is a picture book of the Gower Gulch grade-B oat burners and series. (Alas, their like we will never see again.)

Nachbar, Jack, ed. *Focus on the Western.* Prentice-Hall, 1975.
This anthology of essays defines the purposes, influences, and socio-psychological aspects of the western movie. Illustrated.

Pilkington, William T., and Don Graham, eds. *Western Movies.* University of New Mexico Press, 1979.

Tuska, Jon. *The Filming of the West.* Doubleday, 1976.
Discusses the making of the movies as well as their nature. Marvelous illustrations.

Wright, Will. *Six Guns and Society: A Structural Study of the Western.* University of California Press, 1975.
Horse opera is here sociologically considered.

Western Writers of America

The Western Writers of America has a membership of writers of western fact and westerns. It publishes (since 1953) a monthly journal, *The Roundup*, which includes book reviews and is available for subscription by libraries. At its annual convention, "Spur" awards are given in several categories and the Golden Saddleman Award for an "outstanding contribution to the history and legend of the West." The WWA book club is handled by Doubleday.

Publishers

The western is largely published in paperback as original titles and reprints. The only consistent hardback publisher is Doubleday: the Double-D Westerns, originals, about 24 titles a year. Walker has a regular list of a few titles. Harpers still publishes Zane Grey in hardcover, while St. Martin's regularly issues British western authors. An occasional western or historical novel of the West appears from other houses. There is a trend toward reprinting original paperbacks in hardcover. Lippincott announced the reprinting of some Bantam Book originals; Dutton, the hardcover edition of some Louis L'Amour Bantam Book titles; Bantam Books announced the simultaneous publication (1981) of a Louis L'Amour title in trade paperback and hardcover. Almost all the paperback houses publish some westerns, and a few key authors or series are noted here.

Ace: Has the double-book format. Publishes Elmer Kelton, Giles Lutz, Frank Roderus.

Avon

Ballantine: A new logo, "Western &B," appeared in 1980 for reprints of about 12 titles a year, featuring the following authors:

Elmore Leonard, Dorothy M. Johnson, Brian Garfield, A. B. Guthrie, Lee Leighton, Wade Everett.

Bantam Books: In conjunction with Twentieth-Century Fox, Bantam Books sponsored in 1979 the First Western Novel Competition "to encourage the writing of the kind of quality Western fiction that has entertained readers and moviegoers for decades." Bantam will publish and Fox will purchase the film right. A Bantam editor notes: "We are looking for a novel in the tradition of fast-moving, authentic frontier entertainments by such popular masters of the genre as Zane Grey, Ernest Haycox, Luke Short and Louis L'Amour. We at Bantam have long been aware that sufficient public attention is seldom paid to the quality of writing in the Western genre." The first winner was: *Season of Vengeance*, by W. W. Southard. Among Bantams authors are:

Louis L'Amour, Gary McCarthy's Derby Man series, Clay Fisher, Will Henry, Will Cook, Elmore Leonard, Wayne Overholser, and others.

Bantam publishes the Wagons West series.

Belmont Towers

Berkley: Publishes J. T. Edson's Floating Outfit series.

Dell: Four new series announced 1980.

Fawcett: Publishes Jonas Ward's Buchanan series.

Jove: Publishes Longarm series, by Tabor Evans (house name) and a new series was announced for 1981.

Leisure: Publishes Jack Slade's (house name) Lassiter series and Sundance series.

Manor: Publishes Al Cody's Montana Abbott series.

Pinnacle: Publishes four series: Edge, Adam Steel, Apache, Justice.

Playboy: Publishes Jake Logan and J. D. Hardin series. Both are house names.

Pocket Book: Publishes about 24 titles a year. Authors:

Max Brand, Zane Grey, Matthew Braun, Giles Lutz.

Publishes Zeke Masters's Faro Blake series.

Popular Library

Signet (NAL): Publishes Jon Sharpe's Trailsman series. Authors:

Cliff Farrell, Ernest Haycox, Lee Hoffman, Ray Hogan, Luke Short, Lewis B. Patten, William MacLeod Raine.

Warner: Publishes Renegade series by Ramsey Thorne.

HARDCOVER REPRINT PUBLISHERS

While a great number of paperback westerns are reprints, there has been no extensive hardcover reprinting of westerns since the Grosset & Dunlap line of inexpensive reprints of all types of genre fiction stopped appearing. Some westerns are being reprinted by the large print houses that publish for the library market. These few examples show how little is available:

Aeonian Press: Has reprinted Clarence E. Mulford, Charles Alden Seltzer, and others.

Walter J. Black: For many years has reprinted, at low price, the works of Zane Grey.

Gregg Press: Western Fiction series, 15 titles: David Belasco. *The Girl of the Golden West*; Max Brand. *The Untamed*; Edgar Rice Burroughs. *The War Chief. Apache Devil*; Harvey Fergusson. *Wolf Song. Blood of the Conquerors. In Those Days*; Ernest Haycox. *The Border Trumpet. Bugles in the Afternoon*; Louis L'Amour. *Hondo*; Alan LeMay. *The Searchers. The Unforgiven*; Conrad Richter. *Early Americana and Other Stories*; John Williams. *Butcher's Crossing*; Will Henry. *From Where the Sun Now Stands*.

3 Thriller

If you have an intelligent mind and you like to
read, and you read to escape, then you require an
intelligent literature of escape. I make no distinction
between the novel and the thriller.
— Margery Allingham

Suspense is the code word for the thriller: the characters and the reader are in
a constant state of uneasy anticipation of the worst, which all too often happens.
Why this worst looms — threatening happiness and often life — lies in the mystery
to be analyzed or the adventure to be pursued. If the thriller's suspense derives
naturally from the characters (and their personalities), the situations of hazard
(physical or psychological), and the social or political setting, then this genre
might seem to fall simply within the confines of the standard or mainstream
novel. What distinguishes the thriller into genre status is the imposition of a
pattern (which is the defining characteristic of all genre) clearly labeling the novel
as a work of detection, mystery, espionage, or adventure. This defining pattern
will be noted as each subgenre of the thriller is described.

The label "thriller" is used in fiction reviewing, usually with reference to the
spy/espionage novel. In this book, the term is used to embrace suspense novels
from detection to adventure. The suspense, which derives from a problem to be
solved, is also inherent in genres discussed in later chapters. However, in these
other genres the suspense may be subordinate to romance, horror, or whatever.
Admittedly, then, the groupings in this guide are somewhat arbitrary. All fiction
essentially begins "Once upon a time," and the reader is enticed to read on, filled
with curiosity or tingling with suspense, to find out what happens next.

THEMES AND TYPES

Detective Story and Detectives

If you look at it properly, detective stories are a
sign of civilization. And the investigation of crime is
a sign of all the good in our modern world.
— C. P. Snow
Death under Sail

The mystery tale involving detection to solve a problem through analysis of
clues — physical evidence and the characteristics of persons — has been ever
present in popular literature. What emerged as new in the nineteenth century was
the formal detective. Historians of this genre speculate on the significance of the

formation of France's Sûreté and England's Scotland Yard (and the earlier Bow Street Runners) as a necessary background for the development of the detective as a credible figure in literature.

The writings on the detective story provide a lively literature on its origins and development, and one aspect only needs to be noted here: the genre naturalized in France, England, and the United States, the countries where strongly organized police forces emerged in the nineteenth century. These three countries are still the source of most of the detective novels now being published and translated for readers throughout the world.

Individual fans may prefer a type or types of detective stories but unite in devotion to the particular detective as a personality. Thus, the detective whose cases are continued through a series of short stories or novels never lacks a readership. The series may be referred to not by the author's but by the detective's name. The fan reads them all, ignoring, but not oblivious of, the quality of any single work. (It thus behooves a reader advisor, starting a neophyte reader on an author, to know *the* particular work to be first read to ensure the reader becoming enchanted with the detective.)

The types of detectives are diverse by occupation, and almost all have some defining eccentricity. Police detectives are the most numerous, appearing in what are labeled "police procedurals" or "romans policier." While detectives from the large city forces are the most common — Scotland Yard, the Sûreté, New York or Los Angeles police departments — there are many from the county CID (Criminal Investigation Department) as well as the village constable in England or state police, sheriff, and small town police chiefs and detectives in the United States. Equal in popularity as detectives are the private investigators who may be lone operators or work out of a large agency. Insurance investigators often function as private investigators. Private detectives fall roughly into two types: the straightforward sleuth much like a police detective and the hard-boiled "private eye." The third type of detective is the amateur, characterized by an inveterate nosiness, who may be of either sex or any occupation. (More information will be provided on these types as examples are listed.)

The pattern in detective stories is determined by a series of events expected by the reader — an incident or catastrophe, preferably murder, demanding the attention of the police and perhaps private or amateur detectives as well; the process of detection; the denouement. The manner in which the pattern is developed is limited only by the imagination of the author, but the detective must be the dominant character. The variation in type of detective and background of the plot may determine the readership.

In tone, the detective story varies dramatically from the comic and polite social comedy to harsh realism and horror. Traditionally, a romance has been frowned upon for the detective but is allowed as a minor theme for secondary characters. A few of the series detectives marry or are married, a matter of small interest in most cases to the readers. However, the sexual affairs, particularly of many private eyes, have provided a colorful part of some detectives' characterization, and there is increasing sexual explicitness, with sensationalism, in many private eye novels. The reader has a wide variation of tones to choose from, ranging from the ladylike gentility of Agatha Christie to the savage crudeness of Mickey Spillane.

Some fans read only British detective stories, others only American. Some prefer police procedurals and may read those from any country; some want their private detectives to be hard-boiled private eyes. There are those who delight in the amateur detective, and those who dote on the genteel social comedy of the English country-house murder. Some devotees eclectically try them all but usually end up with favored authors, types of detectives, or backgrounds. The groupings given here suggest the identification needed in reviews and by reader advisors, with a special section for readers who desire a particular background.

The critics ingeniously analyze why the detective story is so popular. Is it simply the fascination of a mystery or puzzle, enticing the reader to match wits with the detective? For the many readers who do not attempt logically to follow the clues, the appeal may be simply in the mounting suspense before all is finally made clear. Does the story satisfy a desire to find in a disorderly world a pattern of rationality that brings order out of chaos? Is there a vicarious solution to original sin: There but for the grace of God am I?

Note must be made of the recurrent and bluntly definite statement that the detective story is dead, worn out, all its variations and plots tiresomely repetitious. Its patterned artificiality is unrealistic and readers now want the more credible crime story or story of psychological suspense deriving from characters of real life. Neither the crime story nor the psychological-suspense novel substitute for the detective story. (Both, incidentally, are more related to the standard novel, particularly of the sensational and sexy best-seller type, than to the genre detective story.) Crime and psychological-suspense stories frequently concern the mentally marred or psychologically deranged. The detective story may concern such defective characters, but its great attraction for many readers is that the perpetrator of the crime is a normal being (even as you and I!) who succumbs to one of the deadly sins through a flaw of character and not of mind. The police procedural is likely to deal with characters of sick mind but is apt to be a bore if this is the only type of criminal involved in the plot.

The detective story continues to be written, published, and read because of the reader's fascination with the personality of the detective. Age does not alter the detective's appeal: Sherlock Holmes is alive after almost 100 years (1887), as are Hercule Poirot (1920), Lord Peter Wimsey (1923), Sam Spade (1930), Jules Maigret (1931), Nero Wolfe (1934), John Appleby (1936), and Philip Marlowe (1939). They are all very much in print in hardcover and paperback, being discovered by succeeding generations of readers. When the devotee of the detective cannot find new detective stories with the type of detective the reader demands, the reader's recourse is clear—back to rereading the old favorites (which may be done periodically anyway). The detective, the more eccentric the better, has become a folk hero.

POLICE DETECTIVES

Police procedurals are a large component in the bibliography of the detective novel. (The French term, *romain policier*, appears frequently in works on the detective story.) The detective of the story usually belongs to an actual named police department, although all personnel are fictional. Scotland Yard, the Sûreté, and the police departments of New York, Los Angeles, and San Francisco are the most commonly used. However, many writers in England use the local police in areas outside London, inventing a rural town or using one of the larger cities, such as Oxford. Authors in the United States gain a distinctively regional tone by using cities or small towns other than New York, Los Angeles, or San Francisco. British and American writers also use countries other than Great

Britain or the United States to provide an exotic setting. As the following listing by country indicates, there are fewer police procedurals from foreign countries, at least available in translation, than for Great Britain and the United States.

The detective in the police procedural must function within the rules of the police department, lacking the freedom of the private detective. Although the pattern may vary because of the personality of the detective, most police detectives work as part of a team, while the private detective is often a loner. Two plot patterns are common. One uses a single murder (or several linked murders) or mystery for the basic plot. The other, in effect, uses the police blotter: every case followed up by the police station staff is observed in varying degrees, although one case is the key focus of detection, and often the other cases are ingeniously linked to the main crime.

As a type, the police detective may seem circumscribed in character by the very nature of police procedures. Nevertheless, writers of police procedurals have been able to create detectives with interesting, often eccentric, personalities so that the readers eagerly follow their cases in book after book. The police detective may be an educated gentleman or a street-wise tough, with a wide range of variations in between. Regional, class, and ethnic backgrounds allow for intriguing diversity in the types of detectives. A recent and welcome addition to the ranks of fictional police detectives has been women; several are noted in the following list.

The authors are listed below by the country to which the police detective belongs. Great Britain is further subdivided; there are several series about the Bow Street Runners, the early nineteenth-century precursors of Scotland Yard; and Scotland Yard detectives are grouped separately from those in the rest of Great Britain. Under the United States heading, a separate section is provided for California, where crime thrives.

Australia

Cleary, Jon (Detective Sergeant Scobie Malone)

Upfield, Arthur (Inspector Napoleon "Bony" Bonaparte, half-caste aborigine)

Brazil

Fish, Robert L. (Captain José da Silva)

Canada

Trevanian (H. Claude LaPointe, Montreal)

China

Van Gulik, Robert (Judge Dee, seventh century)

Denmark

Nielsen, Torben (Superintendent Archer)

Ørum, Poul (Detective Inspector Jonas Morck, Copenhagen)

France

Audemars, Pierre (Inspector Pinaud, Sûreté)

Freeling, Nicolas (Henri Castang)

Grayson, Richard (Inspector Gautier, Sûreté)

Hebden, Mark (Inspector Evariste Clovis Désiré Pel)

Jacquemard, Yves, and Jean-Michel Sénécal (Superintendent Dullac)

Kotzwinkle, William (Inspector Picard)

Simenon, Georges (Inspector Maigret)

Germany

Kirst, Hans Hellmut (Anton Keller, CID, Munich)

Great Britain—Bow Street Runners

Falkirk, Richard (Edmund Blackstone)

Foxall, Raymond (Harry Adkins)

Jeffreys, J. G. (Jeremy Sturrock)

SeBastian, Margaret (Ned Denning)

Great Britain—Scotland Yard

Allen, Michael (Detective Chief Superintendent Ben Spence)

Ashe, Gordon (Patrick Dawlish, freelance before joins the Yard)

Butler, Gwendoline (Inspector Coffin)

Clark, Douglas (Superintendent Masters and Inspector Green)

Cole, G. D. H., and Margaret Cole (Superintendent Henry Wilson)

Crisp, N. J. (Detective Inspector Kenyon)

Crofts, Freeman Wills (Inspector Joseph French)

Deighton, Len (Detective Inspector Douglas Archer, *SS-GB*)

Dickinson, Peter (Inspector James Pibble)

Gardner, John (Detective Inspector Derek Torry)

Garve, Andrew (Chief Inspector Charles Grant)

Heyer, Georgette (Chief Inspectors Hannasyde and Hemingway)

Hill, Peter (Chief Superintendent Robert Staunton and Detective Inspector Leo Wyndsor)

Hilton, John Buxton (Inspector Kenworthy; Detective Thomas Brunt, nineteenth century)

Hunter, John (Chief Superintendent George Gently)

Innes, Michael (Inspector later Sir John Appleby, and also in retirement)

James, P. D. (Commander Adam Dalgliesh)

Jones, Elwyn (Detective Chief Superintendent Barlow)

Kenyon, Michael (Inspector Henry Peckover)

Lemarchand, Elizabeth (Detective Inspector Tom Pollard and Inspector Gregory Toye)

Lewis, Roy (Inspector Crow)

Lovesey, Peter (Sergeant Cribb and Constable Thackeray, nineteenth century)

McKenzie, Donald (Detective Inspector Raven, retired)

Marric, J. J. (Commander Gideon)

Marsh, Ngaio (Inspector Roderick Alleyn)

Martin, Ian Kennedy (Inspector Jack Regan)

Moyes, Patricia (Chief Superintendent Henry Tibbett and his wife Emmy)

Perry, Anne (Inspector Pitt, nineteenth century)

Selwyn, Francis (Sergeant Verity, nineteenth century)

Stubbs, Jean (Inspector Lintott, nineteenth century)

Symons, Julian (Inspector Bland)

Tey, Josephine (Inspector Alan Grant)

Wainwright, John (Chief Inspector Lennox)

Winslow, Pauline (Superintendent Merle Capricorn and Inspector Copper)

Parodies of Scotland Yard

Giles, Kenneth (Inspector Harry James and Sergeant Honeybody)

Porter, Joyce (Inspector Dover)

Great Britain—Other than Scotland Yard

Aird, Catherine (Inspector Sloan)

Anderson, J. R. L. (Chief Constable Pier Deventer)

Ashford, Jeffrey (Detective Inspector Don Kerry)

Burley, W. J. (Chief Superintendent Wycliffe)

Dexter, Colin (Chief Inspector Morse, Oxford)

Gilbert, Michael (Chief Superintendent Charlie Knott)

Hill, Reginald (Superintendent Dalziel and Sergeant Pascoe)

Hoch, Edward D. (Jeffrey Rand, Department of Concealed Communications)

Knox, Bill (Colin Thane and Phil Moss, Glasgow; Webb Carrick, Fishery Protection Service)

McIlvanney, William (Detective Inspector Laidlaw, Glasgow)

Melville, Jennie (Sergeant Charmian Daniels)

Peters, Ellis (Detective Inspector George Felse)

Radley, Sheila (Chief Inspector Douglas Quantrill, Suffolk)

Rendell, Ruth (Chief Inspector Wexford and Inspector Borden)

Great Britain — Other than Scotland Yard (cont'd)

Scott, Jack S. (Detective Sergeant Rosher)

Thomson, June (Detective Inspector Finch: in U.S. editions, Detective Inspector Rudd)

Watson, Colin (Inspector Purbright and Miss Teatime)

Webster, Noah (Jonathan Gaunt, Treasury agent)

Hong Kong

Marshall, William (Chief Harry Feiffer)

Sela, Owen (Chief Inspector Chan)

India

Keating, Henry R. F. (Inspector Ghote, Bombay)

Ireland

Gill, Bartholomew (Chief Inspector McGarr, Dublin)

Kenyon, Michael (Detective Superintendent O'Malloy)

Israel

Klinger, Henry (Captain Shomri Shomar)

Italy

Fruttero, Carlo, and Franco Lucentini. *The Sunday Woman.*

Quinn, Simon (Francis Xavier Killy, Inquisitor series, investigator for the Vatican)

Japan

Melville, James (Superintendent Otani, Tokyo)

Mexico

Blanc, Suzanne (Inspector Menendes, Indian, *The Green Stone*)

Netherlands

Freeling, Nicolas (Inspector Van der Valk)

Wetering, Janwillem van de (Detective Grijpstra and Detective Sergeant de Grier)

New Zealand

Mantell, Laurie (Chief Inspector Peacock)

Norway

Barnard, Robert (Inspector Fagermo, *Death in a Cold Climate*)

South Africa

McClure, James (Lieutenant Tromp Kramer, Afrikaner and Detective Sergeant Zondi, Bantu)

Spain (Mallorca)
Jeffries, Roderic (Detective Inspector Enrique Alvarez)

Sweden
Blom, K. Arne
Högstrand, Olle (Chief Inspector Lars Kollin)
Hubert, Tord
Sjöwall, Maj, and Per Wahlöö (Martin Beck)

Switzerland
, Campbell, R. Wright (Inspector Yves Faucon)

United States
Arrighi, Mel (Detective Romano, New York)

Bagby, George (Inspector Schmidt, New York)

Baxt, George (Pharoah Love, black, New York; Detective Van Larsen)

Biggers, Earl Derr (Inspector Charlie Chan, Honolulu P.D., Territory of Hawaii)

Burns, Rex (Gabriel Wager, Chicano, Denver)

Caspary, Vera (Mark McPherson, New York, *Laura*)

Charyn, Jerome (Isaac Sidel, New York)

Chastain, Thomas (Deputy Chief Inspector Max Kauffman, New York)

Constantine, K. C. (Chief of Police Mario Balzic, Rocksburg, Pennsylvania)

Delman, David (Lieutenant Jacob Horowitz, Nassau Co., N.Y.)

Garfield, Brian (Sam Watchman, Navajo, Arizona Highway Patrol)

The Gordons (FBI agents)

Guthrie, A. B. (Sheriff Chick Charleston and boy, Jason Beard)

Hillerman, Tony (Lieutenant Joe Leaphorn, Navajo Reservation Police)

Himes, Chester (Coffin Ed Johnson and Grave Digger Jones, Harlem)

Hinkemeyer, Michael T. (Sheriff Whippletree, Minnesota)

Jackson, Jon A. (Sergeant Mulheisen, Detroit)

Kamarck, Lawrence (Chief of Police Charles Skagg, black, New England)

King, Rufus (Stuff Driscoll, Florida)

Langton, Jane (Homer Kelly, retired detective, Massachusetts)

Lewin, Michael Z. (Lieutenant Leroy Powder, Indianapolis)

Lockridge, Richard (Captain Heinrich, New York State Police; Lieutenant Nathan Shapiro, New York)

McBain, Ed (Steve Carolla, 87th Precinct, New York)

McDonald, Gregory (Inspector Francis Xavier Flynn, Boston)

United States (cont'd)

O'Donnell, Lillian (Norah Mulcahony, New York; Detective Ed Stiebeck and Mici Anhalt, New York)

Queen, Ellery (Ellery Queen, "amateur" detective son of Inspector Richard Queen, New York)

Reilly, Helen (Inspector McKee, New York)

Rennert, Maggie (Detective Lieutenant Guy Silvestri, Buxford, Massachusetts)

Rifkin, Shepard (Detective Damian McQuaid, New York)

Sanders, Lawrence (Edward X. Delancy, retired Chief of Detectives, New York)

Stern, Richard Martin (Lieutenant Johnny Ortiz, Apache)

Thorp, Roderick (Joe Leland)

Uhnak, Dorothy (Detective Christie Opara, New York)

Waugh, Hillary (Police Chief Fred Fellows, Connecticut; Detective Fred Sessions, New York)

United States—California

Ball, John (Virgil Tibbs, black, Pasadena)

Boucher, Anthony (Lieutenant Jackson, Los Angeles)

Crowe, John (Sheriff Beckett, Buena Costa)

Cunningham, E. V. (Masao Masuto, Nisei, Beverly Hills)

Dunne, John Gregory (Tom Spellacy, Los Angeles, *True Confessions*)

Egan, Lesley (Detective Varallo, Glendale)

Gillis, Jackson (Jonas Duncan, Los Angeles, retired)

Harris, Alfred (Baroni, Southern California)

Lewis, Lange (Detective Tuck, Los Angeles, *The Birthday Murder*)

Linington, Elizabeth (Sergeant Maddox, Hollywood)

Ludwig, Jerry (Detective Sergeant Edward Brenner, Los Angeles)

Pike, Robert L. (Lieutenant Jim Reardon, San Francisco)

Shannon, Dell (Lieutenant Luis Mendoza, Los Angeles)

Wambaugh, Joseph (Los Angeles Police Department)

Weston, Carolyn (Detective Casey Kellog and Sergeant Al Krug, Santa Monica)

Wilcox, Collin (Lieutenant Hastings, San Francisco)

USSR

Litvinov, Ivy (*His Master's Voice*, Moscow, first published 1930, revised 1973)

Smith, Martin Cruz (Chief Homicide Investigator Arkady Renko, *Gorky Park*)

West Indies

York, Andrew (Colonel James Munroe Tallant, black police commissioner, Caribbean Island)

PRIVATE DETECTIVES

The official private detective is of two types—the employee of a large agency; a one- or two-man (or women) operator. Dashiell Hammett created two immortal prototypes: the Continental Op, simply identified for his agency and never named; Sam Spade, a lone-wolf operator after his partner is killed in *The Maltese Falcon.* Sam Spade is also the prototype for the hard-boiled private eye, a type often short on morals but long on integrity. Although not officially labeled private detective, other investigators function as such because of the demands of their occupations: insurance investigators, reporters, psychiatrists, public relations men, bankers. (Lawyers and doctors also qualify and are grouped separately in later sections.) Except for the insurance investigators, these job-related detectives could be considered among the amateur detectives. The distinction is not vital to most readers—what they want is an investigator who acts like a private detective. Readers who prefer the inquisitive amateur as detective may like some of the ones listed below, at least those in which the non-official private investigator acts more like the amateur than the private detective.

France

Demouzon, Alain (Robert Flecheux)

Great Britain

Blake, Nicholas (Nigel Strangeways)

Bush, Christopher (Ludovic Travers, insurance investigator)

Butler, Ragan (Captain Nash, eighteenth century)

Carmichael, Harry (John Piper, insurance investigator; Quinn, crime reporter)

Christie, Agatha (Tuppence and Tommy Beresford, Hercule Poirot)

Copper, Basil (Clyde Beattie, nineteenth century)

Creasey, John (Emmanuel Cellini, psychiatrist)

Doyle, Sir Arthur Conan (Sherlock Holmes)

Francis, Dick (Sid Halley)

Fredman, Mike (Willie Halliday, vegetarian and Buddhist)

Gilbert, Michael (Peter Manciple, insurance investigator, *The Empty House*)

Heald, Tim (Simon Bognor, Board of Trade investigator)

James, P. D. (Cordelia Gray, *An Unsuitable Job for a Woman*)

Kirk, Michael (Andrew Laird, insurance investigator)

Mitchell, Gladys (Dame Beatrice Bradley, psychiatrist)

Norman, Frank (Ed Nelson)

Great Britain (cont'd)

Wentworth, Patricia (Miss Maude Silver)

Williams, David (Mark Treasure, banker)

Yuill, P. B. (James Hazell)

United States

Avallone, Michael (Ed Noon)

Bergman, Andrew (Jack Le Vine)

Bleeck, Oliver (Philip St. Ives, insurance company "go-between")

Block, Lawrence (Scudder, New York)

Box, Edgar (Peter Cutler Sargent III, public relations man. Reprints of the Box novels now reveal the author's real name, Gore Vidal.)

Branston, Frank (Tommy Tompkins, reporter)

Braun, Lilian Jackson (Sim Quilleran, reporter and his Siamese cat)

Burke, J. F. (Sam Kelly, black, house dick, New York)

Chaber, M. E. (Milo March, insurance investigator)

Chesboro, George C. (Dr. Robert "Mongo" Frederickson, dwarf, Ph.D.)

Coe, Tucker (Mitch Tobin, museum night guard, New York)

Coffey, Brian (Harris, clairvoyant, New York)

Collins, Michael (Dan Fortune, one-armed, New York)

Coxe, George Harmon (Jack Fenner, Boston; Ken Murdock, photographer)

Crumley, James (Sughrue, Montana; Milo Milodragovitch, Pacific Northwest)

Daly, Elizabeth (Henry Gammadge, rare book investigator)

DeAndrea, William L. (Matt Cobb, television troubleshooter, *Dead in the Ratings*)

Dewey, Thomas B. (Mac, Chicago)

Downing, Warwick (Joe Reddman, Cheyenne, Denver)

Ellin, Stanley (John Milano, *Star Light, Star Bright*)

Estleman, Loren D. (Amos Walter, Detroit)

Foote-Smith, Elizabeth (Will Woodfield and Mercy Newcastle)

Gunn, James (Kirk "Casey" Cullen, aka Gabriel)

Halliday, Brett (Mike Shayne)

Hansen, Joseph (David Brandstetter, homosexual, insurance investigator)

Hoch, Edward D. (Simon Ark, supernatural, 2000 years old)

Kaplan, Arthur (Charity Bay, New York)

Kaye, Marvin (Hilary Quayle, public relations woman)

Knickmeyer, Steve (Steve Cranmer, Oklahoma City)

Lathen, Emma (John Putnam Thatcher, economic analyst, attorney, executive vice-president of a trust company)

Law, Janice (Anne Peters, Washington, DC)

Leonard, Elmore (Frank Ryan, process server)

Lewin, Michael Z. (Albert Samson, Indianapolis)

Lore, Phillips (Leo Roi, attorney turned private eye, Evanston, Illinois)

MacDonald, John D. (Travis McGee, Florida)

Maling, Arthur (Brockton Potter, stock broker)

O'Neill, Archie (Jeff Pride, travel agent)

Parker, Robert B. (Spenser, Boston)

Pentecost, Hugh (Julian Quist, public relations man)

Philips, Judson (Peter Styles, reporter)

Reed Ishmael (Papa LaBas, "Hoo-Doo" private eye)

Rosten, Leo (Sidney "Silky" Pincus, New York)

Sanders, Lawrence (Joshua Bigg, law firm investigator, *The Tenth Commandment*)

Spillane, Mickey (Mike Hammer)

Stein, Aaron Marc (Matt Erridge)

Stout, Rex (Nero Wolfe, New York)

Tidyman, Ernest (John Shaft, New York)

United States — California

Alverson, Charles (Joe Goodey, San Francisco)

Boucher, Anthony (Fergus O'Breen, Los Angeles)

Chandler, Raymond (Philip Marlowe, Los Angeles)
Chandler, like Hammett, wrote only a few novels (seven, the first in 1939) and short stories, but these established his detective, Philip Marlowe, as a standard aspired to by later writers. Marlowe is the loner, white knight, tough private eye whose personality dominates the novels. Chandler is notable for his image-laden style and for the portrayal, cherished by Angelenos, of Los Angeles and its environs in the thirties. (Chandler's critical essays on detective fiction are listed in the section on criticism.)

Durham, Philip. *Down These Mean Streets a Man Must Go: Raymond Chandler's Knight.* University of North Carolina Press, 1963. The title is a quotation from Chandler.

Gross, Miriam, ed. *The World of Raymond Chandler.* Introduction by Patricia Highsmith. London, Weidenfeld, 1977. Fourteen essays on Chandler's life and work.

MacShane, Frank. *The Life of Raymond Chandler.* Dutton, 1976.

Fenedy, Andrew J. (Detective changes his name to Sam Marlowe, *The Man with Bogart's Face.*)

United States — California (cont'd)
Gault, William (Brock Callahan, ex-guard, Los Angeles Rams)

Gores, Joe (Neal Fargo, San Francisco; Daniel Kearny Associates, San Francisco, skip-tracing agency)

Hammett, Dashiell (The Continental Op; Sam Spade; Nick Charles)
Five novels (the first in 1930) and over 70 short stories made Hammett the great name for the American hard-boiled private eye tradition. (A personal opinion: the Continental Op is *the* master creation in the U.S. hard-boiled detective story.) Fans have organized a three-mile Dashiell Hammett Walking Tour in San Francisco. The members of another group, Continental Detective Agency, hold an annual caper, members garbed in twenties style.

Gores, Joe. *Hammett*. A novel about the young Hammett as a detective in San Francisco which, regrettably, does not evoke Hammett.

Nolan, William F. *Dashiell Hammett: A Casebook*. With an introduction by Philip Durham. McNally & Loftin, 1969. Critical evaluation of the works and good biography.

Wolfe, Peter. *Beams Falling: The Art of Dashiell Hammett*. Bowling Green University Popular Press, 1980.

Harris, Timothy (Thomas Kyd, Los Angeles)

Holmes, H. H. (Mike Duncan, Los Angeles)

Huston, Fran (Nicole Sweet, Los Angeles)

Israel, Peter (B. F. Cage, Los Angeles)

Kaminsky, Stuart (Toby Peters, Los Angeles)

Larson, Charles (Blixen, television executive, Los Angeles)

Lyons, Arthur (Jacob Asch, Los Angeles)

Macdonald, Ross (Lew Archer, Santa Barbara)

Miller, Geoffrey (Terry Traven, Los Angeles, *The Black Glove*)

Platt, Kin (Max Roper, Los Angeles)

Prather, Richard S. (Shell Scott, Los Angeles)

Pronzini, Bill (Nameless detective, San Francisco)

Sadler, Mark (Paul Shaw)

Simon, Roger L. (Moses Wine, Los Angeles)

Solomon, Brad (Fritz Thieringer and Maggie McGuare, Los Angeles, *The Open Shadow*)

Upton, Robert (Amos McGuffin, Los Angeles)

Wager, Walter (Alison Gordon, Los Angeles)

Wilcox, Collin (Stephen Drake, crime reporter)

Humorous Private Eye

The ranks of witty, sardonic, and comic private eyes could be extended at great length. Here is a sampling to indicate that crime or murder is often treated lightly:

Fair, A. A. (Donald Lam and Bertha Cool)

Page, Marco (Joel Glass)

Rice, Craig (Jake Malone, lawyer)

Parody

Because of the eccentric personal characteristics that make the individual detective memorable and the subgenre's formula conventions, the detective is easily parodied. (Some parodies of Sherlock Holmes and Lord Peter Wimsey are noted later.) Some fictional detectives are so eccentric as to become unintentional parodies of the type. The following examples are intentional. (See also the section on parody under detective story criticism.)

Berger, Thomas. *Who Is Teddy Villanova?*

Brautigan, Richard. *Dreaming of Babylon.*

Spencer, Ross H. (Chance Purdue). The epigraphs are inspired lunacy.

AMATEUR DETECTIVES

The amateur detective may be simply nosy, inquisitively becoming involved in mysteries natural to the amateur's ordinary life. Others are in somewhat unusual occupations. Most have their share of eccentricities. Unlike either the police or private investigators, they have no official responsibilities. Indeed they are often an annoyance to the police. Their means of investigation are limited, though they often cooperatively work with the police. Women are often amateur detectives, with the curious spinster being a stereotype (additional examples are found in the later section on women detectives). Here are a few amateurs with their occupation noted, followed by groupings of doctor, lawyer, and rogue or thief:

Asimov, Isaac. *Tales of the Black Widowers.* (Henry, a waiter)

Brett, Simon (Charles Paris, actor)

Delving, Michael (Dave Cannon, Bob Eddison, antiquarian dealers)

Dolson, Hildegarde (Lucy Ramsdale, New England lady, with police Inspector James McDougal)

Dominic, R. B. (Ben Safford, congressman)

Foley, Rae (Hiram Potter, New York society figure)

Forrest, Richard (Lyon Wentworth, juvenile fiction writer)

Francis, Dick (jockey, horse trainer, or whatever connected with British horse racing)

Gash, Jonathan (Lovejoy, antiques dealer)

Kallen, Lucille (C. B. Greenfield, newspaper editor, and Maggie Rome, reporter)

Leather, Edwin (Rupert Conway, art dealer)

Mancini, Anthony (Minnie Santangelo, elderly resident of New York's Little Italy)

Pentecost, Hugh (Pierre Chambrun, hotel manager)

Post, Melville Davisson (Uncle Abner, Virginia rancher)

Scherf, Margaret (Dr. Grace Severance, rich recluse, Las Vegas)

Taylor, Phoebe Atwood (Asey Mayo, New Englander)

Doctor

The doctor is a natural amateur as is the nurse, being often involved with suspicious or unnatural death. (Hospital backgrounds are often used effectively. A classic is Christianna Brand's Inspector Cockrill novel, *Green for Danger*, and P. D. James has used the background effectively in her Commander Dalgleish series.) In the following list, the doctor or nurse is the actual sleuth; all are series characters except Priestley's Dr. Salt:

Bell, Josephine (Dr. David Wintringham)

Duke, Madelaine (Dr. Norah North)

Eberhart, Mignon Good (Nurse Sarah Keate)

Freeman, Lucy (Dr. Ames, psychiatrist)

Freeman, R. Austin (Dr. Thorndyke, scientific medical-jurisprudence)

McCloy, Helen (Dr. Basil Willing, forensic psychiatrist)

Priestley, J. B. (Dr. Salt, *Salt Is Leaving*)

Rinehart, Mary Roberts (Nurse Adams, *Miss Pinkerton*)

Wyllie, John (Dr. Quarshie, black West African physician)

Lawyer

The lawyer might qualify as a private investigator more than an amateur as he seeks to extricate a client from jeopardy. This type of detective story often features scenes of courtroom interrogation in which all is revealed, often dramatically. In some of the following books, the reader is treated to considerable analysis of the law, which is sometimes a bit confusing when the focus is on British jurisprudence.

Cecil, Henry
    The detection and mystery in this British author's novels are urbane social comedy concerning both lawyers and judges. *Daughters in Law* features women lawyers.

Donahue, Jack (Harlan Cole, Texas)

Egan, Lesley (Jesse Falkenstein, Los Angeles)

Gardner, Erle Stanley
Over 80 novels (the first in 1933) celebrate Perry Mason with his aides, Paul Drake and Della Street. Gardner's total is about 103 volumes.

Fugate, Francis L., and Roberta B. Fugate. *Secrets of the World's Best-Selling Writer: The Storytelling Techniques of Erle Stanley Gardner.* Morrow, 1980.

Hughes, Dorothy B. *Erle Stanley Gardner: The Case of the Real Perry Mason.* Morrow, 1978.

Gilbert, Anthony (Arthur Crook, British)

Hare, Cyril (Frank Pettigrew, British)

Hensley, Joe L. (Don Robak)

Kruger, Paul (Phil Kramer, Colorado)

Mortimer, John (Horace Rumpole of the Bailey)

Nielsen, Helen (Simon Drake, Los Angeles)

Thompson, Gene (Dade Cooley, Malibu, *Murder Mystery*)

Traver, Robert (*Anatomy of a Murder*)

Woods, Sara (Antony Maitland, British)

Yarbro, Chelsea Quinn (Charles Spotted Moon, Ojiba, San Francisco)

Rogue or Thief

The tradition of rogue or thief as detective is so well established in detective novels as to negate the amateur status, but this is a convenient niche for listing. Some private investigators skirt the fringes of roguery. The rogues in the following novels are all cheerfully amoral:

Block, Lawrence
Bernard Rhodenbarr is a burglar who runs a bookstore on the side. One of his adventures, *The Burglar Who Liked to Quote Kipling*, will intrigue those who like bibliography and rare books mixed with murder.

Bonfiglioli, Kyril (Honorable Charles Mortdecai, rogue)

Charteris, Leslie (Simon Templar, "The Saint," Robin Hood type)

Creasey, John (The Honorable Richard Rollison, "The Toff," gentleman burglar, "The poor man's Lord Peter Wimsey.")

Hoch, Edward D. (Nick Velvet, thief)

Hornung, E. W.
The exploits of Raffles, gentleman cracksman, have been continued by Barry Perowne.

Morton, Anthony
Reprints reveal the authorship by John Creasey, who used this pseudonym for the cases of John Mannering, "The Baron," jewel thief turned detective.

Parrish, Frank (Don Mallett, poacher, British)

Ecclesiastical

The souls of sinners are one of the responsibilities of the clergy, who are often concerned with proving innocence as well as with finding the guilty. As the listing demonstrates, the practice of detection is open to all religious groups.

Byfield, Barbara Ninde (Simon Bede, Anglican priest and photo-journalist Helen Bullock)

Chesterton, G. K. (Father Brown, Roman Catholic, British)

Holmes, H. H. (Sister Mary Ursula, Order of the Sisters of Martha of Bethany, Los Angeles. Also reprinted under the better known pseudonym Anthony Boucher)

Holton, Leonard (Father Bredder, Franciscan, Los Angeles)

Kemelman, Harry (Rabbi David Small, New England)

Kienzle, William (Father Bob Koesler, Roman Catholic, Detroit)

McInerny, Ralph (Father Dowling, Roman Catholic, Chicago area)

Peters, Ellis (Brother Cadfael, Benedictine monastery, Shrewsbury, twelfth century)

Smith, Charles (Reverend C. P. Randolph, Episcopal Church, Chicago)

English Aristocrat

That everyone loves a lord is a questionable truism, but many detective story readers are intrigued by the aristocrat as amateur detective. There is a similarity to the gentleman detective, whether as police or amateur: Ngaio Marsh's Inspector Roderick Alleyn, Michael Innes's Sir John Appleby, S. S. Van Dine's Philo Vance, and Ellery Queen are a few examples. Members of the British aristocracy appear regularly in the British thriller, often as the corpse, and are natural characters in the popular "English Country House Mystery" (see the division under "Detective Story Settings and Subjects" in a later section). Here are three notable aristocrats as detectives:

Allingham, Margery (Albert Campion)

Dickinson, Peter (King of England, *King and Joker*)

Sayers, Dorothy L. (Lord Peter Wimsey)

Academic

A later section in this chapter lists some novels with an academic background, but professors are not necessarily the detectives. Here are professors who use their scholarly training for crime detection, not always on the campus. That obvious characteristic of academics, eccentricity, is present in most of the detectives listed below:

Arnold, Margot (Penelope Spring and Tobias Glendower, Oxford professors)

Clinton-Baddeley, V. C. (Dr. Davie, Cambridge don)

Crispin, Edmund (Dr. Gervase Fen, Oxford don)

Cross, Amanda (Dr. Kate Fansler, professor of English, New York)

Davey, Jocelyn (Ambrose Usher, philosopher, Oxford don)

Hopkins, Kenneth (Dr. William Blow, 81, and Professor Gideon Munciple, 79, British)

Kemelman, Harry (Professor Nicky Welt, United States)

McCloud, Charlotte (Professor Peter Shandy, New England)

WOMEN DETECTIVES

> The idea seems gaining ground in many quarters
> that in cases of mere suspicion, women detectives are
> more satisfactory than men, for they are less likely to
> attract attention.
> —Catherine Louisa Pirkis,
> nineteenth-century author

The species deadlier than the male appears in all the types of detective stories. In her nineteenth-century origins in the genre, the woman detective tended to lean heavily on intuition but in more modern examples, while often remaining womanly, she uses her wits as ably as the male detective. For many fans there is still identification with the stereotyped, sometimes memorable, spinster sleuth, neatly characterized by the vicar in Agatha Christie's first Miss Marple case, *Murder at the Vicarage* (1930): "There is no detective in England equal to a spinster lady of uncertain age with plenty of time on her hands." (For comment on women detectives, see *The Lady Investigates*, by Craig and Cadogan, in the history section and *Murderess Ink*, compiled by Dilys Winn, in the criticism section under "Topics.")

Several of the listings in this category are repeated from other sections:

Carvic, Heron (Miss Seaton, British spinster)

Christie, Agatha (Miss Jane Marple, spinster)

Cody, Liza (*Dupe*, Anna Lee, private eye, London)

Cross, Amanda (Kate Fansler, professor, New York)

Davis, Dorothy Salisbury (Julie Hayes, amateur)

Dolson, Hildegarde (Lucy Ramsdale with Inspector McDougal)

Eberhart, Mignon Good (Nurse Sarah Keate)

Fraser, Antonia (Jemima Shore, television reporter)

Head, Lee (Lexey Jan Palazoni, rich widow)

Isaacs, Susan (Judith Singer, housewife, *Compromising Positions*)

James, P. D. (Cordelia Gray, private investigator, *An Unsuitable Job for a Woman*)

Kaplan, Arthur (Charity Bay, private eye, New York)

Kaye, Marvin (Hilary Quayle, private eye)

Law, Janice (Anne Peters, private eye)

MacLeod, Charlotte (Sarah Kelling, amateur)

Melville, Jennie (Detective Sergeant Charmian Daniels, British)

Meyer, Lynn (Dr. Sarah Chayse, psychiatrist, Boston, *Paperback Thriller*)

Mitchell, Gladys (Dame Beatrice Bradley, psychiatrist)

Moffat, Gwen (Miss Melinda Pink, mountain climber and justice of the peace, Scotland)

Morice, Anne (Tessa Crichton, actress)

Muller, Marcie (Sharon McCone, private eye, San Francisco)

O'Donnell, Lillian (Detective Norah Mulcahaney, New York Police Department)

Palmer, Stuart (Hildegarde Withers, spinster, with Oscar Piper, New York Police Department)

Peters, Elizabeth (Jacqueline Kirby, middle-aged but sexy librarian)

Porter, Joyce (The Honorable Constance Morrison-Burke, busybody)

Scherf, Margaret (Dr. Grace Severance, retired pathologist)

Tey, Josephine (Miss Pym, *Miss Pym Disposes*)

Uhnak, Dorothy (Christie Opara, New York Police Department)

Wager, Walter (Alison Gordon, private eye, Los Angeles)

Watson, Clarissa (Persis Willum, art curator, New York)

Watson, Colin (Lucille Teatime with Inspector Purbright, British)

Wentworth, Patricia (Miss Maude Silver, private investigator)

By way of a footnote to the women detectives, there have been a fair number of women writers of detective fiction who have featured a hapless young heroine narrator who reiterates too often a variation of "had-I-but-known." In the better versions, the heroine is quite tough but still murmurs the refrain. This heroine became the stereotype in the Gothic romance and frequently in the romantic-suspense novel. The "HIBK" detective novel (also known as the "Fluttering Spinsters" School of Detection) is not a series novel: the heroine narrator is involved in the detecting, but there is usually a formal detective, and the heroine ends up safely married. Mary Roberts Rinehart is the queen of this school, notably in *The Album*, 1933 (her first book was in 1908). Mignon Good Eberhart wrote many indistinguishable ones in this style. Mary Collins (*Dead Center*, 1942), and Lenore Offord (*Skeleton Key*, 1943), each wrote several of good quality. The "masterpiece" of the school is Mabel Seeley's *The Listening House*, 1938.

IMMORTAL INVESTIGATORS

Among the immortals would be Dashiell Hammett's detectives and Chandler's Philip Marlowe, both noted previously. Here, then, are detectives who have become beings in their own right through the devotion of readers (included here are the immortal amateurs: the amateur detectives are listed following this section):

Doyle, Sir Arthur Conan (Sherlock Holmes and Dr. John Watson)
Four novels (*The Hound of the Baskervilles*, 1902; *The Sign of the Four*, 1890; *A Study in Scarlet*, 1887; *The Valley of Fear*, 1915) and 56 short stories, some of novella length, comprise the Canon or sacred writings presented with elaborate notes and period illustrations in the two-volume *The Annotated Sherlock Holmes*, edited by William S. Baring-Gould (Crown, 1967). A host of devout followers have continued the Canon in novel and short story.

Fish, Robert L. *The Incredible Schlock Homes. The Memoirs of Schlock Homes.* (A Bagel Street Dozen)

Gardner, John. *The Return of Moriarity.*

Irvine, R. R. (Short stories about Niles Brundage, actor of Sherlock Holmes roles)

Symons, Julian. *The Three-Pipe Problem.* Novel about an actor of Holmes' roles.

Watson, John H. *The Seven-Per-Cent Solution, Being a Reprint from the Reminiscences of John H. Watson, M.D., as edited by Nicholas Meyer.*
With this 1974 pastiche, Nicholas Meyer (who did two more) incited a flood of imitators. These novels portray Sherlock Holmes either in his own period or (as, of course, he still lives!) in modern times. Many of these are of indifferent quality.

Writings about Sherlock Holmes are more voluminous than the Canon. The association of admirers, the Baker Street Irregulars, publishes the *Baker Street Journal* and hosts events honoring Holmes. A novel by Boucher, *The Case of the Baker Street Irregulars*, has several of the Irregulars involved in and trying to solve a murder in Los Angeles.

Bullard, Scott R., and Michael Leo Collins. *Who's Who in Sherlock Holmes.* Taplinger, 1980.

De Waal, Ronald. *The World Bibliography of Sherlock Holmes and Dr. Watson.* New York Graphic Society, 1973.

De Waal, Ronald. *The International Sherlock Holmes.* Archon/Shoe String Press, 1980. Supplement.

Haining, Peter, ed. *The Sherlock Holmes Scrapbook.* Potter, 1974.

Harrison, Michael. *In the Footsteps of Sherlock Holmes.* London: Cassell, 1958.

Harrison, Michael. *The London of Sherlock Holmes.* London: David & Charles, 1972.

McQueen, Ian. *Sherlock Holmes Detected: The Problems of the Long Stories.* Drake, 1974.

Rosenberg, Sam. *Naked Is the Best Disguise: The Death and Resurrection of Sherlock Holmes.* Bobbs-Merrill, 1974.

Tracey, Jack, ed. *Sherlock Holmes: The Published Apocrypha.* Houghton, 1980.

Christie, Agatha (Hercule Poirot, Miss Jane Marple)
"The first lady of crime" has published 83 titles, including originally appearing collections of short stories. (Over 40 of her titles have been reprinted in large-print editions.) Her dapper detective Hercule Poirot, who said one must "employ the little grey cells," appeared in her first novel (*The Mysterious Affair at Styles*, 1920) and 34 other novels, plus some short stories. Miss Jane Marple, inquisitive village spinster, who insisted "human nature is much the same in a village as anywhere else, only one has opportunities and leisure for seeing it at closer quarters," appeared in Christie's eleventh novel (*Murder at the Vicarage*, 1930) and 11 other novels, plus short stories. A comedy detective couple, Tommy and Tuppence, appeared in her second novel (*The Secret Adversary*, 1922), and 3 other novels, plus short stories, but never rivaled the popularity of Poirot and Marple. In 1926 she successfully broke a sacred detective story law by having her narrator as murderer in *The Murder of Roger Ackroyd.* Her *Autobiography* (London: Collins, 1977) reveals the lady and the writer. Here are a few items from a growing bibliography:

Barnard, Robert. *A Talent to Deceive: An Appreciation of Agatha Christie.* Dodd, 1980.
Barnard, a detective novelist, is both very critical and very appreciative. There is an extensive Christie bibliography. One appendix is a delightfully and critically annotated list of over 80 of her titles.

Jacquemard, Yves, and Jean-Michel Sénécal. *The Eleventh Little Indian.* This detective novel featuring Superintendent Hector Parescot, Sûreté, is a spoof tribute to Christie and her *Ten Little Indians.*

Keating, H. R. F., ed. *Agatha Christie: First Lady of Crime.* Holt, 1977. Thirteen essays by her peers, with delightful illustrations. Among the contributors: Julian Symons, Edmund Crispin, Michael Gilbert, Emma Lathan, Colin Watson, Celia Fremlin, Dorothy B. Hughes, Christianna Brand.

Riley, Dick, and Pam McAllister, eds. *The Bedside, Bathtub, and Armchair Companion to Agatha Christie.* Introduction by Julian Symons. Ungar, 1979.
This lavishly illustrated miscellany does have plot summaries. A comparison of these bland summaries with Barnard's (above) critical annotations is edifying.

Toye, Randall, comp. *The Agatha Christie Who's Who.* Holt, 1980.
All the characters, including the minor, are identified.

Sayers, Dorothy L. (Lord Peter Wimsey; Montague Egg)
Twelve novels (all but one featuring Lord Peter; the first in 1923) and 45 short stories (22 featuring Lord Peter) ensure Lord Peter's immortality. The short stories are to be found in *Lord Peter*, compiled by James Sandoe (Harper, 1972; however, the paperback Avon edition of the same date contains an additional story). This volume also contains an essay by

Carolyn Heilbrun, "Sayers, Lord Peter and God," and a wicked parody by E. C. Bentley, "Greedy Night." Lord Peter is the urbane aristocrat as amateur detective. Sayers' other detective, appearing in 11 short stories, is Montague Egg, a traveling salesman of wine and a delightful character. The many recent books on Sayers deal also with her religious writings, plays, and translation of Dante.

Brabazon, James. *Dorothy L. Sayers: The Life of a Courageous Woman.* With a preface by Anthony Fleming and a foreword by P. D. James. London: Gollancz, 1981.
> The "authorized" (by her son) biography, published early (Sayers stipulated no biography until 50 years after her death) puts into limbo the disgraceful book by Hitchman (below). Brabazon knew Sayers, had access to all her papers, and was given complete editorial freedom. In style, wit, intelligence, and spirit, he matches his subject to perfection.

Durkin, Mary Brian. *Dorothy L. Sayers.* Twayne, 1980.
> About half the volume is criticism on the detective writings.

Gaillard, Dawson. *Dorothy L. Sayers.* Ungar, 1981.
> This critical appraisal of the detective works adds a distinctly feminist viewpoint.

Hannay, Margaret P., ed. *As Her Whimsey Took Her: Critical Essays on the Work of Dorothy L. Sayers.* Kent State University Press, 1979.
> Five of the 15 essays in this collection are on Sayers as a detective story writer.

Hitchman, Janet. *Such a Strange Lady: A Biography of Dorothy L. Sayers.* Harper, 1975.
> This is a *very* strange book; the author has neither taste nor grace.

Hone, Ralph E. *Dorothy L. Sayers: A Literary Biography.* Kent State University Press, 1979.
> The life and all the works are intertwined.

Scott-Giles, C. W. *The Wimsey Family: A Fragmentary History Compiled from Correspondence with Dorothy L. Sayers.* London: Gollancz, 1977.
> The author, Fitzalen Pursuivant of Arms Extraordinary, has supplied heraldic drawings. Both Scott-Giles and Sayers obviously enjoyed this fanciful creation.

Stout, Rex (Nero Wolfe and Archie Goodwin)
> "Wouldn't it be funny if we turned out to be a kind of female Holmes and Watson?" Julie asked.
> "Hilarious," Doctor [her psychoanalyst] said without a smile. "Wouldn't Nero Wolfe and Archie Goodwin be better models?"
> "I don't think I know them" Julie said.
> "That is the most depressing thing I've heard today."
> —Dorothy Salisbury Davis
> *A Death in the Life*
> (Reprinted with permission of Dorothy Salisbury Davis)

Nero Wolfe's bulk is not matched by the number of published books about his detective genius: 46 titles (the first in 1934, of these 12 are collections of novellas, 36 in all). He never leaves his house willingly—legman and witnesses bring him the information and *he* thinks. He loves food, orchids, language, and his privacy. In *Gambit*, Archie informs a prospective client, who has been told Wolfe is indignantly burning a copy of Webster's Third, "Once he burned up a cookbook because it said to remove the hide from a ham end before putting it in the pot with lima beans. Which he loves most, food or words, is a tossup." Nero Wolfe has an enthusiastic following: the Wolfe Pack (700 members) held its third annual Black Orchid Banquet in New York in 1980; there is a *Rex Stout Newsletter* (appearing in *The Armchair Detective*) and a Nero Wolfe Award for Mystery Fiction. Archie, his assistant, is in the hard-boiled detective mold. In *Make out with Murder*, by Chip Harrison, the amateur investigator, the world's most devoted mystery fan, believes Nero Wolfe is alive and living in Manhattan.

Baring-Gould, William S. *Nero Wolfe of West Thirty-Fifth Street: The Life and Times of America's Largest Private Detective*. Viking, 1969.

McAleer, John L. *Rex Stout, a Biography*. Little, Brown, 1977.

Stout, Rex. *The Nero Wolfe Cook Book*. Viking, 1973.
This is a delicious introduction to the novels. Eating well is more important than detection, and the meals in the novels are meticulously described. Here are the recipes along with the passages from the novels in which Wolfe and Archie, and sometimes guests, dined.

DETECTIVE STORY SETTINGS AND SUBJECTS

Just as many readers of detective fiction prefer a type of detective, others seek those stories with a particular background of country, social order, activity, organization, or profession. Two bibliographies cited later (Barzun and Taylor, Hagen) provide some subject indexing. (Hagen also provides a very limited "Scene of the Crime.") *The Poisoned Pen* published a subject guide by Richard Emery in Volume 3, Number 1 (Jan.-Feb. 1980), which has been continued with very active supplementation by subscribers, three supplements in 1980. The index terms are not yet standardized, but here are some groupings from all sources of subjects to be found.

Advertising, banking, computers, factories, insurance.

Antiques and collecting, archaeology, art and art forgery, rare coins, Egyptology, fashion designers, jewelry, museums and galleries.

Ballet, burlesque, motion pictures and Hollywood, music, opera, theater.

Academia, authors, books and publishing, booksellers, libraries.

Sports: baseball, basketball, boxing, cricket, flying, golf, hockey, horse racing, hunting, skiing, tennis.

Boarding houses, country houses, pubs, motels, restaurants, seaside resorts, villages.

Railroads, ships, and cruises.

Doctors, hospitals and nursing homes, amnesia.

Birds, cats, dogs.

Africa, Australia, Brazil, China, India.

Churches, clergy.

Witchcraft, magic.

Gourmet cooking, gardening.

Courtrooms, lawyers.

The possibilities are intriguing as the following miscellaneous topics show: butlers, occult detectives, Victorian and Edwardian settings, chess, rogues, mysteries about detective fiction (*The Undetective*, by Bruce Graeme). History buffs would enjoy Robert Player's *Oh, Where Are Bloody Mary's Earrings*, and two on Richard II, Elizabeth Peters's *The Murders of Richard III* and Josephine Tey's *The Daughter of Time*. The British Parliament is the background for *Who Goes Hang?*, by Stanley Hyland, in which the detectives are a committee of members. (Incidentally, this is an extreme example of changes made when a British mystery is published in the United States—about 100 pages of text were deleted, including all the passages describing library and historical research of fascinating interest to librarians.) For Jane Austen devotees there is T. H. White's *Darkness at Pemberley*—a twentieth-century Elizabeth Darcy at the Pemberley of *Pride and Prejudice*. Dr. Johnson and, of course, Boswell are the detectives in Lillian De La Torre's period detective stories. Two recent novels by Robert Barnard, *Death of a Mystery Writer* and *Death of a Literary Widow*, indicate the substantial list to be made on the literary life in detective fiction. For those interested in Greek philosophy, there is Margaret Doody's *Aristotle Detective*.

An interesting list could be made of detective stories by authors not associated with the subgenre: C. P. Snow, whose first published novel was a detective story, *Death under Sail*, as was his last, *A Coat of Varnish*; Kingsley Amis with *The Riverside Villas Murder*; Charles Dickens, whose unfinished *The Mystery of Edwin Drood* has tempted several authors to try a conclusion, the latest being Leon Garfield in 1980.

Here are a few examples of subject groupings with very selective listings:

Locked Room
Carr, John Dickson
> Carr wrote several of these. In *The Three Coffins* (British title: *The Hollow Man*), his detective, Dr. Gideon Fell, gives a neat discourse on the problem of the locked room.

Santesson, Hans Stefan, ed. *The Locked Room Reader: Stories of Impossible Crimes and Escapes.* Random, 1968.
> Sixteen stories, including "The Locked Room" by Carr.

English Country House

> Murder can be so much more charming and enjoyable,
> even for the victim, if the surroundings are pleasant and the
> people involved are ladies and gentlemen—like ourselves.
> —Alfred Hitchcock

Aird, Catherine. *The Stately Home Murders.*

Anderson, James. *The Affair of the Blood-Stained Egg Cosy.*

Heyer, Georgette. *Envious Casca. No Wind of Blame. The Unfinished Clue.*

Innes, Michael. *Hamlet, Revenge!*

Peters, Elizabeth. *The Murders of Richard III.*

Libraries and Librarians

Blackstock, Charity. *Dewey Death.*

Bosse, Malcolm. *The Man Who Loved Zoos.*

Dolson, Hildegarde. *Please Omit Funeral.*

Filstrup, Jane Merrill. "The Shattered Calm: Libraries in Detective Fiction." *Wilson Library Bulletin* 53(12/78):320-27; (1/79):392-98.
   The bibliography is in two parts: "The Librarian as Victim"; "The Librarian as Sleuth."

Goodrum, Charles A. *Dewey Decimated.*

Holding, James
   Hal Johnson, a library sleuth for overdue books, appeared in several short stories in *Ellery Queen's Mystery Magazine.*

Johnson, W. Bolingbroke. *The Widening Stain.*

Langton, Jane. *The Transcendental Murder.*

Peters, Elizabeth. *The Seventh Sinner. The Murders of Richard III.*

Valin, Jonathan. *Final Notice.*

Book Trade and Publishing

Allingham, Margery. *Flowers for the Judge.*

Asimov, Isaac. *Murder at the ABA.*

Blackburn, John. *Blue Octavo.* (U.S. title: *Bound to Kill*)

Blake, Nicholas. *End of Chapter.*

Clarke, Anna. *The Lady in Black.*
   Chapman & Hall are the publishers; the reader is George Meredith.

Delving, Michael. *Smiling the Boy Fell Dead.*

Farmer, Bernard J. *Death of a Bookseller.*

Hallahan, William H. *The Ross Forgeries.*

Hamilton, Henriette. *The Two Hundred Ghost.*

Hodgkin, M. R. *Dead Indeed.*

Monteilhet, Herbert. *Murder at the Frankfurt Book Fair.*

Moore, Doris Langley. *My Caravaggio Style.*

Morley, Christopher. *The Haunted Bookshop.*

Page, Marco. *Fast Company.*

Reno, Marie R. *Final Proof.*

Rhode, John, and Carter Dickson. *Fatal Descent.*

Sims, George. *The Terrible Door.*

Stern, Richard Martin. *Manuscript for Murder.*

Symons, Julian. *The Narrowing Circle.*

College and University

Bernard, Robert. *Deadly Meeting.*

Blake, Nicholas. *The Morning after Death.*

Boucher, Anthony. *The Case of the Seven of Calvary.*

Clinton-Baddeley, V. C. *My Foe Outstretched beneath the Tree.*

Cole, G. D. H., and Margaret Cole. *Off with Her Head.*

Constantine, K. C. *The Blank Page.*

Cross, Amanda. *Poetic Justice. Death in a Tenured Position.*
The second title has a strong women's liberation tone.

Dillon, Eilis. *Death in the Quadrangle.*

Eustis, Helen. *The Horizontal Man.*

Fiske, Dorsey. *Academic Murder.*

Graham, John Alexander. *The Involvement of Arnold Wechsler.*

Hodgkin, M. R. *Student Body.*

Innes, Michael. *Death at the President's Lodging. Old Hall, New Hall.*

Johnson, W. Bolingbroke. *Widening Stain.*

Levin, Ira. *Juliet Dies Twice.*

MacKay, Amanda. *Death Is Academic.*

MacLeod, Charlotte. *Rest You Merry. The Luck Runs Out.*

Masterman, J. C. *An Oxford Tragedy.*

Mitchell, Gladys. *Fault in the Structure.*

Rees, Dilwyn. *The Cambridge Murders.*

Rennert, Maggie. *Circle of Death.*

Robinson, Robert. *Landscape with Dead Dons.*

Sayers, Dorothy L. *Gaudy Night.*

Vulliamy, C. E. *Don among the Dead Men.*

Mystery-Suspense, Psychological-Suspense

Those genre novels the publishers often label "A Novel of Suspense" fall into an amorphous catchall. What they have in common is abundant suspense. Some mystery-suspense novels may seem to differ little from the detective novel: there is a crime and its investigation. However, the formal detection, by police or private investigator, is secondary. The narration is not by the detective but by a character disturbingly involved in the mystery or by a potential victim. The author and the reader are concerned with the background of the mystery, along with the emotions and personal and private relationships of the characters. Suspense heightens as the narrator becomes more and more dangerously involved, distrusts feelings of trust or love, or comes close to disaster. It may be that the detection is wholly the function of the involved narrator. Occasionally, the narrator is a detached observer or one in love with the central character in the mystery.

Psychological-suspense novels follow somewhat the same pattern. They may, however, center on the background or build-up of the crime. Usually there is some aspect of psychological abnormality as a causal factor. The narrator may be warped, and the plot develops as the narrator's compulsion leads to the crime. Occasionally, there may be suggestions of the supernatural.

Both these types of suspense novels may seem indistinguishable from some types to be described later. The psychological-suspense novel merges into the crime novel—in the first, the compulsions to crime are psychological; in the second, the crime is cold-bloodedly planned, however psychopathic the schemer. Mystery-suspense novels are often full of romance and seemingly akin to the novel of romantic-suspense—in the first, the mystery is the important story line; in the second, the romance dominates, with the Gothic romance, which incorporates elements of horror and the supernatural, being the extreme example.

What differentiates these thriller novels is largely the intent of the author. Genre authors are quite canny about the type of reader they want to entice. Atmosphere and background, style of narration, and the manner of characterization vary in each genre. Sometimes, however, the variations are so diluted as to be almost imperceptible: this frequently occurs among authors who write in more than one genre, but usually more successfully in one than the other or others.

A thriller author, who can vary writing style to suit different subgenres and appeal to different readers, will frequently further differentiate by using a pseudonym distinctive to each subgenre. The reader, then, does not have the same expectation from each pseudonym, and the author can, in effect, become a different author for each. Indeed, the reader may be unaware of reading the same author in different guises. (A good example is Erle Stanley Gardner writing as A. A. Fair.) When the author uses the same name for more than one genre, the author's own distinctive style is usually a constant, allowing for the pattern characteristic of each genre.

Selections in this subgenre begin with authors best known for this subgenre, followed by a list of authors who are better known for books in another genre.

Armstrong, Charlotte
Blackstock, Charity
Brandel, Marc

Carpenter, Margaret. *Experiment Perilous.*

Clarke, Anna

Cook, Robin

Davis, Mildred

Ellin, Stanley

Eustis, Helen. *The Horizontal Man.*

Fremlin, Celia

Hallahan, William H.

Hitchens, Dolores

Hubbard, P. M.

Hughes, Dorothy B.

Kiefer, Warren

Mackintosh, May

Meyer, Lynn. *Paperback Thriller.*

Player, Robert

Potts, Jean

Roueché, Berton

Detective Story Writers

Bell, Josephine

Berckman, Evelyn

Block, Lawrence

Davis, Dorothy Salisbury

Dickinson, Peter

Disney, Doris Miles

Eberhart, Mignon Good

Ferrars, E. X. (Elizabeth)

Fleming, Joan

Garve, Andrew

Gilbert, Michael

Irish, William

McCloy, Helen

McMullen, Mary

Peters, Elizabeth

Peters, Ellis

Rendell, Ruth

Symons, Julian

Waugh, Hillary

Wilcox, Colin

Woolrich, Cornell

Crime/Caper Writers
Bloch, Robert

Cain, James M.

Highsmith, Patricia

Spy/Espionage Writers
Albrand, Martha

Thomas, Ross

Romance Writers
Whether to label Mary Stewart's novels as mystery-suspense or romantic-suspense is a tossup. Her novels have been reviewed by reviewers of mystery and detective stories (Anthony Boucher asked, "Is anybody writing better adventure-suspense-romance than Miss Stewart?"). Stewart and Elizabeth Peters are listed in both sections for the same books; they are read equally by fans of both. The novels of the other romance writers tend to be simpler to label—all belonging in romantic-suspense and some also qualifying as mystery-suspense.

Aiken, Joan

Butler, Gwendoline

Cadell, Elizabeth

Daniels, Dorothy

Graham, Winston

Hodge, Jane Aiken

Holland, Isabelle

Mackintosh, May

Michaels, Barbara

Peters, Elizabeth

Stewart, Mary

Whitney, Phyllis A.

Crime/Caper

The line between a straight novel and a crime
novel is sometimes very thin.
—Newgate Callendar

The label "crime" is used quite generally in publishing and reviewing to encompass all thrillers. In this book it is used for the novel that centers on the perpetrator of a crime, whether a professional criminal or an amateur—the ordinary person who is pushed to the limits of endurance in a situation and who decides a criminal act is the only solution. Between the two extremes lies a plethora of rogues of both sexes, all degrees of education, varying social classes, and all sharing the trait of cunning, whether they be stupid or highly intelligent. Among the private eyes are found a number of rogues, but their criminous acts are usually for a good cause—the epithet for them is amoral rather than criminal.

The day of the master criminal is past, although Sax Rohmer's Dr. Fu Manchu stories are finding some new fans. *Ellery Queen's Crookbook* (Random, 1974) celebrates the genre. These crime novels vary from harshly realistic to picaresque or comic.

UNDERWORLD

A few write with harsh realism of the underworld of crime: Burnett, Greene, and Higgins are listed here. (One might include Dashiell Hammett.) Other authors treat the underworld and its criminals with realism but combine criminals and amoral rogues to allow for a character with whom the reader can sympathize.

Arrighi, Mel

Bloch, Robert

Burnett, W. R. *Little Caesar. The Asphalt Jungle.*

Cain, James M.

Canning, Victor

Freeborn, Brian

Greene, Graham. *This Gun for Hire.*

Higgins, George V.

Leonard, Elmore

MacKenzie, Donald

Scott, Jack S.

Wainwright, John

Westheimer, David

ROGUE

The cheerfully amoral rogue is, with a few exceptions, a likeable character whose contravening of the law doesn't seem *that* serious to the reader. Several rogues among those listed here appear in series:

Block, Lawrence (Bernard Rhodenbarr)

Bonfiglioli, Kyril (Honorable Charles Mortdecai)

Chase, James Hadley

Drummond, Ivor (a trio of rogues: Lady Jennifer, Colley and Count Sandro)

Fish, Robert L. (Kek Huuygens)

Furst, Alan (Robert Levin)

Highsmith, Patricia (Tom Ripley)

Hornung, E. W. (Raffles)

Leblanc, Maurice (Arsène Lupin)

McDonald, Gregory (Fletch)

Meynell, Laurence (Hooky Hefferman)

Norman, Frank

Perowne, Barry (Raffles)

Stark, Richard (Parker)

CAPER

Here are all the thieves, con men, and the shady rogues who pull off their deals with a blithe disregard of law and, usually, morality. Many of the following authors write other types of thrillers, and the title noted is an example from their novels that distinctively involves a caper:

Andress, Lesley. *Caper.*

Buckman, Peter. *The Rothschild Conversion.*

Butterworth, Michael. *X Marks the Spot.*

Carson, Robert. *The Golden Years Caper.*

Cecil, Henry. *Much in Evidence.*
  Many of his law court comedies are also comic capers.

Cleary, Jon. *Peter's Pence.*

Cox, Richard

Crichton, Michael. *The Great Train Robbery.*

Dodge, David. *To Catch a Thief.*

Erdman, Paul E.

Garve, Andrew

Godey, John. *The Taking of Pelham One Two Three.*

Goldman, James. *The Man from Greek and Roman.*

Harris, MacDonald. *The Treasure of Sainte Foy.*

Hunter, Evan

Kenrick, Tony

Kwitny, Jonathan. *Shakedown.*

Lambert, Derek

Lehman, Ernest. *The French Atlantic Affair.*

Lowden, Desmond

Maling, Arthur

Moore, Robin. *The French Connection.*

Roudybush, Alexandra

Thomas, Ross. *Chinaman's Chance.*

Underwood, Michael

COMIC CAPER

Among the authors previously listed for crime-caper are several who use comedy, either broadly or sardonically (Frank Norman's cockney crooks being a lovely instance). Donald Westlake has made the caper into farce so successfully that each new title is greeted with cheers. Nan and Ivan Lyons joined the comic caper field with *Someone Is Killing the Great Chefs of Europe*, followed by *Champagne Blues*, and may make a special line of cookery capers.

Spy/Espionage

The spy or secret agent has never been a respectable figure. He appears seldom in literature as a major figure before the twentieth century. The pattern for this genre was set in the few early classics listed below:

Buchan, John. *The Thirty-Nine Steps* (1915).
This introduces Richard Hannay, spy-catcher and spy who appears in several novels. *The Thirty-Nine Steps* has one of the great and long chase scenes in the genre. It became a classic motion picture.

Childers, Erskine. *The Riddle of the Sands* (1903).
Introduces the theme of the German plot to invade England, complete with British traitor and amateur hero.

Conrad, Joseph. *The Secret Agent* (1907). *Under Western Eyes* (1911).
The Secret Agent brings in the world of revolutionaries and anarchists. *Under Western Eyes* introduces the double agent.

Kipling, Rudyard. *Kim* (1901).
"The Great Game" as Kim calls his spying for British intelligence in India, introduces the exotic background, an aspect that adds greatly to the appeal of the genre. How Kim, as a boy, is trained for his work is marvelously described.

Maugham, W. S. *Ashenden: Or, The British Agent* (1928).
Maugham was an agent during World War I, probably the first of the agents to turn his experience into a novel. He introduces the antihero as agent. His tone is realistic and sardonic, and the outrageous or sensational is toned down to the ordinary.

Oppenheim, E. Phillips. *The Great Impersonation* (1920).
This is the only one of Oppenheim's many spy novels to survive. His first published novel of international intrigue was issued in 1898 and several more appeared during World War I. He introduced the spy world of elegant high society and exotic European cities; Monte Carlo with its gambling setting was often used.

Orczy, Baroness. *The Scarlet Pimpernel* (1905).
The aristocratic fop as a disguise for the highly intelligent agent is here at its most romantic. The theme is introduced of daring rescues from enemy countries, in this case aristocrats saved from the guillotine during the French Revolution.

The early classic authors have successors in a small group of writers who have set the tone for the spy/espionage novel and have been imitated, if rarely excelled. Among the successors are:

Ambler, Eric
He began with a novel in 1936 and is still at it with *The Care of Time* in 1981. The antihero and the amateur, unwittingly caught up in the spy network, are featured. His portrayal of agents and spymasters is sardonic and unromantic; there is a general atmosphere of disillusionment in an unpleasant game. Backgrounds are exotic, especially the Balkans and the Middle East.

Fleming, Ian
James Bond, 007, the British Secret Service agent is, of course, among the immortals. Fleming had experience in naval intelligence during World War I. The first Bond adventure, *Casino Royale*, 1953, established his flamboyant characteristics. Sex and sadism in an international setting were ingredients for some outrageous adventures with Cold War spies. Linked to him is the tag: Licensed to Kill. Attempts to continue the Bond legend after Fleming died have not been successful.

Greene, Graham. *Our Man in Havana* (1958).
Greene is not considered a genre fiction author but has written three spy novels important to the genre, his first being *The Confidential Agent* (1939). During World War II he was in intelligence and undoubtedly drew from his experience for *the* classic parody of the genre, *Our Man in Havana*, which reduces everything to the ridiculous. *The Quiet American* (1955) is a somber spy novel.

Household, Geoffrey. *Rogue Male* (1938).
This is the prototype story of the private individual who undertakes his own spy mission, encountering extreme danger and exciting chases.

Innes, Michael
Best known for his detective stories, Innes wrote several spy novels notable for sometimes outrageously fantastical plots and characters: *The Secret Vanguard* (1940); *Appleby on Ararat* (1941); *The Journeying Boy* (1949); *Operation Pax* (1951); *The Man from the Sea* (1955).

Le Carré, John
The Spy Who Came in from the Cold (1963) set the classic pattern for the unheroic spy, the pattern of double agents, and the anatomization of the bureaucracy of intelligence headquarter operations. Le Carré's experience was in the British Foreign Office. In *Tinker, Tailor, Soldier, Spy* (1975) and *Smiley's People* (1979), the main character is George Smiley, the antithesis of James Bond.

Marquand, John P.
Mr. Moto, the Japanese super-spy, first appeared in *No Hero* (1935). He is the complete professional spy. Marquand uses the plot device of a young American man and woman involved in intrigue by chance and, during many thrilling adventures, falling in love. The locale is usually the exotic Orient, with one story set in Hawaii. The use of the romantic amateur pair became a standard device in the genre.

Simmel, Johannes Mario. *It Can't Always Be Caviar: The Fabulously Daring Adventures and Exquisite Cooking Recipes of the Involuntary Secret Agent Thomas Lieven* (1965).
The amoral rogue amateur as reluctant spy in this novel, translated from

the German, brings to the genre the picaresque antihero. Read it to know why the menus and recipes are vital to his espionage career as, successively, a German, British, French, American, and Russian spy.

Sulzburger, C. L. *The Tooth Merchant* (1973).
While Michael Innes used the wildest fancifulness in his spy novels, Sulzburger has gone one better and spoofed the genre by blandly making mythology real in this picaresque novel of irreverent political commentary.

The host of authors writing the spy novel follow the patterns set by the early authors and imitate the later successful ones. Commonly used are the international scene, the more exotic the better; intelligence departments, the more corruptible the more realistic; exotic characters with an atmosphere of sexuality and sadism; political commentary, frequently jaundiced; the hazardous chase; the competent professional who may have a conscience. There are several spies in series. The following list is selective, as the number of authors writing spy novels grows steadily larger. Many of these authors also write in other subgenres of the thriller.

Aarons, Edward S. ("Assignment" series)

Allbeury, Ted

Anderson, J. R. L. (Colonel Peter Blair)

Ardies, Tom

Bagley, Desmond

Buckley, William F. (Blacky Oakes)

Canning, Victor

Coles, Manning. *Drink to Yesterday.*

Condon, Richard. *The Manchurian Candidate.*

Creasey, John (Peter Ross, Gordon Craigie, Bruce Murdoch, and Mary Dell)

Deighton, Len

Dickinson, Peter. *Walking Dead.*

Egleton, Clive

Forsyth, Frederick

Freemantle, Brian. *Goodby to an Old Friend.* (Charlie Muffin).

Gardner, John (Boysie Oakes)

Garfield, Brian. *Hopscotch.*

Garner, William. *A Big Enough Wreath.* (Michael Jagger).

Gilbert, Michael

Haddad, C. A. (David Haham)

Haggard, William. *Hard Sell.*

Hamilton, Donald (Matt Helm)

Hall, Adam (Quiller)

Harvester, Simon (Dorian Silk)

Hughes, Dorothy B.

Hunt, E. Howard

Kyle, Duncan

Ludlum, Robert

MacLean, Alistair

Marks, Ted. *The Man from ORGY.*
A pornographic spy story.

Marlowe, Derek. *A Dandy in Aspic.*

Mason, F. Van Wyck

Masters, John

Mather, Berkely

Mitchell, James

Perry, Ritchie (Phillis)

Price, Anthony (Dr. David Audley)

Sela, Owen

Thomas, Ross

Trevanian. *The Eiger Sanction.*

Underwood, Michael

Wheatley, Dennis

York, Andrew

Spy stories tend to be quite grim. There are, however, a few inept and comic spies as follows (the classic parody of the spy novel is Graham Greene's *Our Man in Havana* listed above):

Benchley, Nathaniel. *Catch a Falling Spy.*

Mikes, George. *The Spy Who Died of Boredom.*

Porter, Joyce (Eddie Brown)

Women as spies appear frequently as secondary characters. Here are a few examples in which the woman is the lead (including two as series characters):

Albrand, Martha
Strongly romantic story usually involving a woman innocently caught up in spying.

Bosse, Malcolm. *The Man Who Loved Zoos.*
The woman involved in chasing a spy is a librarian.

Gilman, Dorothy (Mrs. Pollifax)

MacInnes, Helen
> With *Above Suspicion* (1941) MacInnes began a best-selling line of novels of romantic international intrigue. Her female spy is usually an amateur and often paired romantically with another amateur — all in the most exotic spots in Europe.

O'Donnell, Peter (Modesty Blaise)
> Modesty began in the comic strips in 1962 and appeared first in book form in 1965. She is the female James Bond.

Financial Intrigue/Espionage

Paul Erdman probably set this subgenre going in 1973 with *The Billion Dollar Sure Thing*, and authors have gleefully taken on the world of international banking, oil cartels, and multinational corporations as well as lesser businesses. Political chicanery is often involved along with crooked doings among the rich and powerful. The following examples show wide variation in pattern, but money is the prime factor in the plots:

Ambler, Eric. *Send No More Roses.*

Black, Gavin. *The Golden Cockatrice.* (Paul Harris).

Blankenship, William. *The Programmed Man.*

Brady, James. *Paris One.*

Duncan, Robert L. *Temple Dogs.*

Erdman, Paul E.

Fowlkes, Frank. *The Peruvian Contracts.*

Haig, Alec. *Sign on for Tokyo.*

Keagan, William. *A Real Killing.*

Law, Janice. (Ann Peters, oil company troubleshooter)

Lehman, Ernest. *The French Atlantic Affair.*

Maling, Arthur. *Schroeder's Game.*

Rhodes, Russell L. *The Styx Complex.*

Sanders, Lawrence. *The Tangent Objective.*

Stewart, Edward. *Launch.*

Thomas, Ross. *The Money Harvest.*

Political Intrigue and Terrorism

This is a newly emerging subgenre. Common to it are many of the characteristics of the spy/espionage subgenre and the disaster subgenre, with frequent overtones of science fiction. The intent of the author is usually to make angry comment about the international political scene. Some of the books are national in background, usually with international political implications. Agencies such as the CIA are often featured. The threat of terrorism is pervasive. This subgenre is not yet defined by prototypes, but until time tells, this writer would pick Robert Littell's *The Amateur* and Ross Thomas's *The Mordida Man*. The examples below show how involved these stories are with current political problems and situations. It will be interesting to observe how changing world politics affect surviving interest in some of these novels.

Alexander, Patrick. *Show Me a Hero.*

Allbeury, Ted. *The Twentieth Day of January.*

Archer, Jeffrey. *Shall We Tell the President?*

Borchgave, Arnaud de. *The Spike.*

Cole, Burt. *Blood Note.*

Collins, Larry, and Dominique Lapierre. *The Fifth Horseman.*

Coppel, Alfred. *The Hastings Conspiracy.*

Forsyth, Frederick. *The Devil's Conspiracy.*

Garve, Andrew. *Counterstroke.*

Henissart, Paul. *Margin of Error.*

Littell, Robert. *The Amateur.*

Ludlum, Robert. *The Bourne Identity.*

Nelson, Walter. *The Siege of Buckingham Palace.*

Orde, Lewis, and Bill Michaels. *The Night They Stole Manhattan.*

Paul, Barbara. *Liars and Tyrants and People Who Turn Blue.*

Seymour, Gerald. *The Harrison Affair.*

Thomas, Ross. *The Mordida Man.*

West, Morris. *Proteus.*

Washburn, Mark. *The Armageddon Game.*

Williamson, Tony. *The Samson Strike.*

Disaster

> All the scenarios are either very low in probabil-
> ity, or very distant in the future.
> —Isaac Asimov
> *A Choice of Catastrophes*

This, also, is a newly emerging subgenre: the reviewers are labeling several types of novels as "disaster" thrillers. The catastrophe may be either natural, i.e., nature's fury or acts of God, or man-made. Natural disaster may be earthquake, volcanic eruption, tidal wave, meteor strike, new ice age, flood, plague, aberrational behavior of bird or animal life—the only limit is the author's imagination. (However, not within that imaginative limit is the matter of the supernatural.) Man-made disasters may include nuclear explosions, accidents caused by experimenting with bacteria or with man's biological heritage, accidents in aircraft or ocean vessels, or accidents caused by tampering with nature's equilibrium (e.g., destroying the ozone layer)—again, the author's imagination has a wide range. Frequently, the disaster has a political link, relating this type of book to the spy/espionage subgenre. There is also a science fiction aspect in the themes of apocalypse, doomsday, and worlds in collision. Only a few authors are now specializing in disaster novels.

The rise of this subgenre is paralleled by the popularity of the disaster motion picture in the sixties and seventies, such as *The Towering Inferno, Earthquake, Airport, The Last Wave,* and *The Poseidon Adventure.* Of the last named, the producer commented: "In the first six minutes, 1,400 people are killed and only the stars survive."

Why is the subgenre so popular? This writer refuses to conjecture in a world tottering on the brink of disaster! In any case, the reader has a wide choice among the following books of ways to contemplate catastrophe:

Block, Thomas H. *Mayday.*

Canning, Victor. *The Doomsday Carrier.*

Corley, Edwin. *The Genesis Rock.*

Cravens, Gwyneth. *The Black Death.*

Cussler, Clive. *Raise the Titanic.*

Godey, John. *The Snake.*

Hailey, Arthur. *Airport.*

Herbert, James. *The Rats.*

Herzog, Arthur. *IQ 83. The Swarm. Earthsound. Heat.*

Hyde, Christopher. *The Wave.*

Johnson, Stanley. *The Doomsday Deposit.*

MacLean, Alistair. *Goodbye California.*

Moan, Terrance. *The Deadly Frost.*

North, Edmund H., and Franklin Coen. *Meteor.*

Orgill, Douglas, and John Gribbin. *The Sixth Winter.*

Page, Thomas. *Sigmet Active.*

Racine, Thomas. *The Great Los Angeles Blizzard.*

Rubens, Howard, and Jack Wasserman. *Hambro's Itch.*

Scortia, Thomas N., and Frank M. Robinson. *The Nightmare Factor. The Prometheus Crisis. The Glass Inferno.*

Slater, Ian. *Firespell.*

Smith, Martin Cruz. *Nightwing.*

Stone, George. *Blizzard.*

Warner, Douglas. *Death on a Warm Wind.*

Adventure

Actually all thrillers can be labeled adventures, as can the western and much of science fiction. But in this specific subgenre, the adventurer is one who seeks adventure on land, sea, or in the air, following the old tradition of the hero who matches strength against the powers of natural elements and enjoys the danger. Not included here are war stories as such, although war is often involved. The exception is the naval warfare series, largely derivative from the prototype Hornblower series by C. S. Forester.

Many of these books are set in wild and primitive areas of the world, often feature treasure hunts or lost mines, may involve piracy, and are full of combat with villains of all sorts. They may or may not eschew romance—there may be, as for Ulysses, a patiently weaving Penelope welcoming the hero home after his dalliance with Circe and others. (Paul Zweig in *The Adventurer* [Basic Books, 1972] analyzes the lure of adventure and the character of the adventurer, tracing the literature from Ulysses, the medieval romances, Robinson Crusoe, and others. He notes "the unrelenting masculinity of adventure literature—from the Iliad to James Bond ..." and considers the adventurer as being "in flight from women.")

There is a political angle to adventures as many concern revolutionary action in non-European countries, gun-running, or mercenary activities. The story may concern the search for a friend or relative lost in strange circumstances, a ship or plane wreck, hijacking, hunting wild animals, pioneering treks, exploration expeditions, the overcoming of natural disasters, an escape and the ensuing chase—the plot possibilities are varied.

There is a notable parody of the subgenre in the Flashman series by George MacDonald Fraser.

The adventure is considered the subgenre of male interest as Romance is identified for women, with the sweet-and-savage romance providing women with their adventure element.

Here are a few classic adventure authors, followed by those currently prolific in the field:

Burroughs, Edgar Rice. Tarzan series.

Conrad, Joseph

Curwood, James Oliver

Falkner, J. M. *Moonfleet.*

Haggard, H. Rider. *She. The Return of She. King Solomon's Mines.*

Hughes, Richard. *A High Wind in Jamaica.*

Kipling, Rudyard. *Kim.*

London, Jack

Verne, Jules

White, Stewart Edward

Wren, P. C. *Beau Geste.*

In the tradition of these classic adventure authors are the following writers, several of whom write largely only in this subgenre:

Adler, Warren. *Trans-Siberian Express.*

Bagley, Desmond

Becker, Stephen. *The Chinese Bandit.*

Buchan, John

Cleary, Jon

Cussler, Clive

Drummond, Ivor

Forbes, Colin

Forester, C. S. *The African Queen.*

Forsyth, Frederick

Gann, Ernest K.

Garfield, Brian

Garve, Andrew

Higgins, Jack

Household, Geoffrey

Innes, Hammond

Knox, Alexander

Logan, Mark (Nick Minnett, Scarlet Pimpernel tradition)

Longstreet, Stephen

Ludlum, Robert

Lyall, Gavin

MacLean, Alistair

MacNeil, Duncan (Captain James Ogilvie)

Masters, John

Mather, Berkely

Meyer, Nicholas. *Black Orchid.*

Murray, W. H.

Sela, Owen. *The Portuguese Fragment.*

Selwyn, Francis. *Sergeant Verity and the Imperial Diamond.*

Shute, Nevil

Smith, Wilbur. *The Eye of the Tiger.*

Thomas, Donald. *The Flight of the Eagle.*

Westheimer, David

Woodhouse, Martin

ADVENTURE BOOKS IN SERIES

Most books of the naval warfare series concern the Napoleonic wars. The imitated prototype is C. S. Forester's Hornblower series, which follows his career from midshipman to admiral. The life of Hornblower is the subject of a "biography" by C. Northcote Parkinson, *The Life and Times of Horatio Hornblower* (Little, Brown, 1970), so authentic as to persuade the unwary he really existed. Parkinson so regretted the end of the series, he started a series of his own, noted below. A few of the series deal with World Wars I and II naval warfare. While similar lists might be made for other types of adventure (e.g., airplane stories), few would prove as extensive as the following group on sea and naval adventure:

Beach, Edward L.

Callison, Brian

Forester, C. S. Hornblower series.

Gilpatric, Guy (Glencannon)

Hartog, Jan de. *The Captain.*

Hayden, Sterling. *Voyage.*

Jennings, John

Kent, Alexander (Captain Richard Bolitho)

McCutchan, Philip (Lieutenant Halfhyde)

Mason, F. Van Wyck

Meacham, E. K. (Captain Perceval Merewether, East India Co.)

Monsarrat, Nicholas. *The Cruel Sea.*

Nordhoff, Charles B. *Mutiny on the Bounty.*

O'Brian, Patrick (Captain Jack Aubrey)

Parkinson, C. Northcote (Lieutenant Richard Delancey)

Pope, Dudley (Lieutenant Lord Ramage)

Rayner, R. A.

Reeman, Douglas

Sabatini, Rafael. *Captain Blood. The Sea Hawk.*

Trew, Antony. *The Zhukov Briefing.*

White, Simon (Captain Jethro Cockerill)

Wouk, Herman. *The Caine Mutiny.*

Specifically aimed at the male audience are a number of paperback "action/adventure" series, in the trade parlance, with several new titles announced for 1981. The western has always been considered action/adventure as have some of the thriller series (detectives, spies). These new series offer he-men who function as vengeance squads, martial arts experts, mercenaries, and the like. The following list is not exhaustive, and new series are announced frequently:

Ace Books

Nick Carter Detective series and The Saint series (featuring Simon Templar). A newer line is the Casca series, featuring novels about mercenaries, vengeance, and similar subjects.

Bantam

A new series (1981), the Sergeant series by Gordon Davis, was taken over from Zebra, which published numbers one to three. The series character is Sergeant C. J. Mahoney in World War II adventures. Bantam announced there would be one each month, and number nine had appeared early in 1982. Bantam also publishes a War Book series of nonfiction adventures.

Berkley

The Raven series, by Donald MacKenzie (1981), features adventures by playboy ex-cop John Raven. Walter Wager's Alison Gordon series about a "female James Bond" is aimed at a male audience.

Dell

Announced for 1982 is a new series: American Aviation Saga.

Fawcett

Travis McGee detective books, by John D. MacDonald, and the Matt Helm secret agent books, by Donald Hamilton, are considered male-oriented action/adventure. New line (1981) the Arms series, by Kenneth L. Cameron.

NAL (New American Library)

Three new series in 1981 depicting "strong male characters": Dusky MacMorgan series, featuring an adventurous fishing captain off the Florida Keys and worldwide waters; Americans at War series; The Mercenary series. In 1980 the adult western, the Trailsman series, was started.

Playboy Press

Publishes a nonfiction War Book series. New in 1981, the Bounty Hunter series. Already publishes C. N. Parkinson's Lt. Richard Delancy sea adventure series and two adult western series: Jake Logan and J. D. Hardin.

Pinnacle

Don Pendleton's The Executioner series, "the granddaddy" of the action/adventure type. Publishes 10 male-oriented action/adventure series: The Destroyer series, by Warren Murphy; Death Merchant series; Edge (western) series; Penetrator series. New series (1981): The Nazi Hunter and Six Gun Samurai, a "sushi Western."

Warner

Men of Action line announced for 1981: six series of original, contemporary action/adventure novels (to be four titles each month): Dirty Harry series, by Dune Hartman, based on the "character made popular by the Clint Eastwood films"; S-Com Strategic Commando series; Ninja Master series; Ben Slayton: T-Man series; The Hook series; Boxer Unit-OSS series. "Violence and sex can be more graphically described in a novel [than on film]. None of this is gratuitous. We don't pander to people who want to read pornography or sadistic action. Our heroes aren't psychopaths, they're mature adults — like our readers."

TOPICS

Detective Story and Detectives

BIOGRAPHY OF FICTIONAL DETECTIVES

The detective as a fictional character is given a biographical write-up in some studies on the detective story with a blandly literal tone as though the detectives were indeed actual living beings. Some books with biographical listing are noted later, but here are three works simply on the detectives:

Pate, Janet. *The Book of Sleuths.* Contemporary Books, 1977.
The lives of 40 detectives (including a few from comic strips, motion pictures, and television) are presented with emphasis on their careers. Bibliography and filmography are added with illustrations from the films. Among the detectives are: C. Auguste Dupin, Nick Carter, Sherlock Holmes, Father Brown, Bulldog Drummond, Hercule Poirot, Peter Wimsey, Charlie Chan, Philo Vance, Ellery Queen, Miss Marple, Sam Spade, The Saint, Nick Charles, Inspector Maigret, Perry Mason, Nero Wolfe, Philip Marlowe, Mike Hammer, Commander Gideon, and Piet Van der Valk.

Penzler, Otto, ed. *The Great Detectives.* Little, Brown, 1978.
Twenty-six detectives are described by their creators: Roderick Alleyn (Ngaio Marsh); John Appleby (Michael Innes); Lew Archer (Ross Macdonald); Father Bredder (Leonard Holton); Flash Casey (George Harmon Coxe); Pierre Chambrun (Hugh Pentecost); Inspector Cockrill (Christianna Brand); Captain José Da Silva (Robert L. Fish); Nancy Drew (Carolyn Keene); the 87th Precinct (Ed McBain); Fred Fellows (Hillary Waugh); Inspector Ghote (H. R. F. Keating); Matt Helm (Donald Hamilton); Duncan Maclain (Baynard H. Kendrick); Mark McPherson (Vera Caspary); Lieutenant Luis Mendoza (Dell Shannon); Mr. and Mrs. North (Richard Lockridge); Patrick Petrella (Michael Gilbert); Superintendent Pibble (Peter Dickinson); Quiller (Adam Hall); Inspector Schmidt (George Bagby); The Shadow (Maxwell Grant); Michael Shayne (Brett Halliday); Virgil Tibbs (John Ball); Dick Tracy (Chester Gould); Inspector Van der Valk (Nicholas Freeling).

Penzler, Otto. *The Private Lives of Private Eyes, Spies, Crimefighters, & Other Good Guys.* Grosset, 1977.
Twenty-five lives are illustrated from books and motion pictures, with bibliography and filmography for each: Lew Archer, Modesty Blaise, James Bond, Father Brown, Nick Carter, Charlie Chan, Nick and Nora Charles, Bulldog Drummond, C. Auguste Dupin, Mike Hammer, Sherlock Holmes, Jules Maigret, Philip Marlowe, Miss Jane Marple, Perry Mason, Mr. Moto, Hercule Poirot, Ellery Queen, The Shadow, John Shaft, Sam Spade, Dr. Thorndyke, Philo Vance, Lord Peter Wimsey, Nero Wolfe.

BEST-SELLING AUTHORS

In 1975 the leading authors in order of most sales (2 million or more for each title) were Mickey Spillane (8 titles), Erle Stanley Gardner (25 titles), Robert Traver (*Anatomy of a Murder*), Joseph Wambaugh (*The New Centurions*), and John D. MacDonald (*The Damned*). Ten years earlier, Joseph Wambaugh did not appear and MacDonald was eleventh in order. Following Spillane, Gardner, and Traver were Ellery Queen, Agatha Christie, Richard S. Prather, A. A. Fair (Erle Stanley Gardner's pseudonym), Dashiell Hammett, Raymond Chandler, Earl Derr Biggers, Leslie Charteris, and Marco Page.

What type of detective has the greatest appeal? Spillane's private eye is notorious for sex and sadism. Gardner's lawyer Perry Mason is a suave gentleman. Wambaugh's Los Angeles policemen are realistic. Ellery Queen, the investigator, is a sophisticated gentleman. Christie's Poirot and Miss Marple are genteel figures suitable to social comedy detection. Prather, Fair, Hammett, Chandler, MacDonald, and Page feature private eyes in the hard-boiled tradition. Bigger's Charlie Chan is unique. Charteris' The Saint is a rogue and a gentleman. The readers, then, take their popular choice.

In sheer volume of titles, which collectively have a large sale, John Creasey's books belong among the best-sellers. Creasey used some 28 pseudonyms to produce about 650 titles, largely mystery, detective, and spy stories and some westerns (under three pseudonyms). He averaged about 12 titles a year. Reprints now appear with the pseudonymous works revealing the Creasey authorship. The Toff series was written under Creasey. His best-known pseudonyms are Kyle Hunt (psychiatrist Emmanuel Cellini series); Anthony Morton (The Baron, John Mannering, series); J. J. Marric (Commander Gideon of Scotland Yard series); Gordon Ashe (Pat Dawlish of Scotland Yard series); Jeremy York (Superintendent Folly of Scotland Yard series).

ANTHOLOGIES

Almost all of the early and current writers of detective stories have used the short-story form, and the anthologies provide a satisfactory introduction for the reader in choosing those authors whose style in the subgenre is pleasing to the individual reader's taste. Many of the anthologies also include other types of thrillers: spy, psychological-suspense, crime, and the like. The following listing is selective. Included are several annual series.

Barzun, Jacques, ed. *The Delights of Detection*. Criterion, 1961.
The anthology is delightful, beginning with Barzun's essay, "Detection and the Literary Art," and followed by 17 stories written by Ernest Bramah, G. K. Chesterton, Kenneth Livingston, Dorothy Sayers, E. C. Bentley, H. C. Bailey, R. Austin Freeman, Harry Kemelman, Daniel Pattiward, John D. MacDonald, Edmund Crispin, Bayard Wendell, Michael Gilbert, Rex Stout, P. C. de Beaumarchais, William Leggett, Alexandre Dumas.

Best Detective Stories of the Year. 1945- .
Includes list of award winners and bibliography of nonfiction for the year. Thirty-fourth in 1980.

Best of the Best Detective Stories. Dutton, 1971.

Clute, Cedric E., Jr., and Nicholas Lewin, eds. *Sleight of Crime: 15 Classic Tales of Murder, Mayhem and Magic.* Regnery, 1977.
All stories involve magicians and magic.

Conklin, Groff, ed. *Great Detective Stories about Doctors.* Collier, 1965.

Crime Writers Association Annual.
Sampling of titles: *Butcher's Dozen; A Pride of Felons; Crime Writers' Choice; Choice of Weapons; Some Like Them Dead; Planned Departures.*

Gilbert, Elliot L., ed. *The World of Mystery Fiction.* Publisher's Inc., 1978.
There is an introductory history of the genre to this selective anthology.

Greene, Hugh, ed. *The Rivals of Sherlock Holmes: Early Detective Stories.* Pantheon, 1970.

Greene, Hugh, ed. *The Further Rivals of Sherlock Holmes.* Pantheon, 1973.

Haycraft, Howard, and John Beecroft, eds. *A Treasury of Great Mysteries.* Simon & Schuster, 1947. 2v.
Includes four novels: Agatha Christie, *Murder in the Calais Coach*; Eric Ambler, *Journey into Fear*; Raymond Chandler, *The Big Sleep*; Daphne Du Maurier, *Rebecca*; and stories by Erle Stanley Gardner, Edgar Wallace, Georges Simenon, Patrick Quentin, Mary Roberts Rinehart, John Dickson Carr, Ellery Queen, Margery Allingham, William Irish, Dorothy L. Sayers, Leslie Charteris, Ngaio Marsh, Rex Stout, Stuart Palmer and Craig Rice, Carter Dickson.

Hitchcock, Alfred. *Alfred Hitchcock's Tales to Keep You Spellbound.* Vol. 1. Dial, 1977.
From *Alfred Hitchcock's Mystery Magazine.*

Kahn, Joan, ed. *Hanging by a Thread.* Houghton, 1969.

Kahn, Joan, ed. *Some Things Dark and Dangerous.* Harper, 1970.

Kittredge, William, and Steven M. Krauzen, eds. *The Great American Detective.* NAL, 1978.
The detectives: Nick Carter, Race Williams, Sam Spade, The Shadow, Philip Marlowe, Ellery Queen, Dan Turner, Susan Dare, Jerry Wheeler, Hildegard Withers, Nero Wolfe, Perry Mason, Michael Shayne, Lew Archer, Mack Bolan, the Executioner.

Mystery Writers of America Annual.
Sampling of titles: *Crime across the Sea; Sleuths and Consequences; With Malice toward All; Crime without Murder; Murder Most Foul; Dear Dead Days; Mirror Mirror, Fatal Mirror; Every Crime in the Book; When Last Seen.* The thirty-third, 1980, *The Edgar Winners*, presents 23 stories, winners of the Edgar Award for the Best Mystery Short Story of the Year, 1947-1978.

Queen, Ellery, ed. *Ellery Queen's Champions of Mystery.* Dial, 1977.

Queen, Ellery, ed. *Ellery Queen's Murdercade.* Random, 1975.

Queen, Ellery, ed. *Ellery Queen's Poetic Justice: 23 Stories of Crime, Mystery and Detection by World-Famous Poets from Geoffrey Chaucer to Dylan Thomas.* NAL, 1967.

Queen, Ellery, ed. *Ellery Queen's Napoleons of Mystery.* Davis, 1978.

Queen, Ellery, ed. *Ellery Queen's Windows of Mystery.* Dial, 1980.
Semiannual anthologies from *Ellery Queen's Mystery Magazine.*

Sayers, Dorothy L., ed. *Great Short Stories of Detection, Mystery and Horror.* Series one to three. London: Gollancz, 1929-1934.
Also published as *Omnibus of Crime.*

Sayers, Dorothy L., ed. *Great Tales of Detection.* Everyman, 1936.
Both titles have notable introductions, cited with criticism in a following section.

Winter's Crimes. Macmillan.
A British annual, the twelfth in 1980.

Hard-Boiled Detectives

The hard-boiled detective had his first glory in the pulp magazines in the United States in the 1920s. Many of the authors of note in the history of the detective story in the United States first appeared in the pulp magazines. They wrote largely of the underworld of crime in which their tough detectives held their own. Although a few British authors created hard-boiled detectives, the anthologies below present stories by the originators of the type in the United States:

Goulart, Ron, ed. *The Hardboiled Dicks: An Anthology and Study of Pulp Detective Fiction.* Sherbourne, 1965.

Ruhm, Herbert, ed. *The Hard-Boiled Detective: Stories from Black Mask Magazine, 1920-1951.* Vintage Books, 1977.
There is an introduction by the editor to stories by Carroll John Daly, Dashiell Hammett, Norbert Davis, Frederick Nebel, Raymond Chandler, Lester Dent, Erle Stanley Gardner, George Harmon Coxe, Merle Constiner, William Brandon, Curt Hamlin, Paul W. Fairman, and Bruno Fischer.

Shaw, Joseph T., ed. *The Hard-Boiled Omnibus: Early Stories from Black Mask.* Simon & Schuster, 1946.
There is an introduction by Shaw, editor of *Black Mask.* The authors included: Lester Dent, Reuben Jennings Shay, Raoul Whitfield, Raymond Chandler, Dashiell Hammett, Norbert Davis, Paul Cain, Thomas Walsh, Ed Lybeck, Roger Torrey, and Theodore Tinsley.

Women Detectives

Women appeared as fictional detectives as early as 1861. The following anthologies show the varieties in types of women detectives and that their modern role has changed dramatically:

Manley, Seon, and Gogo Lewis, comps. *Grand Dames of Detection: Two Centuries of Sleuthing Stories by the Gentle Sex.* Lothrop, 1973.
Among the authors are Baroness Orczy, Carolyn Wells, Agatha Christie, Dorothy L. Sayers, and Margery Allingham.

Queen, Ellery, ed. *The Female of the Species*. Little, Brown, 1943.
This early short-story anthology includes women both as detectives and criminals.

Slung, Michele B., ed. *Crime on Her Mind: Fifteen Stories of Female Sleuths from the Victorian Era to the Forties*. Pantheon, 1975.
The introduction presents a critical history, and an appendix lists the lady detectives in chronological order from 1861 to 1973, with annotations.

Slung, Michele B., ed. *Woman's Wiles: The 1979 Mystery Writers of America Anthology*. Harcourt, 1979.
Each annual MWA anthology has a theme.

Detection and Science Fiction

In the chapter on science fiction, there is a section on the detective in space, a neat combination of genres. Here are two anthologies to indicate that the conjunction of the genres is not new:

De Ford, Miriam Allen, ed. *Space, Time and Crime*. Paperback Library, 1964.

Santesson, Hans, ed. *Crime Prevention in the 30th Century*. Walker, 1970.

Plays

Agatha Christie and Dorothy L. Sayers, among others, have written plays of detection. Christie's *The Mousetrap* is London's longest-running play. Dorothy L. Sayers first wrote *Busman's Honeymoon* as a play, which had a successful run and was later made into a motion picture. Mary Roberts Rinehart's *The Bat* was also a stage success. Many of the plays of mystery and detection in the following anthologies were made into motion pictures. (See the later section on film.)

Cartmell, Van H., and Bennett Cerf, eds. *Famous Plays of Crime and Detection*. Blakiston, 1946.

Richards, Stanley, ed. *Best Mystery and Suspense Plays of the Modern Theatre*. Dodd, 1971.

Richards, Stanley, ed. *Ten Classic Mystery and Suspense Plays of the Modern Theatre*. Dodd, 1973.

BIBLIOGRAPHY

These bibliographies vary in coverage. Some are of the authors in the genre, some include material on allied genres, some are of secondary works, and several embrace a number of aspects.

Barnes, Melvin. *Best Detective Fiction: A Guide from Godwin to the Present*. London: Bingley, 1975.
Critical and highly selective, with surprising omissions, e.g., P. D. James.

Barzun, Jacques, and Wendell Hertig Taylor. *A Catalogue of Crime.* Harper, 1971.
> Selective, idiosyncratic, and delightful for the personal annotations by two devoted academic fans who sometimes disagree in opinion, this is a bibliography to read for its critical flavor and bite. The scope encompasses ghost stories and true crime. There are sections on the short story and play, critical works on the genre, and all aspects of Sherlock Holmes. The bibliography is currently being continued in *The Armchair Detective.*

Breen, Jon L. *What about Murder? A Guide to Books about Mystery and Detective Fiction.* Scarecrow Press, 1981.
> Two-hundred and thirty-nine books are listed and critically annotated. There are seven sections: General Histories, Reference Books, Special Subjects, Collected Essays and Reviews, Technical Manuals, Coffee-Table Books, Works on Individual Authors. The annotations are extensive and reveal Breen's wide reading and obvious enjoyment of the genre. Indispensable for serious fans.

Hagen, Ordean A. *Who Done It? A Guide to Detective, Mystery and Suspense Fiction.* Bowker, 1969.
> Now replaced by Hubin (below) but still of interest for the subject and background sections, the bibliography of secondary material, and the like.

Hubin, Allen J. *The Bibliography of Crime Fiction.* Publisher's Inc., 1979.
> The author listing notes series detectives and all pseudonyms. Series characters are indexed as are titles. The most comprehensive bibliography available. There are no annotations.

Johnson, Timothy W., and Julia Johnson, eds. *Crime Fiction Criticism: An Annotated Bibliography.* Garland, 1981.
> The annotations are concise and critical. "General Works," 530 items, includes reference works, monographs, dissertations, and articles and portions of books. There are 1,480 items on over 250 individual authors.

Melvin, David Skene, and Anne Skene Melvin, comps. *Crime, Detective, Espionage, Mystery and Thriller Fiction & Film: A Comprehensive Bibliography of Critical Writing through 1979.* Greenwood Press, 1980.
> An alphabetical listing without annotation. Omitted is "Holmesiana," for which the compilers refer the user to De Wall's bibliography, and the following genres: macabre, fantasy, ghosts, supernatural, Gothic, science fiction. *The Armchair Detective* is not indexed, and they note the index to the first 10 volumes published in 1979. There are title and subject indices.

Mundell, E. H., Jr., and G. Jay Rausch. *The Detective Short Story: A Bibliography and Index.* Kansas State University Library, 1974.
> The Library's Bibliographic Series, No. 14. Comprehensive and invaluable guide to finding stories in collections.

Reilly, John M., ed. *Twentieth-Century Crime and Mystery Writers.* London: Macmillan, 1980.
> Some 600 writers are given bibliographical and critical coverage. Works listed include nongenre titles. The critical essays vary greatly in length and quality and are signed. Occasionally the author has also supplied a brief personal essay. The appendix adds nine nineteenth-century writers and 16 foreign writers.

HISTORY

There is now a voluminous body of history and criticism on the detective subgenre. Many titles include material on the mystery, crime, spy, and horror story as well. Although there is a division in this book between history and criticism, this categorization reflects each book's formal organization: both provide history *with* criticism. Despite the many works of history and criticism on the detective story, the definitive history is still to be written. The examples listed here, excepting Haycraft's, are too specialized and idiosyncratic to be definitive:

Craig, Patricia, and Mary Cadogan. *The Lady Investigates: Women Detectives and Spies in Fiction*. London: Gollancz, 1980.
> The history starts with Mrs. Paschal in *The Revelations of a Lady Detective* (1861) and describes the variety of women detectives to date, with stringent criticism of their quality as detectives. The chapter "Spouses, Secretaries and Sparring Partners" acknowledges the women whose role was secondary to the male detective's. "A Sweet Girl Sleuth: The Teenage Detective in America" discusses the tribe of Nancy Drews (" 'You're a regular detective, Nancy!' "). There's lots of lovely quotation.

Haining, Peter. *Mystery! An Illustrated History of Crime and Detective Fiction*. Souvenir Press, 1977.
> The history is sketchy but the illustrations are voluminous and imaginative.

Haycraft, Howard. *Murder for Pleasure: The Life and Times of the Detective Story*. Appleton, 1941.
> Still the basic history despite its date. It includes a list of "Cornerstones," 1841-1938, and a guide to characters, "Who's Who in Detection."

LaCour, Tage, and Harold Mogensen. *The Murder Book: An Illustrated History of the Detective Story*. Herder, 1974.
> This is translated from the Danish and contains interesting European references. The history is presented topically. The illustrations are varied and wonderful.

Murch, A. E. *The Development of the Detective Novel*. London: Owen, 1958.
> Useful for the early history.

Ousby, Ian. *Bloodhounds of Heaven: The Detective in English Fiction from Godwin to Doyle*. Harvard, 1976.
> Main coverage is on William Godwin, Vidocq, Dickens, Collins, and Doyle.

Routley, Erik. *The Puritan Pleasures of the Detective Story*. London: Gollancz, 1972.
> Emphasis is on the British story.

Scott, Sutherland. *Blood in Their Ink: The March of the Modern Mystery Story*. London: Stanley Paul, 1953.
> His interest is largely in the detective story.

Stewart, R. F. *... And Always a Detective: Chapters on the History of Detective Fiction*. London: David & Charles, 1980.

Not a standard history but a fascinating discussion of the origins of the sensational thriller in the nineteenth century and the development of the image of the detective. This is for the knowledgeable fan.

Symons, Julian. *Mortal Consequences: A History—From the Detective Story to the Crime Novel.* Harper, 1972.
The British title: *Bloody Murder.* His history leads to the conclusion that the detective story is played out, and the more realistic, psychological, sociological crime novel is in ascendance.

CRITICISM

The section on bibliography provides a guide to the voluminous critical material on the detection and mystery subgenres, including works on individual authors. The selection given below from this voluminous literature indicates many of the types of criticism available:

Allen, Dick, and David Chacko, eds. *Detective Fiction: Crime and Compromise.* Harcourt, 1974.
This is an anthology of stories, with a section on criticism, meant to be used as a textbook. There are questions, suggested topics, and a reading list for students. The scope is extended to include writers not generally considered detective authors.

Ball, John, ed. *The Mystery Story.* Publisher's, Inc., 1976.
Noted writers here comment on aspects of the subgenre: amateur, women, ethnic, police, and private detectives; locked rooms; spies; "Gothic Mysteries"; series characters; "The Great Crooks"; use of pseudonyms. There is also an annotated subject bibliography.

Chandler, Raymond. *Raymond Chandler Speaking.* London: Hamilton, 1962.

Chandler, Raymond. *The Simple Art of Murder.* Norton, 1968.
The first title contains letters, many pungently critical, on a variety of subjects relating to his writings and the detective story. The second is a collection of his short stories and includes the title essay, a classic statement much anthologized.

Eames, Hugh. *Sleuths, Inc. Studies of Problem Solvers: Doyle, Simenon, Hammett, Ambler, Chandler.* Lippincott, 1978.

Geheim, David. *Sons of Sam Spade. The Private-Eye Novel in the 70s: Robert B. Parker, Roger L. Simon, Andrew Bergman.* Ungar, 1980.

Gilbert, Michael, ed. *Crime in Good Company: Essays on Criminals and Crime-Writing.* London: Constable, 1959.
This excellent collection "on behalf of the Crime Writers' Association" both defines and criticizes. Among the contributors: Josephine Bell, Michael Underwood, Maurice Procter, Cyril Hare, Raymond Chandler ("The Simple Art of Murder"), Michael Gilbert, Julian Symons, Jacques Barzun, Stanley Ellin, Eric Ambler.

Haycraft, Howard, ed. *The Art of the Mystery Story: A Collection of Critical Essays.* Simon & Schuster, 1946.

The best all-round anthology of the classic essays by both authors and fans of the genre. Includes "The Detection Club Oath"; "Who Cares Who Killed Roger Ackroyd?," by Edmund Wilson; "The Locked-Room Lecture," by John Dickson Carr; "Watson Was a Woman," by Rex Stout and a treasure of others.

Keating, H. R. F., ed. *Crime Writers. Reflections on Crime Fiction, by Reginald Hill, P. D. James, H. R. F. Keating, Troy Kennedy Martin, Maurice Richardson, Julian Symons, Colin Watson.* Additional material by Mike Pavell. London: BBC, 1978.
Includes essays on Sherlock Holmes, Dorothy L. Sayers, Dashiell Hammett, Georges Simenon, Patricia Highsmith, and others.

Landrum, Larry. "Detective and Mystery Novels." In Inge, M. Thomas, ed. *Handbook of American Popular Culture*, 1978. Vol. 1, pages 103-120.

Landrum, Larry N., Pat Browne, and Ray B. Browne, eds. *Dimensions of Detective Fiction.* Popular Press, 1976.
Twenty-three essays by academics cover diverse aspects of the genre and a number of individual writers.

Larmoth, Jeanne. *Murder on the Menu.* Recipes by Charlotte Turgeon. Scribner's, 1972.
Seemingly every possible situation in the English mystery, particularly in the country house or village setting, at which food could be served is described, complete with recipes. Along with the fun is some witty criticism of the genre and appropriate quotations.

Madden, David, ed. *Tough Guy Writers of the Thirties.* Southern Illinois Press, 1958.
Includes essays on the *Black Mask* authors, Dashiell Hammett, James M. Cain, and Raymond Chandler.

Mann, Jessica. *Deadlier Than the Male: An Investigation into Feminine Crime Writing.* London: David & Charles, 1981.
"Why is it that respectable English women are so good at murder?" asks the author who then seeks elucidation through the lives and works of Agatha Christie, Dorothy L. Sayers, Margery Allingham, Josephine Tey, and Ngaio Marsh. Her long first part is an intriguing definition of the subgenre and its heroes and heroines. Her conclusion is that these authors reflected a stable and, to them, desirable society; that in the present society of angry chaos, authors will reflect not a background received with pleasure but a background that will terrify the readers. Jessica Mann sees the subgenre becoming not an entertainment but virtually indistinguishable from the anguishedly realistic mainstream novel.

The Mystery and Detection Annual. 1972 and 1973.
Donald Adams edited and published these two exemplary volumes of essays and reviews, beautifully printed and illustrated.

Nivens, Francis M., Jr., ed. *The Mystery Writer's Art.* Bowling Green University Popular Press, 1970.
Twenty-one essays by authors and fans of the genre. Included are two essays by Frank McSherry on detection in San Francisco.

Panek, LeRoy. *Watteau's Shepherds: The Detective Novel in Britain, 1914-1940*. Bowling Green University Popular Press, 1979.

With introductory materials, here are critical chapters on E. C. Bentley, Agatha Christie, A. A. Milne, Dorothy Sayers, Anthony Berkeley Cox, Margery Allingham, John Dickson Carr, and Ngaio Marsh. Appendix I provides an intriguing analysis of the detective story plot through the use of detailed flowcharts.

Rosenberg, Bernard, and David M. White, eds. *Mass Culture: The Popular Arts in America*. Free Press, 1957.

Includes: Edmund Wilson, "Who Cares Who Killed Roger Ackroyd?"; George Orwell, "Raffles and Miss Blandish"; Charles J. Rolo, "Simenon and Spillane: The Metaphysics of Murder for the Millions"; Christopher LaFarge, "Mickey Spillane and His Bloody Hammer."

Sayers, Dorothy L. "Introduction" to her *Great Short Stories of Detection, Mystery and Horror*.

This classic critical history on the origins and development of the detective story is often reprinted. There is also an excellent shorter introduction to the second series and one to her other anthology, *Tales of Detection*. (See listing of anthologies.)

Watson, Colin. *Snobbery with Violence: Crime Stories and Their Audience*. London: Eyre, 1971.

The subgenre, sociologically considered, suffers badly, but the sophisticated fan will enjoy the writing.

Winks, Robin W., ed. *Detective Fiction: A Collection of Critical Essays*. Prentice-Hall, 1980.

Among the 17 essays are several of the classics: W. H. Auden, "The Guilty Vicarage"; Dorothy L. Sayers, "Aristotle on Detective Fiction"; Edmund Wilson, "Who Cares Who Killed Roger Ackroyd?"; Joseph Wood Krutch, "Only a Detective Story"; Gavin Lambert, "The Dangerous Edge"; Sayers's Introduction to *The Omnibus of Crime*; Jacques Barzun, "Detection and the Literary Art." The appendix includes a description of university courses on the detective story, a critical bibliography, and "A Personal List of 200 Favorites" that includes some spy genre titles.

Winks, Robin W., ed. *The Historian as Detective: Essays on Evidence*. Harper, 1969.

The editor admits he compiled these 26 essays for fun, and the reader with tastes for historical research will share the fun as Winks draws parallels from detective stories to preface each historian's account of sleuthing for evidence.

Winn, Dilys. *Murder Ink: The Mystery Reader's Companion*. Perpetrated by Dilys Winn. Workman, 1977.

The founder of the New York bookstore, Murder Ink, presents a delightful and irreverent miscellany, profusely illustrated, celebrating her favorite subgenre in all its guises.

Winn, Dilys, comp. *Murderess Ink: The Better Half of the Mystery*. Workman, 1979.

This is a lighthearted potpourri on women mystery writers, women in mystery stories, and women detectives. All in fun and lots of illustrations. There is, fortunately, an index to the miscellany.

Criticism — Parody

So formalized a subgenre is readily parodied. To enjoy parody, the reader must be familiar with the authors parodied. Except for the book by Gorey, these examples are detective stories in which the style of each author named is parodied. The last two are listed (perhaps discreetly) by Anonymous.

Bruce, Leo. *Case for Three Detectives.*
Sergeant Beef solves the murder handily while Lord Simon Plimsoll (Peter Wimsey), Monsieur Amer Picon (Hercule Poirot), and Monsignor Smith (Father Brown) conjecture deviously and vainly.

Christie, Agatha. *Partners in Crime.*
Tommy and Tuppence, Christie's husband and wife detective team, solve a series of cases and, in each, approach the problem as would one of the classic detectives. They mock the detectives' eccentricities of manner and speech. All the detectives were popular before 1929 when *Partners in Crime* was first published. (It is still available in paperback reprint.) Among the detectives are Dr. Thorndyke, Bull Dog Drummond, Sherlock Holmes, Father Brown, The Old Man in the Corner, Hanaud, Inspector French, Roger Sheringham, Dr. Fortune, and Poirot.

The Floating Admiral [by] Certain Members of the Detection Club. With a new introduction by Christianna Brand. Gregg Press, 1979.
First published in 1932. Thirteen authors successively wrote a chapter, none knowing the final solution (although each in the appendix provides one, not revealed to the other authors). Among the familiar creators of this pseudoparody are G. K. Chesterton, G. D. H. and M. Cole, Henry Wade, Agatha Christie, Dorothy L. Sayers, Ronald A. Knox, Freeman Will Crofts, Edgar Jepson, and Anthony Berkeley ("Clearing Up the Mess").

Gorey, Edward. *The Awdrey-Gore Legacy.* Dodd, 1972.
The inimitable drawings reveal all the tricks of the subgenre.

Mainwaring, Marion. *Murder in Pastiche; Or, Nine Detectives All at Sea.* Macmillan, 1954.
Seeking to solve the murder on the luxury liner are passengers Atlas Poireau, Sir Jon. Nappleby, Jerry Pason, Broderick Tourneur, Trajan Beare, Miss Fan Sliver, Spike Bludgeon, Mallory King, Lord Simon Quinsey.

Six against Scotland Yard: In Which Margery Allingham, Anthony Berkeley, Freeman Wills Crofts, Father Ronald Knox, Dorothy L. Sayers, Russell Thorndike Commit the Crime of Murder Which Ex-Superintendent Cornish, C.I.D., Is Called Upon to Solve. Doubleday, 1936.

The Smiling Corpse. Wherein G. K. Chesterton, S. S. Van Dine, Sax Rohmer, and Dashiell Hammett Are Surprised to Find Themselves at a Murder. Farrar, 1935.

ENCYCLOPEDIAS

Still needed is an exhaustive encyclopedia for mystery and detection, but the following is a promising beginning:

Steinbrunner, Chris, and Otto Penzler. *Encyclopedia of Mystery and Detection.* McGraw-Hill, 1976.
Entries are largely under authors and fictional detectives or other important characters. There are a few encyclopedic articles: "*Black Mask*"; "Collecting Detective Fiction"; "Comic Art Detectives"; "Dime Novels"; "Had-I-But-Known School"; "Locked Room Mysteries"; "Organizations"; "Orientals, Sinister"; "Pulp Magazines"; "Radio Detectives"; "Scientific Detectives"; "TV Detectives." Author bibliographies include full stage, screen, radio, and television versions. The author essays are usually critical. Illustrations are from books and films; there are also many portraits.

WHO'S WHO: PSEUDONYMS AND CHARACTERS

Many of the reference works provide references to pseudonyms and lists of characters, particularly the detective. Hubin (above) lists all pseudonyms, provides cross-references, and indexes the series characters. The book by Penzler et al. (below) provides little that is not in Steinbrunner (above), but the organization of the material is appealing as is the tone.

Penzler, Otto; Chris Steinbrunner; Charles Shibuk; Marvin Lachman; and Francis M. Nevins, Jr., comps. *Detectionary: A Biographical Dictionary of Leading Characters in Detective and Mystery Fiction, Including Famous and Little Known Sleuths, Their Helpers, Rogues Both Heroic and Sinister, and Some of Their Memorable Adventures, as Recounted in Novels, Short Stories, and Films.* Overlook Press, 1977.
There are four sections: "Detectives" lists the fictional detective with a biographical sketch. "Rogues & Helpers" gives a biographical sketch for criminals and villains as well as for all types of Dr. Watsons, including police detectives secondary to the major private or amateur detective. "Cases" gives a summary of selected mystery novels. "Movies" annotates under detective or movie title a selection of movies, particularly those in series. An author index gives detective and titles of novels. Illustrations are from motion pictures.

WRITERS' MANUALS

While meant for the writer of mysteries to improve both style and economy, these manuals are informative, critical, and interesting reading for the detective/mystery fan:

Burack, A. S., ed. *Writing Suspense and Mystery Fiction.* The Writer, 1977.
Some 30 genre authors comment on how to do their craft (includes remarks from a few critics, one being Ogden Nash bemoaning the had-I-but-known school).

Mystery Writers of America. *The Mystery Writer's Handbook: A Handbook on the Writing of Detective, Suspense, Mystery and Crime Stories.* Edited by Herbert Brean. Harper, 1956.

Mystery Writers of America. *The Mystery Writer's Handbook.* Newly Revised Edition. Writer's Digest, 1976.
> The revised edition is edited by Lawrence Treat. Both editions are needed as only a few of the articles are carried over. The authors in both editions are practitioners in the genre.

FILM

Film versions have made many detectives into folk heroes, often identified with the actor who characterized the detective in a series of motion pictures or in television series. Many of the books on the detective subgenre emphasize the relationship between fiction and film through illustrations from the films. Renewed interest in a writer usually follows the release of a motion picture or television show — examples are found in Agatha Christie and Dorothy L. Sayers. As often happens among critics of the subgenre in book form, there are radically different evaluations of the subgenre in film (and individual films) by the two authors listed below:

Everson, William K. *The Detective in Film.* Citadel, 1972.
> He starts with Sherlock Holmes (1903) and ends with the private eyes, with fine critical evaluations of treatments by both U.S. and British filmmakers and a few foreign producers. The illustrations are a delight.

Tuska, Jon. *The Detective in Hollywood.* Doubleday, 1978.
> Tuska also begins with Sherlock Holmes but treats only U.S. films. There is much about the actors and directors interviewed by Tuska. Profusely illustrated.

MAGAZINES AND FANZINES

The pulp magazines that made the fame of many detective story writers are long gone. Two magazines are now important for the detective short story: the venerable *Ellery Queen's Mystery Magazine* (since 1941) and *Alfred Hitchcock's Mystery Magazine* started in 1956.

Mystery had its first bimonthly issue at the end of 1979 and is a commercial glossy magazine with articles and interviews of popular appeal, book reviews, publishing news and comment on the genre in motion pictures and on television. There have been occasional short stories. It is fully illustrated.

Three fanzines have, fortunately, achieved a permanence and regularity to support their importance. All have interesting and varied articles, critical and bibliographical. All carry both current and retrospective reviews, and all are enlivened by long, enthusiastic, and critical letters from subscribers. *The Armchair Detective*, a quarterly in its fourteenth volume (1981), has published an index to the first 10 volumes (invaluable as a reference for reviews) and regularly includes the *Rex Stout Newsletter* and the supplementation for Barzun and Taylor, *Catalogue of Crime.* It also provides a checklist of current fiction in the subgenre. *The Mystery Fancier* is a bimonthly in its fifth volume (1981). *The*

Poisoned Pen is a bimonthly in its fourth volume (1981) and has as a continuing feature the "Subject Guide to Mystery Fiction."

Clues: A Journal of Detection (volume 1, 1980) is published by the Bowling Green University Popular Press twice yearly and gives the academic mind a showcase.

ASSOCIATIONS AND CONVENTIONS

Associations of mystery and crime writers serve to further the status and publishing of the subgenre and the economic welfare of writers. The U.S. and British associations present annual prizes. The prestige of these three associations is recognized by publishers who note an author's prize-winning status in advertisements and book jacket blurbs.

Detection Club
British honorary association founded in 1928. It has a delightful oath to which new members subscribe. Has published several anthologies to benefit the club.

Crime Writers' Association
British group founded in 1932. The "Gold Daggers" are the annual awards.

Mystery Writers of America
Founded in 1945. "Edgars" (Edgar Allan Poe Awards) are presented in several categories at the annual dinner. An annual anthology (first one in 1946) is published for the benefit of the association. The thirty-third annual anthology, *The Edgar Winners* (Dial, 1980), has an appendix listing "Edgar and Special Awards, 1945-1978": Grand Master, Best Novel, Best First Novel, Best Short Story, Best Paperback Original, Best Juvenile, Best Fact-Crime, Best Critical/Biographical Study, Outstanding Mystery Criticism, Best Motion Picture, Special Awards.

There are two conventions:

International Congress of Crime Writers
The first was held in London in 1975; the second, New York, 1978; the third, Stockholm, 1981. (The last brought out the statement that crime really pays in Sweden — both Swedish and translated authors sell extremely well.)

BoucherCon
The annual Anthony Boucher memorial convention. The first was in 1969 and the twelfth in 1981. Anthony Boucher, a pseudonym, wrote detective and science fiction stories and was notable as a critic and reviewer. A selection of his criticism and reviews was edited by Robert E. Briney and Francis M. Nevins, Jr.: *Multiplying Villainies: Selected Mystery Criticism, 1942-1968* (A BoucherCon Book, 1973, limited to 500 copies). In the book are found the annual lists of the best mysteries, with brief annotations, published in the "Criminals at Large" column in the *New York Times Book Review*, which he wrote from 1951 to 1968. The neophyte reader of mysteries will benefit from the reviews and the use of the lists

as a reading guide. In *Rocket to the Morgue* (1942), published under the pseudonym H. H. Holmes and reprinted in paperback under Anthony Boucher, is found the neat combination of his detection and science fiction interests — the suspects are science fiction writers, amusingly articulate about the genre, and a science fiction character seemingly come to life.

There are many fan clubs, several publishing a journal. Among the authors cherished by fans: Dorothy L. Sayers, John D. MacDonald, Rex Stout, Edgar Wallace, Sax Rohmer, Ellery Queen, and, of course, Sir Arthur Conan Doyle.

BOOK CLUBS

Mystery Guild (Doubleday) distributes book club editions of selected current thrillers. *Mystery Guild* also stocks for distribution some older titles and omnibus volumes (usually three titles in one volume, by a single author). The *Detective Book Club* reprints current titles by three authors in a three-in-one volume. All are good buys for public libraries.

PUBLISHERS

Almost all major U.S. houses publish some mystery (thriller) novels, and a few have large lines or named series: Dial; St. Martin's; Random House; Scribner's; Little, Brown; Viking, and others. The following are some well-known series:

Crime Club (Doubleday)

Red Badge (Dodd, Mead)

Cock Robin (Macmillan)

Red Mask (Putnam)

Inner Sanctum (Simon & Schuster)

Harper Novels of Suspense
(The long-time editor, Joan Kahn, resigned in 1980 then issued "Joan Kahn Books" through a newly established publisher, Ticknor & Field, and in 1982 switched to Dutton.)

Midnight Novels (Houghton Mifflin)

Seagull Library of Mystery and Suspense (Norton)

Collins does extensive publishing in Great Britain in its Crime Club line, as does Gollancz, while other publishers also have sizeable lists of thrillers: Jonathan Cape, Hutchinson, Heinemann, Hodder, Hamish Hamilton, Weidenfeld, Michael Joseph, Secker & Warburg, Macmillan, Robert Hale. It is notable that many U.S. titles appear promptly on British lists, while, in proportion, fewer British titles are issued in the United States.

Many paperback houses, both U.S. and British, regularly reprint new thrillers soon after hardcover editions. Some titles are originally published in paperback, but fewer titles than appear for other genres. Harlequin House's new (1981) line Raven House Mysteries includes original titles, the first group by pseudonymous authors, all labeled as members of the Mystery Writers of America. Paperback publishers tend to reprint many titles by a popular author, including quite old ones. For example, Bantam, Dell, Pocket Books, and Popular Library reprint Agatha Christie; some 80 titles are currently (as of 1981) available. Dorothy B. Hughes, whose thrillers were among the Pocket Books reprints in the forties and then were long out of print, has recently appeared again in paperback. The "Checklist" in *The Armchair Detective* gives current new and reprint titles and is a useful alert as more early writers are being reprinted: for example, Philip Macdonald and S. S. Van Dine, first published in the twenties and thirties.

Several of the paperback houses have regularly scheduled reprints: the Penguin Crime Monthly series is in its fourth year (1981) as is Harper's Perennial Library; Bantam Books has issued two a month for the last two years. Dell Books started two new series in 1980, each issuing two titles per month: Murder Ink Mysteries, selected by Carol Brener of Murder Ink mystery bookstore, and Scene of the Crime series, selected by Ruth Windfeldt of Scene of the Crime bookstore. The 18 titles in both series available in April 1981 date from 1922 (A. A. Milne, *The Red House Mystery*) to 1978 (Robert Barnard, *Death of a Mystery Writer*; and Pauline Glenn Winslow, *Copper Gold*). All are in traditional detective story pattern.

Dover has been reprinting in quality paperback classic mystery and detective novels of the nineteenth and early twentieth centuries: Mary E. Braddon, Ernest Bramah, Wilkie Collins, Freeman W. Crofts, R. Austin Freeman, Jacques Futrelle, Emile Gaboriau, Maurice Leblanc, Gaston Leroux, Arthur Morrison, Melville Davisson Post, Sax Rohmer, T. S. Stribling, Robert Van Gulik, H. E. Wood, and others.

Fifty Classics of Crime Fiction, 1900-1950, edited by Jacques Barzun and Wendell Hertig Taylor (Garland Publishing, 1976), is an ambitious reprint set. (A second set is announced for classics to 1975.) Its list forms a desirable basic reading guide to the detective story (to which almost all authors belong). Many of these authors have been recently reprinted in paperback editions, although the particular title may not be currently available. (There are 49 names as the first volume of the set is an introduction and only includes short stories.) This list, of course, includes the recognized classic authors in the field. Also reprinted in the set are some little remembered authors, and this notice has led to other titles by several of the authors being reprinted in paperback editions.

Allingham, Margery. *Dancers in Mourning.* 1937.

Bailey, H. C. *Mr. Fortune: Eight of His Adventures.*

Barton, Miles (aka John Rhode). *The Secret of Hugh Eldersham.* 1930.

Bentley, E. C. *Trent's Last Case.* 1912.

Blake, Nicholas. *Minute for Murder.* 1947.

Bramah, Ernest. *Max Carrados.* 1914.

Bullett, Gerald. *The Jury.* 1935.

Chandler, Raymond. *The Lady in the Lake.* 1943.

Chesterton, G. K. *The Innocence of Father Brown.* 1911.

Christie, Agatha. *The Murder of Roger Ackroyd.* 1926.

Cole, G. D. H., and Margaret Cole. *The Murder at Crome House.* 1927

Crispin, Edmund. *Buried for Pleasure.* 1949.

Doyle, Arthur Conan. *The Hound of the Baskervilles.* 1902.

Eustis, Helen. *The Horizontal Man.* 1946.

Fearing, Kenneth. *The Big Clock.* 1946.

Freeman, R. Austin. *The Singing Bow.* 1912.

Gardner, Erle Stanley. *The Case of the Crooked Candle.* 1944.

Garve, Andrew. *No Tears for Hilda.* 1950.

Gilbert, Michael. *Smallbone Deceased.* 1950.

Grafton, C. W. *Beyond a Reasonable Doubt.* 1940.

Green, Anna Katherine. *The Circular Study.* 1900.

Hare, Cyril. *When the Wind Blows.* 1949.

Head, Matthew. *The Congo Venus.* 1950.

Heyer, Georgette. *A Blunt Instrument.* 1938.

Hilton, James. *Was It Murder?* 1935.

Huxley, Elspeth. *The African Poison Murders.* 1939.

Innes, Michael. *The Daffodil Affair.* 1942.

Kindon, Thomas. *Murder in the Moor.* 1929.

Lewis, Lange. *The Birthday Murder.* 1945.

McCarr, Pat. *Pick Your Victim.* 1946.

Macdonald, Ross. *The Drowning Pool.* 1950.

McGuire, Paul. *A Funeral in Eden.* 1938.

Marsh, Ngaio. *A Wreath for Rivera.* 1949.

Milne, A. A. *The Red House Mystery.* 1922.

Morrah, Dermot. *The Mummy Case.* 1933.

Onions, Oliver. *In Accordance with the Evidence.* 1915.

Page, Marco. *The Shadowy Third.* 1946.

Perdue, Virginia. *Alarum and Excursion.* 1944.

Phillpotts, Eden. *"Found Drowned."* 1931.

Sayers, Dorothy L. *Strong Poison.* 1930.

Snow, C. P. *Death under Sail.* 1932.

Stout, Rex. *Too Many Cooks.* 1938.

Upfield, Arthur. *The Bone Is Pointed.* 1938.

Wade, Henry. *The Dying Alderman.* 1930.

Webster, Henry Kitchell. *Who Is Next?* 1931.

Wilkinson, Ellen. *The Division Bell Mystery.* 1932.

Witting, Clifford. *Measure for Murder.* 1945.

Crime/Caper

FILM

The two titles on films listed previously under detective stories contain notice of some of the rogue caper films. The two noted here are on the crime films that were long a staple in Hollywood:

Cameron, Ian. *A Pictorial History of Crime Films.* London: Hamlyn, 1975.

Clarens, Carlos. *Crime Movies: From Griffith to the Godfathers—and Beyond.* Norton, 1979.

Spy/Espionage

ANTHOLOGIES

In addition to the following, spy stories may be found in anthologies of mystery and detective stories.

Ambler, Eric, ed. *To Catch a Spy: An Anthology of Favorite Spy Stories.* Atheneum, 1965.
　　The authors included are John Buchan, Somerset Maugham, Compton Mackenzie, Graham Greene, Eric Ambler, Ian Fleming, Michael Gilbert. Ambler's introduction is a historical definition of the subgenre, with its lovely comment on "The early clock-and-dagger stereotypes—the black-velveted seductress, the British secret-service numbskull hero, the omnipotent spymaster...."

Bond, Raymond T., ed. *Famous Stories of Code and Cipher.* Holt, 1947.
　　Only a few in this anthology are spy stories, but codes and ciphers are always identified with the genre.

Dulles, Allen, ed. *Great Spy Stories from Fiction.* Harper, 1969.
　　A classic anthology of 32 stories with critical introductions.

BIBLIOGRAPHY

As many of the authors of the spy novel also write mystery and detective novels, material on them, in addition to that in the two bibliographies listed below, may be found among some of the bibliographies and other reference books in the detective story section.

McCormick, Donald. *Who's Who in Spy Fiction.* Taplinger, 1977.
　　The biocritical annotations list the works. The introduction is historical and critical. Appendix: "List of Abbreviations, Titles and Jargon Used in Espionage in Fact and Fiction"—the definitions are often amusing.

Smith, Myron J. *Cloak-and-Dagger Bibliography: An Annotated Guide to Spy Fiction, 1937-1975.* Scarecrow Press, 1976.
　　The annotations are briefly descriptive and not critical. Only one or a few of the titles by an author are annotated.

HISTORY AND CRITICISM

Additional material on the spy novel will be found in some of the books in the detective story section.

Harper, Ralph. *The World of the Thriller*. Johns Hopkins University Press, 1974 [1969].
   Through an analysis of the hero and the situations of the spy subgenre, the author seeks to understand why readers become so engrossed in the books. He concludes that the subgenre, despite its sensationalism, exposes our nature to ourselves.

Merry, Bruce. *Anatomy of the Spy Thriller*. London: Gill, 1977.
   The analysis of the books is idiosyncratic; to be critical, the reader should be a fan of the subgenre. The book contains a wealth of quotation.

Palmer, Jerry. *Thrillers: Genesis and Structure of a Popular Genre*. London: Edward Arnold, 1978.
   An eccentric book—the author's reading seems largely of Mickey Spillane and Ian Fleming. Included here as an object lesson in distrusting titles.

4 Romance

Man's love is of man's life a thing apart,
'Tis woman's whole existence.
>   — Byron
>   *Don Juan*

Who, at present, could name the volumes of horror and romance that set Emma Bovary to mortal dreaming?
>   — George Steiner

"Why, Sir," said Johnson, "if you were to read Richardson for the story, your impatience would be so much fretted that you would hang yourself. But you must read him for the sentiment."

It is a truth universally acknowledged, that a single man in possession of a good fortune must be in want of a wife.
>   — Jane Austen
>   *Pride and Prejudice*

"There is no happiness in love, except at the end of an English novel."
>   — Signora Neroni
>   (a character in Anthony Trollope's
>   *Barchester Towers*)

Silly novels by Lady Novelists are a genus with many species determined by the particular quality of silliness that predominates in them — the frothy, the prosy, the pious, or the pedantic. But it is a mixture of all these — a composite order of feminine fatuity, that produces the largest class of such novels, which we shall distinguish as the mind-and-millinery species.
>   — George Eliot

Be suspicious of Women. They are given to the Reading of frivolous Romances....
>   — *The Old Librarian's Almanac*

THE APPEAL OF ROMANCE

Critics of Literature, suitably capitalized, avert their eyes disdainfully from the popular romance or dismiss its authors and readers with witty contempt. Yet the devoted readers, blissfully unaware their taste is lamentable, have ensured by their demand the steady supply of romantic fiction since Henry Richardson's *Pamela* staunchly defended her virtue and attained her heart's desire. *Pamela*, the novels of Jane Austen, of Charlotte and Emily Brontë, and of Anthony Trollope are soberly treated by critics of Literature. However, these types of books get a better reception in two books by British authors:

> Anderson, Rachel. *The Purple Heart Throbs: The Sub-Literature of Love.* London: Hodder, 1974.
>
> Cecil, Mirabel. *Heroines in Love, 1750-1974.* London: Michael Joseph, 1974.

The Purple Heart Throbs analyzes the popular romantic fiction of the nineteenth and twentieth centuries, noting plot and themes and the changing attitudes of society affecting both. Full plot summaries and extensive quotations reveal the constant appeal of the genre, regardless of how women's ideas and position in society were being transformed. Emotional experiences might be tinged with religious spirituality or aimed at sexual fulfillment, but the desired ending was marriage. No fundamental difference, except in adaptation to current sexual mores, distinguishes these novels from those popular today. There are chapters on the soap opera type of romance, the desert sheik epic, the doctor-nurse, and newly independent working woman romances. Why women read romances is discussed, the rules governing the genre analyzed, and members of the Romantic Novelists Association are given their say in defense of the genre. "Although they may no longer believe in God, readers do still believe in love" — the abundant quotations are a delight.

Heroines in Love provides nine stories from magazines, the first dated 1780 and the last 1969. Each is extensively and critically prefaced to form a history of the romantic heroine in magazine fiction. Each of the chapters comments on the stories published in the period, e.g., "The Horrors, 1794-1833"; "The Pure, 1830-1870"; "The Happy-Housewife Heroine, 1950-1965." There is much quotation and summary of typical plots. Illustrations from magazines of each period are included.

Martin Lewin, whose reviews of popular romances in the *New York Times Book Review* were a constant delight, provides an anthology, *Love Stories* (New York: Quadrangle, 1975), not of the pulp or popular romance authors but by "serious" authors (e.g., Willa Cather, Vladimir Nabokov, Shirley Jackson, Isaac Bashevis Singer, Elizabeth Spencer). He says simply, "Love is an idea whose time has come back."

"What does a woman want?" asked Freud, and did not read romances to find the answer. (What do men want? The local V.A. hospital reports an ardent readership for Barbara Cartland.) What women read for dream-escape into emotional fulfillment varies in the trappings of historical period, place, and social milieu but not in the essential element — true love triumphant against all odds.

Why do women read romances so voraciously? One of this author's students began her paper on popular romances thus: "I stopped reading Romances when I started having them." She probably began reading them again when the routine monotony of daily living caught up with her. Women know the escape from reality or frustration in the reading of romances is an escape into fantasy, whether innocent or erotic. They are not deluded but delighted. They identify with a heroine and a world beyond their attainment but not their dreams.

(Similarly, men who read adventure stories identify with the competent and virile hero, Walter Mittys all.) Romances are read by women of all ages, occupations (lawyers or housewives), and economic status. "Obviously, for a large share of the female population, equal rights and liberation are one thing, fantasies quite another," a reviewer commented on one of Rosemary Rogers' sweet-and-savage romances. "All passion spent," we know we will live happily ever after.

Within the romance genre are several quite distinctive subgenre, differentiated for appeal to disparate audiences by setting, types of characters, and handling of sexual relations, i.e., is love holy and discreet as in the womanly romance or replete with violence and explicitness as in the sweet-and-savage romance? The publishers (particularly of paperbacks) aware that readers choose by type, label the books explicitly by phrase (nurse romance, Gothic romance, Regency romance, historical romance, saga), or by a series title that immediately identifies the type for the reader, or by a readily recognized kind of cover illustration (notably for the Gothic romance), or by suggestive titles (*Wicked Loving Lies*), or by length (sweet-and-savage romances are seldom less than 400 pages and often 600).

THEMES AND TYPES

Womanly Romances

The classic encompassing type of romance is the womanly romance (dominant, for example, in the Harlequin romances), contemporary in setting, with home and marriage the goals for living happily ever after. (The period romance—notably Barbara Cartland—may be in essentials a womanly romance, but the historical setting adds a glamour appealing to a readership different from those who want the everyday present romantically rendered.) The world depicted may be of a small town or metropolis: in it girl meets boy, they misunderstand each other, and, ultimately, blissfully reconcile. Many books of this genre are set in the business world (marrying the boss' son or the boss himself). Others, particularly in smaller communities, center on the relationships of several families. A more exotic setting is obtained by having the girl take a job abroad and, occasionally, by having the hero be of that country. The foreign setting may frequently be linked to sports, e.g., a ski resort.

The following are authors of the prototype womanly romance:

Ayres, Ruby M.
  British author, over 140 novels, her first published in 1917.

Baldwin, Faith
  In her eighties, she is "the First Lady of the Love Story": currently in hardcover and paperback, about 100 novels.

Bloom, Ursula
  British, "The Queen of the romantic novel," over 500 titles.

Dell, Ethel R.
  British, her first work published in 1912, and on the best-seller list in 1916, several reprinted and condensed in Barbara Cartland's "Library of Love" series. " 'Yes, I am mad,' he said, and the words came quick and passionate, the lips that uttered them close to her own. 'I am mad for

you, Anne I worship you. And swear that while I live no other man shall ever hold you in his arms again. Anne — goddess — queen woman — you are mine — you are mine — you are mine.' "

Hill, Grace Livingston
Over 50 novels (20 million copies) reprinted by Bantam Books and written from 1882 to 1947: "Mrs. Hill's novels of romance are about wholesome people whose profound faith and generous hearts let them cope with the problems of the modern world."

Montgomery, Lucy Maude
The Anne of Green Gables (first published in 1908) and the Emily series. Now considered for the young adult audience.

Norris, Kathleen
The American Woman's dream in best-selling novels, her first published in 1911 and on the best-seller list in 1916.

Webster, Jean. *Daddy-Long-Legs* (1912).
Now considered for young adult audience.

The tried-and-true romance patterns, providing a story in which happy endings are obligatory, are pursued faithfully by a large number of women authors. (The several hundred who turn out the Harlequin romances are noted in discussing that publishing house. Several have written over 50 novels.) The authors continuing the traditions of womanly romance are myriad. The following listing is selective. To extend it to include the many authors now writing for original paperback series would be futile until time proves which ones will survive.

> "Have you a story about a shy young heroine who meets a rich handsome aristocrat and they get married and live happily ever after — but without sexist overtones?"
> — Caption to a cartoon by Hector Breene

Cadell, Elizabeth
British, thirty-third novel in 1979. Light comedy and suspenseful romance. "Presents a love story bound to warm the coldest heart."

Caldwell, Taylor
Thirty-fifth novel, 1980. Twenty-five paperback titles, 25 million copies. Often a religious aspect, "liberally peopled by villains and schemers, and often ... deal with family dynasties." " 'But you can't marry me. You are — Jeremy Porter — and a rich man and a lawyer, and I am only a servant girl.' " *Ceremony of Innocence.*

Cookson, Catherine
British, over 40 novels. Forty-two novels in British paperback, 20 million copies. "A long juicy woman's novel full of a great deal of sentiment and suffering, nobility and nonsense...." *Katie Mulholland.* Mary Ann series, eight novels to date.

Duncan, Jane

"My Friends" series, over 20 novels: "homely account of lives and life patterns, gently told and shot through with ... perceptive observations about ordinary people."

Dwyer-Joyce, Alice

"Romantic escapism with a touch of mystery" — *The House of Jackdaws.* "I knew that eternity itself would not be long enough to love Patrick. I had found a magic world where nobody walked but he and I ... where he was king and I was queen and we walked in Paradise together" — *The Moonlit Way.*

Eden, Dorothy

Over 30 novels (including Gothic and historical romances). "If you put Dorothy Eden's name on a seed catalogue it would sell" — Ace Books editor.

Gaskin, Catherine

Lofts, Norah

Loring, Emilie

Marchant, Catherine

"... A wonderfully engrossing tale, a heroine with just the right amounts of innocence, honesty, loyalty and spirit, and a couple of heroes imperfect enough to be attractive and very human" — *The Slow Awakening.*

Pilcher, Rosamunde

"I don't know where Rosamunde Pilcher has been all my life — but now that I've found her, I'm not going to let her go. The reason being that she writes romantic novels that are nearly perfect little *bon-bons*: not too much sugar, very little artificial coloring, lots of natural ingredients, ingeniously blended" — *Sleeping Tiger.* "... It is warmed with honest sentiment, lubricated with tears of happiness and souped up by an ace romanticist" — *Under Gemini.*

Read, Miss

"Warm-hearted story of English village life." "Miss Read's sure sentimental touch has again created a warm novel filled with her familiar characters" — *Return to Thrush Green.*

Stevenson, D. E.

British, over 50 novels. "Funny, entertaining and clean." Mrs. Tim series: "With her usual charm and friendly understanding, Mrs. Tim makes friends, influences people and straightens out a lot of problems, including her own." Several titles available in large print, G. K. Hall & Co.

Thirkell, Angela

British, 35 novels. Barsetshire series: cosily snobbish upper-class village doings.

Van Slyke, Helen

Her nine novels sold six million copies. "It's all soap opera and it's all grand" — *The Best Place to Be.* "... When did you last feel you really knew the people in a book ... that you shared their pain and pleasure, in some form, in your own life? When did you find yourself smiling at something on one page and staining the next one with nice therapeutic tears? ...

Millions of readers want the kind of reality they can interpret in terms of their own experience, or within the scope of their own imagination. They don't scoff at sentiment; it never goes out of style. They believe in good and evil, in love and loyalty, and in bitterness and betrayal. This is the stuff real life is made of...." " 'Old-fashioned' and 'Up-to-the-Minute.' " by Helen Van Slyke — *The Writer*, November 1975, page 14.

SOAP OPERA

Within the definition of womanly romance must be included a type with gloomy overtones — the "soap opera" romance. Sin, suffering, and retribution permeate the pages, with an occasional relief of joy or spiritual uplift. The pattern was set in the nineteenth century with *East Lynne* ("Next week *East Lynne*" — the touring stock company's placard was seldom missing in small towns in both England and the United States in the first quarter of this century for the stage version) and notably continued in *Stella Dallas* (book, radio serial, motion picture) — the wife who strayed, the unforgiving husband who keeps the child, and so forth. Included also are romances with excessive attention to anguish. Some of the older prototypes include:

Finley, Martha. Elsie Dinsmore series (first in 1868).

Porter, Gene Stratton. *Freckles* (1904).

Prouty, Olive Higgens. *Stella Dallas* (1923).

Wood, Ellen Price. *East Lynne* (1861).

Examples of more recent prototypes are:

Metalious, Grace. *Peyton Place* (1956).

Segal, Erich. *Love Story* (1970).

The sob-sister kin of this type of romance is the pulp magazine and radio and television soap opera series. All are heavy on problems and afflictions, divorce and love triangles, illness and suffering, with mixed-up and messed-up being fixed attributes of emotions. For those who missed the pulps, here is an anthology, complete with the original advertisements and illustrations:

Moriarity, Florence, ed. *True Confessions: Sixty Years of Sin, Suffering and Sorrow, 1919-1979, from the Pages of True Confessions, True Story, True Experience, True Romance, True Love, Secrets, Modern Romance*. Simon & Schuster, 1979.

If you are not a soap opera fan, here are a few readings to tune into some lustily sinful plots:

Edmondson, Madeleine, and David Rounds. *From Mary Noble to Mary Hartman: The Complete Soap Opera Book*. Stein, 1976.

Kinzer, Nora Scott. "Soapy Sin in the Afternoon." *Psychology Today*, August 1975, pages 46-48.

LaGuardia, Robert. *The Wonderful World of Soap Operas*. Ballantine, 1974.

"Sex and Suffering in the Afternoon." *Time*, November 12, 1976:46-48, 51-53.

Time notes that about a quarter of the students at Princeton "drop everything to watch 'The Young and the Restless' each afternoon," and this writer has known students to schedule classes around their favorite series. *Time*'s most trenchant comment: "It appears that the facts of ordinary life must be abandoned when watching the soaps." (Announced in 1980 are novelizations in several volumes of three daytime serials, drawing on the scripts by several authors. Also, in 1980 appeared a photonovel soap opera: Winifred Wolf's *And Baby Made Three*, dealing with parenthood, divorce, and reconciliation in 338 black-and-white photographs of sequential action using actors, with wisps of dialogue in the margins.)

DOCTOR

A goodly part of the action in these soap operas occurs in hospitals (two of the popular series are "The Doctors" and "General Hospital") with doctors and nurses aboundingly present. The doctor is a natural hero for romance, deriving power and mystery from his godlike control of life and death. The nurse, being also intimately involved in these great dramas of human existence, derives an emotional intensity of characterization from her occupation. Doctor and nurse romances may share soap opera plot elements but, despite the current number featuring malpractice, are usually moral and uplifting. Recently the doctor romance has been disturbingly intermingled with mad scientist and horror aspects, *not* a subgenre appealing to the romance reader. (The novels of Robin Cook and Irving Sobel illustrate this type.) Prototypes of the doctor romance are the British author A. J. Cronin's *The Citadel* (1937) and Morton Thompson's *Not as a Stranger* (1954). Other authors have written occasional doctor romances (e.g., Mary Roberts Rinehart's *The Doctor*, a long soap opera first published in 1935 and reprinted in paperback in 1966), but the following listing is for those authors specializing in this subgenre:

Douglas, Colin
    Three novels to date about young Dr. Campbell in a hospital in Scotland; serious but with touches of comedy.

Gordon, Richard
    British, "Doctor in the house" series.

Seifert, Elizabeth
    Over 60 novels on doctors in love.

Slaughter, Frank
    Over 55 novels. "At the end of the trail for Dr. Reed is a possible Nobel Prize and the love of his lab assistant. 'The warmth of her kiss told him that she was now his and his alone...' " — *Plague Ship*. "The ingredients include: doctors, their wives, hospital work, marital crises, drugs, adultery, murder and scandal" — *Doctors Wives*.

NURSE

The litter of paperback originals labeled by their publishers "Nurse Romance," are indistinguishable from each other: young nurse and romantic doctor, finding love among the bedpans amidst the heavy drama of their misunderstandings and patients' traumas. Arlene Hale has seemingly written hundreds: a typical title — *Nurse Julia's Tangled Loves*. A British nurse, Lucilla Andrews, has written some 20 hospital romances, not published in the United States. Three established nurse series are decidedly for young adults: Helen D. Boylston's Sue Barton series, Dorothy Deming's Penny Marsh series, and Helen Wells' Cherry Ames series.

FANTASIES OF PASSION

Firmly in the subgenre womanly romance are fantasies of passion, erotic and purple but not wallowing in the sexual adventures filling the sweet-and-savage romance. These two prototypes have influenced many writers and have been imitated but never surpassed:

Glyn, Elinor. *Three Weeks.*
Her only erotic romance, published in 1907, treats illicit love with a high moral tone ("And so, as ever, the woman paid the price.") The young hero is initiated into the rites of love by a mature woman (and on a tiger-skin rug).

> Would you like to sin
> With Elinor Glyn
> On a tiger skin
> Or would you prefer
> To err with her
> On some other fur?

Elinor Glyn coined the sex term "It" and also taught Rudolph Valentino how to kiss the palm not the back of a woman's hand.

Hull, Ethel M. *The Sheik* (1919).
"The first romantic heroine to be sexually assaulted, to learn during three hundred pages of it to enjoy it, and to marry the man who did it." Rachel Anderson, *The Purple Heart Throbs.*

Diana's eyes passed over him slowly till they rested on his brown, clean-shaven face, surmounted by crisp, close-cut brown hair. It was the handsomest and the cruellest face that she had ever seen. Her gaze was drawn instinctively to his. He was looking at her with fierce burning eyes that swept her until she felt that the boyish clothes that covered her slender limbs were stripped from her, leaving the beautiful white body under his passionate stare.

She shrank back, quivering, dragging the lapels of her riding jacket together over her breast with clutching hands, obeying an impulse that she hardly understood.

"Who are you?" she gasped hoarsely.

"I am the Sheik Ahmed Ben Hassan."

The "sand-and-tit" epics inspired by *The Sheik* usually descend into sweet-and-savage romance.

Romantic-Suspense

The subgenre romantic-suspense frequently eludes easy labeling. Novels in this category may blend into the thriller subgenre mystery-suspense (in which the mystery dominates the romance, making the novel of equal interest to both sexes) and into spy/espionage in the hands of such as Helen MacInnes (in whose novels romance and espionage share billing). Most clearly defined is the Gothic novel, but the publishers often label it a suspense novel rather than a Gothic, seeking to evade the negative attitude toward the Gothic because so much ridicule has been directed towards its stereotyped plot.

Romantic-suspense novels are a woman's novel — while full of adventure and suspense, neither is allowed to diminish the heroine's romantic involvement. Many other types of romance have elements of suspense and mystery, and authors of romantic-suspense novels usually write in several other subgenres of romance as well. (Some of the authors listed below are also listed for other types of romance.) Plot background may be basically domestic (girl marries, goes to family estate, husband dies or disappears; family secret leads to murder, scandal, and so forth) or with exotic foreign background (an archaeological dig) or with the trappings of the period romance. Mary Stewart, the "Queen" of this subgenre, is very satisfactorily high in romantic appeal and so strong in suspenseful adventure in foreign parts involving both romantic leads as to be the one author in this category of interest to men as well as women readers. Most of the authors listed below appear in hardcover editions as well as paperback reprints:

Aiken, Joan
"Another top-notch confection from a first-class pastry cook" — *The Smile of the Stranger*. "Tale of dicey doings in the 19th century is an agreeable if frothy diversion" — *The Five-Minute Marriage*.

Anthony, Evelyn
"Cleverly turned out romantic suspense, sparked with the flavor of contemporary horseracing" — *The Silver Falcon*.

Butler, Gwendoline

Conway, Laura
"For those who enjoy a touch of the occult in their romances" — *Take Heed of Loving Me*.

Eberhart, Mignon Good
Fifty-two mysteries, first in 1929, equally romantic and mysterious. "As is to be expected, the mystery is thickly sauced with sensitivity and the love interest is more important than the solution. The story is, however, not a whit the worse for it" — *Two Little Rich Girls*.

Eden, Dorothy

Foley, Rae
"At least Foley tells her story without the sentimentality that so often afflicts stories of romantic suspense" — *Where Helen Lies*.

Gaskin, Catherine

Gilman, Dorothy
"All ends well, girl gets boy, and the wicked are suitably punished" — *The Tightrope Walker.*

Hodge, Jane Aiken
"Cafe expresso reading with all the attractive scenic touches" — *One Way to Venice.*

Holland, Isabelle

Holt, Victoria
"... In Australia, where Jessica encounters a jealous rival, a missing gem, and a couple of murders before finding true love — with her husband" — *The Pride of the Peacock.*

Howatch, Susan

Johnston, Velda
"Star-crossed lovers, two suspicious deaths, and a dash of period flair...." — *The Silver Dolphin.*

Lofts, Norah

Marlowe, Ann

Mayberry, Ann

Michaels, Barbara
"... The ending is a zonker and very, very romantic" — *Wait for What Will Come.*

Peters, Elizabeth
"Vicky's adventures and misadventures are wonderfully amusing and tongue-in-cheek suspenseful" — *Street of the Five Moons.*

Stewart, Mary
The queen of the genre to whom others are compared.

Whitney, Phyllis A.

GOTHIC

The most enduring subgenre within romantic-suspense is the Gothic novel, now somewhat eclipsed by the historical romance in its several guises. Many of the Gothic novel authors have turned to other forms of romance, notably the period romance, and are simply using variations of the Gothic plot, often with supernatural aspects. The publishers still issue a few Gothics, but the paperback publishers have let up on their series that flooded the stands, and those issued are with less stridently Gothic covers. Much issued under the label romantic-suspense is unabashedly in the Gothic mode.

That Gothic is often applied to novels of supernatural horror and terror stems from the historically dual sources of the Gothic novel. The literary Gothic novel of the eighteenth and nineteenth centuries, the Gothic in the Radcliffe tradition (Ann Radcliffe whose *Mysteries of Udolpho* set the pace), featured a heroine, young orphan or widowed, whose life, lover, child, and wealth are threatened by wicked uncles et al., abetted by necromancers, amidst the prisons of ruined and haunted castles, with scenes of terror threatening the heroine's sanity. The Radcliffe type of Gothic is in the romance tradition, while the type patterned after Horace Walpole's ("Mystery is the wisdom of blockheads.") *The Castle of Otranto* emphasizes supernatural terror, usually in a medieval setting.

These early Gothic novels contributed some characteristics to the modern Gothic, but story and characters belong to a type of novel quite unlike the modern Gothic. "The characters in the fictions themselves, like their authors and their early readers, are not merely people who lived before Freud; they are still innocent of exposure to human nature as Jane Austen understood the term. The best Gothic story, therefore, remains the one which produces instantaneous sensations of surprise, fear and bewilderment; and it is this that the Gothic novels of the eighteenth century still so satisfyingly do.... The quasi-innocent world of nightmare with which the circulating libraries beguiled the rainy afternoons of girls like Catherine Morland" (The heroine of Jane Austen's *Northanger Abbey*) (from the *Times Literary Supplement* review by A. N. Wilson, of Elizabeth McAndrew's book *The Gothic Tradition in Fiction* [Columbia University Press, 1980]). An anthology edited by Seon Manley and Gogo Lewis, *Ladies of the Gothics: Tales of Romance and Terror by the Gentle Sex* (Lothrop, 1975), is largely in the Radcliffe tradition and illustrates the differences between early and modern Gothic novels.

The modern Gothic novel derives from Charlotte Brontë's *Jane Eyre* and Daphne Du Maurier's *Rebecca*. Two basic plots emerge. From *Jane Eyre*: a young heroine, alone in the world, takes a post as governess, companion, nurse, or secretary; goes to an isolated house where suspicious, mysterious, perhaps supernatural, events occur, threatening the heroine who snoops; she falls in love with her employer, his/her son, a friend/relative of the family; there is doubt as to which of the two men to whom she is attracted is villain or hero, the latter usually acting in the more dastardly fashion for much of the book. From *Rebecca*: a young heroine, alone in the world, marries, often under odd circumstances; goes to the ancestral mansion where mysteries concerning her husband or his family prove threatening to the heroine's life and sanity; there is often confusion as to identity of hero and villain. A third type derives loosely from Emily Brontë's *Wuthering Heights* with elements of the supernatural, star-crossed lovers, and evil immanent in house, jewels, or other objects. Authors sometimes mix elements from all three variations.

The heroine is typically naive (often to the point of imbecility), but occasionally there is a strong-minded (liberated?) heroine, greatly enhancing the quality of the novel. It is notable how often the reviewers comment on the heroine's mental capability: "a relatively intelligent heroine," "a young woman of surprising innocence," "girl's deliberate denseness makes the book seem longer than it is." A happy ending is obligatory, however bittersweet, but sexual explicitness is forbidden: "The villain can want to beat her, torture her, or even kill her. But he mustn't contemplate rape!" (from D. R. Koontz's *Writing Popular Fiction*, Writer's Digest, 1972). The heroine narrator belongs to the she-suppressed-a-shudder school and shares the characteristics of the thriller's had-I-but-known narrator. For both types of novel, suspense is necessarily lessened as the heroine *is* narrating the events, so she did survive!

Misleadingly to the romance fan, the Gothic label may appear on supernatural tales of ghosts and horror. Some called occult Gothic are determinedly decadent, with emphasis on sex and satanism. Many novels of romantic suspense indulge in Gothic characteristics, and the readership interest is usually satisfied by either subgenre.

These three prototypes have never lost their magic and popularity, remaining ever in print in hardcover and paperback editions. All became classic motion pictures.

Brontë, Charlotte. *Jane Eyre* (1847)
" 'You, poor and obscure, and small and plain as you are—I entreat you to accept me as your husband.' " "Reader, I married him."

Brontë, Emily. *Wuthering Heights* (1847).

Du Maurier, Daphne. *Rebecca* (1938).
"Last night I dreamt I went to Manderley again."

The deluge of Gothic novels, particularly in original paperbacks, no longer appears from the publishers, but these authors still write variations of the Gothic, often labeled romantic suspense, as well as other types of romance:

Aiken, Joan
"It would seem that Aiken, clearly a witty woman of good sense, has tried to do a Gothic, but is much too sprightly and amusing to bring it off"—*A Cluster of Separate Sparks*. "A ghost-ridden Scottish castle, the 'Beast of Bermondsey' prowling the streets of London, a wife's amputated hand found in her husband's luggage..."—*Castle Barebane*.

Astley, Juliet
"... Eccentrics who are as fascinating as the atmospheric castle and the dark passions that lurk within it"—*Copsi Castle*.

Berckman, Evelyn

Carr, Philippa

Coffman, Virginia
"Romy Becker's marriage ... seemed to be having adverse effects. Romy's memory began playing tricks on her. People claimed they'd seen her in places she couldn't remember being. Then there were the near fatal accidents. Was she insane? Or was she the victim of some terrifying hoax?"—*The High Terrace*.

Daniels, Dorothy
"Was there any escape for a lovely young woman lured into a stronghold of unspeakable evil?"—*House of Silence*. "Yet if Amy had known the terror that awaited her in a place where her only ally was charming Jess Foster, a sworn enemy of all the Paiges, she would have boarded the first train back North, leaving Death to rule unchallenged at Greenlawn"—*Bridal Black*. "Soon Tidemill was no longer her gracious home, but a grim prison—and unless she discovered its evil secret, it would destroy her body and possess her soul"—*Bride of Terror*. "Though I still knew very well that some mysterious and harsh force was working against me, what I faced wasn't worth going through ... there was the ever-present threat of those ghosts"—*The Spanish Steps*.

DeWeese, Jean
"It was over. The link with the past was broken and past was once again only the past. The dead were once again the dead, and their ranks had been increased by one"—*Cave of the Moaning Wind*.

Eden, Dorothy
"Lightning flashed across the windows and there was a distant crack of thunder. Miss O'Riordan peered out into the dark night" — *Whistle for the Crows.*

Ford, Hilary
"The author has taken a shopworn Gothic formula and fashioned it into a delightful novel that captures the *bon ton* of speech and manners of post-Regency London and Guernsey, and she even makes her nice-Nelly heroine a thoroughly likeable character" — *Sarnia.*

Heyer, Georgette
Cousin Kate: The Gothic among her Regency romances.

Hill, Pamela
"The heroine is a governess and properly masochistic; the hero is dark, saturnine and properly hag-ridden and vengeful, if not actually sadistic. Though the wife is not mad to begin with...." — *The Devil of Aske.*

Hodge, Jane Aiken
"The author of many Gothics has pulled a small switcheroo — the heroine is not a lovely 21-year-old hired as a companion to a single lady, but instead a single lady hired as a companion to a lovely 21-year-old. The beautiful setting is Greece" — *Strangers in Company.*

Holland, Isabelle
"What Miss Holland brings to her Gothics that is so sorely lacking in many of them is a tongue-in-cheek sense of humor and an awareness that the women involved are often much stronger than the men" — *Trelawney.* "It takes courage to do a take-off on 'Jane Eyre' in modern guise...." — *Darcourt.* "Hints of dark sexual misdeeds in the past come to light and there is a climactic fire scene in which Barbara comes to the rescue of the hero, a nice twist" — *Kilgaren.* "Holland is the new queen of the intelligent Gothic novel....". *The de Maury Papers.*

Holt, Victoria

Howatch, Susan

James, Margaret
"She discovers that the old house has an unsavory reputation and that a murder has occurred there" — *Ring the Bell Softly.*

Johnston, Velda
"A spirited young governess encounters danger and terror in a massive medieval castle in France" — *I Came to a Castle.* "An enjoyable spooky bit of black magic focusing on a contest of wills, and a satisfactory deciphering and exorcism of the past" — *A Presence in an Empty Room.*

Leonard, Phyllis G.
A proper Bostonian librarian in Mexico in 1881 struggles "against the lure of desire and the finality of death" — *Prey of the Eagle.*

Mackintosh, May
"... A Scottish schoolteacher ... a wicked but glamorous actress, a valuable stolen diamond, any number of good-looking men, and, as a lagniappe, lots of expensive clothes and exotic interior decoration" — *Appointment in Andalusia.*

Maybury, Anne

"There had been no meaning in his kiss, but she clung to the feel of it on her mouth as though it were the fire at which she could warm herself" — *Whispers in the Dark.* "And I am warning you! What we heard was a scream of real terror. We have a right to investigate" — *I Am Gabriella.* "You weren't crying from grief. You're scared to death some one will find out what really happened up at Maladieu. That's why you're crying" — *The Moon Is Down.*

Michaels, Barbara

"Nobody in the business plots the Gothic novel with more abandon." "Both girls wind up imprisoned in a ruined abbey, guarded by fierce dogs, their virtue threatened by the wicked Wolfsons" — *Sons of the Wolf.* "... An old house in the back country of Virginia ... haunted by an 18th century witch and her cat familiar.... Cat lovers will especially enjoy this one" — *Witch.*

Norton, Andre

The science fiction author "has a flair for Gothic romance as well" — *The Opel-Eyed Fan.*

Randall, Rona

"With one swift movement I was off the couch, restoring order to my disarranged skirts, smoothing my hair, turning my back upon him as I drew my torn bodice over my breast and hid from him the tears which disillusion brought." "The kind of rubbish that gives the Gothic a bad name" — *Dragonmede.*

Ross, Marilyn

"Is it any wonder our heroine has trouble sleeping" — *Curse of Black Charlie.*

Stafford, Caroline

"Elizabeth, fortunately, seems to have the proverbial nine lives as she negotiates her uneasy and risky days at Ravensholme" — *The Honor of Ravensholme.*

Stevenson, Florence

Stewart, Mary

"... Fairy-tale castle of a dream, something remote and romantic and impossible." A classic Gothic among her novels of romantic suspense — *Nine Coaches Waiting.*

Tattersall, Jill

"... A gorgeous but poor orphan goes as a governess to a gorgeous big house where lives a gorgeous wicked man.... This just might have been conceived as a parody" — *Midsummer Masque.*

Whitney, Phyllis A.

"... The brooding English manse, the innocent yet resourceful young heroine, the potentially dangerous lover — with a modern London background" — *Hunter's Green.*

Parody

So stereotyped a novel is ripe for parody. The classic is Jane Austen's *Northanger Abbey*, in which the heroine interprets all situations as though she were in one of Mrs. Radcliffe's romances. The hero assures her, "I have read all Mrs. Radcliffe's works and most of them with great pleasure. The *Mysteries of Udolpho*, when I had once begun it, I could not put down again.... I remember finishing it in two days ... my hair standing on end the whole time." (The "Horrid Seven" mentioned in the novel were reprinted by the Folio Society as *Horrid Novels: Castle of Wolfenbach. Clermont. The Mysterious Warning. The Necromancer of the Black Forest. The Midnight Bell. The Orphan of the Rhine. Horrid Mysteries.*) In Margaret Atwood's *Lady Oracle* (Simon & Schuster, 1976), the heroine writes costume Gothics, with passages enticingly quoted, and their stories entwine with her own. Georgette Heyer's *Sylvester, Or, The Wicked Uncle*, itself a delightful Regency novel, has a heroine who writes a Gothic novel in the Radcliffe tradition, published anonymously, a roman à clef satirizing the ton. A recent (1980) Gothic romance is so pure an example of the genre as to be almost a parody, *The Court of Silver Shadows*, by Beatrice Brandon. It has a modern castle in Florida, all the stock characters and plot devices and surmounts them all by ingenious variations, sophisticated dialogue, humor, and an enchanting gimmick. All the characters are steeped in Hollywood movies of the thirties and forties, quote from the dialogue (identifying with the actor who originated the role), and the castle is wired so that tapes of sound track voices speak from waxwork figures or echo in the rooms, with intent, of course, to frighten or scare one to death. For readers unacquainted with the genre in its modern style, this book is a delightful introduction.

Historical Romance

Historical pulp, a genre spawned by romantic melodrama and the high example of Sir Walter Scott, leads a prodigal, unembarrassed existence. It has its ephemeral masters and Stakhanovites, adroitly turning out reams of the stuff on a fundamentally honest level of research. The cloaks and daggers are authentic; the laird's moorland, the plantation, the gabled street stand up to the historian's inspection, candidly miniature in detail. A stylized archaism, which renders the antique feel of things without obstructing the reader, spangles the dialogue and narrative. As in a New England oil-lard-and-rocking-chair emporium (authentic hot buns next door), there is enough patina of the past to make up for the spurious. To a degree that only Marxist literary critics have investigated, it is from this order of pulp narrative that a major part of the common readership derives its image of history. Sometimes the form is exploited with such innocent vim that a queer case of near-greatness occurs: "Quo Vadis?" "The Last Days of Pompeii," "Gone With the Wind" endure in the frontier zone between discarded daydreams and rooted archetypes.

    —George Steiner
    (*New Yorker*, September 23, 1976)

History sealed with a kiss.
— Anonymous

The historical romance can be divided into two groupings. The first presents authentic historical background, characters, and events, although fictitious characters and events are often, perhaps usually, introduced either as conjecture or to make a full and lively tale. The degree to which fictionalization is used and the seriousness of the author's historical attitude may provide the criteria differentiating the historical *novel* from the historical *romance*, although this writer's criteria are derived from the intelligence shown by the author in interpreting history and the quality of the writing. Many novels hover uneasily between the two types. Therefore, the serious reader devoted to the historical *novel* may find some historical *romances* of interest and the reader of historical *romances* may enjoy some historical *novels*, the latter dependent on readability in a popular sense.

The second group is more properly labeled *period* romance. Although these romances may introduce historical characters as part of the background, their intent is the creation of a dream of romance safely in another time far distant from the mundane present: the romance is then more believable in a society detached from the reader's. The reader escapes into a past world of glamour recreated skillfully in all details of life — speech, clothing, food, furnishings, and the like — so that a time and place are evoked in which the reader can live vicariously.

The characteristics of the types of historical romance can be contrasted in essentials. All recreate a historical period and atmosphere, usually with great detail — in the historical romance/novel, the period is essential to that particular novel; in the period romance, the atmosphere is merely the romantic aura of another time within which lovers may play out their story. The historical characters and events — kings, queens, wars — in the historical novel/romance are the plot essentials: in the period romance they merely add to the background.

The reader with a strong interest in history will welcome extensive description of background, the way of life and incidents of the time, while the romance reader may find such description excessive. One reader's insistence on being given the "real" story of authentic characters and events contrasts with another reader's desire for a "romantic" plot and hang the facts of history. The most successful writers of historical romance know the exact mixture of fact and fiction to satisfy the genre fans. (In the subgenres sweet-and-savage and plantation romances, the only necessity is sex in an exotic setting.) Present in all types of romance fiction is adventure, given a fuller scope the less the plot is restricted by historical authenticity.

(Similar comparisons may be made for the western and some thriller subgenres. The reader of westerns may be interested in the authentic history of the American West as well as in a story of adventure. The reader of spy/espionage and the political-terrorist thrillers may be drawn to the depiction of international affairs and political intrigue as well as the more sensational story lines.)

The "history" in the books, following the four prototypes, that are labeled "historical romance" may have been based on real events or invented:

Haggard, H. Rider. *She* (1887).

Hope, Anthony. *The Prisoner of Zenda* (1894).

McCutcheon, George Barr. *Graustark* (1901).

Orczy, Baroness. *The Scarlet Pimpernel* (1905).

Many authors of historical romance also write other types of romance using a historical setting: romantic suspense, Gothic, period romance.

Allen, Hervey. *Anthony Adverse.*

Bellah, James Warner

Caldwell, Taylor
"... Greek tragedy reduced to the level of soap opera"—*Glory and the Lightning.*

Carr, Philippa
"... Murder, witchcraft, and romance ... in Elizabethan England ... will entertain ... the most seasoned Gothic fan"—*The Witch from the Sea.*

Coffman, Virginia

Costain, Thomas

Dunnett, Dorothy
"The intricate plotting and counter-plotting make it as much a game of detection as an exercise in historical fiction"—*The Disorderly Knight.* Part of a six-volume series with a sixteenth-century Scottish adventurer hero.

Esler, Anthony
Purple prose and passion and touches of sweet-and-savage romance. "... Spirited and unashamed costume romantic"—*Blade of Castlemayne.*

Gedge, Pauline
"... The enforced conquest of ancient Britain by Imperial Rome"—*The Eagle and the Raven.*

Gellis, Roberta
The Roselynde Chronicles, four volumes. "... Her historical romances are carefully researched costume dramas...."—*Joanna.*

Gluyas, Constance
For "those who like their historical romances more romantic than historical....".*Born to Be King.*

Goldman, James

Golon, Sergeanne
"... Filled with adventure, coincidence, narrow escape, mystery, period background—all the things that make up a nicely old-fashioned historical novel." "Plunging once more into the turbulent adventure of gorgeous, sensuous, heroic, psychic crackshot Angelique...."—*Angelique and the Ghosts.* Ninth in the Angelique series.

Hardwick, Mollie

Heyer, Georgette
"Simon rises from page to lord and advisor to King Henry by dint of hard work and real ability. His singleminded quest for advancement leaves no room in his life for women — until he meets the Lady Margaret" — *Simon the Coldheart.*

Hill, Pamela

Hodge, Jane Aiken

Holland, Cecelia

Holt, Victoria
"An accurate portrayal of the intrigue of the Elizabethan court." "For those addicted to ruffles and flourishes and gossipy travails...." — *My Enemy the Queen.* "... A young British schoolmistress becomes involved with an arrogant French count and is caught up in the terror of the opening days of the revolution" — *The Devil on Horseback.*

Irwin, Margaret

Jarman, Rosemary Hawley
"... Manages to convey the lush, devious bawdy ambiance of her chosen century, makes lively a time, place and society that once were and still seem passing strange" — *The King's Grey Mare.*

Kaye, M. M.
"... Leisurely, panoramic ... rich in adventure, heroism, cruelty and love, rich in India." "An Indian *Gone with the Wind*" — *The Far Pavilions.*

Keyes, Frances Parkinson

Lancaster, Bruce

Leslie, Doris

Lewis, Hilda
"Like several of her previous novels this takes as its subject the woman at the side of one of history's great men" — *Wife to the Bastard.*

Lofts, Norah
"Our knight's adventures in the land of the Moors, his lady's struggle at home during his long absence make delightfully dramatic reading and provide a superficial but intriguing portrait of one way of English life as it was lived 500 years ago" — *Knight's Acre.* Volume of a trilogy. "I do not want to be a lady. I want to be a wool merchant." "A gentle fifteenth-century tale of Women's Liberation" — *The Maud Reed Tale.*

Marshall, Edison

Mason, F. Van Wyck

Mitchell, Margaret. *Gone with the Wind.*

Plaidy, Jean
"Queen of popular historical novels." Norman trilogy. Plantagenet saga. Stuart saga.

Roberts, Kenneth

Rofheart, Martha
"The author moves easily through castles, festivals, and trysts...." — *Fortune Made His Sword.*

Sabatini, Rafael
"He was born with a gift of laughter and a sense that the world was mad." [Opening sentence of *Scaramouche*.] "Delightfully courtly, flowery, old-fashioned but not dated.... Nobody writes historical romances like this anymore — more's the pity" — *Scaramouche*. "Why is a book by Sabatini almost impossible to stop reading?" — *Time*, March 9, 1976. "From the neck down [his heroines] might as well be buried in moth balls" — *Time*, March 9, 1976.

Schoonover, Lawrence

Seton, Anya

Shellabarger, Samuel

Thane, Elswyth
Williamsburg series.

Vaughan, Carter A.

Winsor, Kathleen. *Forever Amber.*

Yerby, Frank
"... It swashes where it ought to swash.... And there's this beautiful Greek slave girl Zenobia...." — *The Saracen Blade.*

HISTORICAL NOVEL

The following authors display a serious respect for history. Many will appeal to costume romance readers as they often supply adequate dollops of romance. Indeed, some, like Sabatini, allow the costume romance characteristics to dominate the history.

Dumas, Alexandre
The *Three Musketeers* includes a spy/espionage plot.

Scott, Sir Walter

Some selective modern examples are:

Barnes, Margaret Campbell

Bryher

Druon, Maurice

Duggan, Alfred

Fast, Howard

Forester, C. S.
Hornblower series.

Graves, Robert

Hackett, Francis

Heyer, Georgette. *The Spanish Bride. An Infamous Army. Lord John.*

Oldenbourg, Zoe

Renault, Mary
"The historical novelist recognizes man's need to transmit his tradition of the past and feels a responsibility for doing so with a respect for factual truth. This attitude distinguishes the historical novelist from the costume romanticist" — Renault.

Sabatini, Rafael. *Scaramouche.*

Sutcliffe, Rosemary

Treece, Henry

Undset, Sigrid. *Kirsten Lavransdatter.*

Yourcenar, Marguerite. *The Memoirs of Hadrian.*

PERIOD ROMANCE

The period or costume romance places the love story within the romantic aura of another time, the dream given credibility by its remoteness from the reader's own experience, and enhanced, for women readers, by great detail on dress, food, and mannered social activity. (Harlequin Books in publicity for its Masqueraders series notes that five out of ten women read romances and four out of the ten read historical romances, undoubtedly of the costume variety.) The most popular period romance and the one commonly labeled by publishers is the Regency romance. However, all periods are used—the medieval, eighteenth century, and Victorian England being among the dominant periods—and a trend is noticed for publishers to label as "a delightful Georgian" (Playboy Press) or Victorian romance as well as Regency. The Edwardian period (turn of the century to World War I) has become popular following the television series "Upstairs, Downstairs." The background of social history is often colorfully and extensively developed, particularly by those writers who use one period almost exclusively. These examples attest to the popularity of the period romance and its almost infinite variety:

Aiken, Joan

Allardyce, Paula

Astley, Juliet

Bristow, Gwen

Cartland, Barbara
"The world's all-time best-selling romantic novelist." About 300 novels to date, at the rate of 14 to 20 a year. A biography: Henry Cloud, *Barbara Cartland: Crusader in Pink* (London: Weidenfeld, 1979).

"My heroines are all pure. They'll never go to bed with a man until they have a ring on their fingers.... I'll wager [1976] you that in ten years, it will be fashionable again to be a virgin." "... As I write a story with a virgin heroine, we *know* the story is always going to be very much the same, because the girl is pure and the man isn't." "We all want beauty, love, and more than that, we want assurance that we are loved." "The touch of sharp reality in the lemon mellowed by the golden glory of the orange should make him realize that only in marriage will he find the true perfection and fulfillment of love" — *Recipes for Lovers*. (Menus, recipes, and advice for romantic dinners.)

"The Cartland formula is costume romance, fairy tales with passive heroines, men who are never less than perfection, and love that is spiritual. Although Cartland always finds a way to titillate her readers by maneuvering the lovers into bed, sex is never consummated without marriage."

Her period romances are now a United Features Syndicate comic strip, daily and Sunday, run in newspapers in Atlanta, Baltimore, Chicago, Dallas, Houston, Miami, Cleveland, San Francisco, and other cities.

Some happy endings: (All "..." in the quotations are Barbara Cartland's — distinctively her style, as are the one sentence paragraphs.)

With his mouth holding her captive, he carried her away into a glorious secret kingdom of their own where there was no pride ... only a fiery, uncontrolled ecstatic love — *The Proud Princess*.

Then there were only the mountain peaks and the 'knife-edge' of ultimate joy — *The Magnificent Marriage*.

"I love ... you ... too," she whispered against the Marquis's lips and there was no need for words — *The Bored Bridegroom*.

On the sea the reflection of light from the rising moon touched softly moving waves with silver as if they caressed the body of the goddess of love — *Kiss the Moonlight*.

They were one and he carried her towards the burning glory of the sun — *The Devil in Love*.

Our lives will be so beautiful that we will attain a perfection that is known only to the gods — *The Perfection of Love*.

The Earl looked at Baptista, thinking it would be impossible for any woman to look more lovely or so pure and untouched.

Then as if he could not help himself, his arms tightened and slowly, as if it was a moment he would savor and remember, his lips came down on hers.

He could feel the ecstasy she was experiencing vibrate from her lips to his, and awaken in him sensations he had never known before.

It was so perfect that for a moment he was dazzled by it, as if they were enveloped by a light divine — *Signpost of Love*.

"I want you ... as a man wants a woman ... I can no longer protect you from myself."

"How stupid you are dear, dear Guardie! ... I want to feel your arms around me ... your lips against mine ... I want to be yours, yes, really and truly ..." — *The Innocent Heiress*.

Carr, Philippa

Cleeve, Brian
"Lively characters of all classes, combined with love, torture, heroism, and a blend of social satire and social uplift, make this—like Cleeve's others—several hundred cuts above the usual historical flimflam"—*Judith.* "Her youthful man-hating is dissolved into healthy sexuality through the offices of a young male librarian whom she loves and nearly loses during her subsequent trial for high treason"—*Kate.*

Coffman, Virginia
"He kissed me. His rifle came between us and he said: 'I seem to have the most incredible bad luck in trying to kiss you. There is forever some obstacle.'
'Not forever,' I promised him"—*The Alpine Coach.*

Cookson, Catherine
"... But now of her own accord she put her arms about him and when his mouth covered hers and his hands moved down over her hips and she responded to him he moaned his joy, and it was in this moment her love for him was born"—*Tilly Trotter.*

Courtney, Caroline

Eden, Dorothy

Fitzgerald, Nancy
"The story is lots of frothy fun, increased by the appearance of Wilde, Swinburne and other luminaries who play bit parts"—*Chelsea.*

Gibbs, Mary Ann

Gilbert, Anna
"A decorous, agreeable tale about love and loss in England of the 1880's"—*The Look of Innocence* (winner of Britain's Romantic Novel of the Year Award).

Gluyas, Constance

Hardwick, Mollie, and Michael Hardwick
Write separately also. Together: a series of novels on the characters in the television series "Upstairs, Downstairs."

Heaven, Constance

Heyer, Georgette
" 'Leonie, you will do well to consider. You are not the first woman in my life.'
She smiled through her tears.
'Monseigneur, I would so much rather be the last woman than the first,' she said"—*These Old Shades.*

Hill, Pamela

Hodge, Jane Aiken
"By day the governess to [Lord] Hawth's bastards, Kate roves the countryside on horseback at night, masquerading as Kit a male.... The book is a virtual spoof of historical romances...."—*Red Sky at Night, Lovers' Delight.*

Holland, Sheila

Laker, Rosalind

Lofts, Norah

McBain, Laurie

Michaels, Barbara

Paradise, Mary

Payes, Rachel Cosgrove

Randall, Rona
"Our little Cinderella finds her Prince Charming and marries him, but, alas too late, discovers that charming is as charming does" — *The Mating Dance.*

Rayner, Claire
The Performers series.

Roberts, Janet Louise

Russell, Ray
"The sexual realities of pre-Victorian London" — *Princess Pamela.*

Salisbury, Carola

Stubbs, Jean

Winston, Daoma

Period Romance — Regency

The most popular period romance features the Regency period (England in the first third of the nineteenth century) and is, for many readers, epitomized by the novels of Georgette Heyer. She is, in the diction of the Regency, "The Nonpareil," and all other authors using the period are "poor drab" imitators. (Publishers note on jackets or paperback covers: "In the grand tradition of Georgette Heyer" or "The best since Georgette Heyer." A reviewer denigrated Barbara Cartland as the "poor woman's Georgette Heyer.") The Friends of the English Regency, a California association of devotees of Georgette Heyer and the Regency romance, holds an annual Assemblee at which there is period dancing in costume, publishes a newsletter, and presents a "Georgette" award for the best new Regency romance.

The Regency world is one of high society, the London Season of the wealthy and titled enjoying the assemblies at Almack's, the dandies in their fashionable garb. The country estate is also featured as are the fashionable doings at Bath. Frequently, the heroine is impoverished, the daughter of a poor country parson, an orphan, but always a lady. Manner and dress are of utmost importance. The moral tone is licentious, but love reforms all rakes. (*The Dandy: Brummell to Beerbohm*, by Ellen Moers [Viking, 1960], devotes the first hundred pages to the Regency period.)

These prototypes differ in style, but all reflect a mode of life immediately recognizable as characterizing the Regency. Fanny Burney's *Evalina*, published prior to the Regency, foreshadows the Regency tone.

Austen, Jane

"It is a truth universally acknowledged, that a single man in possession of a good fortune must be in want of a wife"—*Pride and Prejudice* (1813).

Bulwer-Lytton, Edward

"... The season was unusually dull, and my mother, after having looked over her list of engagements, and ascertaining that she had none worth staying for, agreed to elope with her new lover"—*Pelham; Or, Adventures of a Gentleman.* First published in 1828 but revised in 1840 as the libertine Regency tone offended Victorian taste.

Burney, Fanny

"We have been a-shopping, as Mrs. Mirvan calls it, all this morning, to buy silks, caps, gauzes, and so forth"—*Evelina; Or, The History of a Young Lady's Entrance into the World* (1778).

Farnol, Jeffery

"He took the standard ingredients [of the Regency]—bucks, duellists, pugilists, smugglers and haughty ladies—and fitted them into variations of the standard nineteenth-century plot based on usurped or disputed birthrights.... [A novelist] wearing his heart on his sleeve but writing with his tongue in his cheek." Many have as a solver of mysteries Jasper Shrig, the Bow Street Runner. His first novel was published in 1910.

Authors listed below capitalize on the sure-fire plot in which a spirited heroine captures a rakish hero in an aristocratic social setting.

> These spiritual descendents of Jane Austen have a wit and elegance, a sophistication that Harlequin's contemporary romances lack.
> —Leona Neuler (Fawcett Books editor quoted in *New York Times Book Review*'s "Paperback Talk," February 24, 1980)

Aiken, Joan

Allardyce, Paula

Arnett, Caroline

Baldwin, Rebecca

"For him it is a marriage of convenience, but for Cassie it is a love match"—*The Cassandra Knot.*

Blanshard, Audrey

Cartland, Barbara

"Spunky young orphan heiress Petrina Lyndon climbs over the wall of her school to run away to London and become a lady-bird...."—*Loves, Lords, and Lady-Birds.*

Clark, Gail

"There is added delight in the thoroughness with which the author presents a full picture of the Regency period—dress, manners, mores, even slang"—*Dulcie Bligh.*

Cleeve, Brian

"He tries to make Sara his mistress but she rebuffs him"—*Sara.*

Darcy, Clare
"The best since Georgette Heyer."

"The heroine masquerading as a boy, is befriended by the elegant, proud Redmayne. She is running away, he thinks he is in search of another beauty...." — *Elyza*. " 'The neighborhood is *very* thin of eligible men.... Obviously I have raised three daughters with more hair than wit' " — *Gwendolyn*.

Faire, Zabrina

Fellows, Catherine

Gray, Vanessa

Harkness, Judith

Heyer, Georgette
Her style and use of period language are inimitable: all the examples are from *The Quiet Gentleman*.

"Providence has decreed that he should succeed to his dear father's honours," pronounced the Dowager, thinking poorly of Providence.

. . . . .

"Well, now you come to ask me," said Mr. Warboys, with the air of one making a discovery, "I don't know what I mean! Spoke without thinking! Often do! Runs in the family: uncle of mine was just the same. Found himself married to a female with a squint all through speaking without thinking."

. . . . .

"Parrot-faced is she?" said the viscount, interested. "Lay you a monkey she don't peck me! Dear boy, did you ever *see* my aunts? Three of 'em, all parrot-faced, and all hot at hand! Father's frightened of 'em — m'mother's frightened of 'em! Freddy won't face 'em. Only person who can handle 'em's me! No bamming — true as I stand here! Ask anyone!"

. . . . .

"Phantom! Let me assure you that we have nothing of that sort at Stanyon! I should not countenance it; I do not approve of the supernatural."

. . . . .

"My father was a great reader, though not, of course, during the hunting season."

. . . . .

"You would become disgusted with my odious common sense. Try as I will, I *cannot* be romantic!" said Miss Morville.
His eyes danced. "Oh, I forbid you to try! Your practical observations, my absurd robin, are the delight of my life!"
Miss Morville looked at him. Then, with a deep sigh, she laid her hand in his. But what she said was: "You must mean a sparrow!"
"I will not allow you to dictate to me, now or ever, Miss Morville! I mean a robin!" said the Earl firmly, lifting her hand to his lips.

Hill, Fiona
"A Georgette Heyerish bit of flummery—with considerably more wit and pizazz than the legendary Georgette herself"—*The Autumn Rose*. [The type of review that leads the Heyer fan astray: alas, *not* true!] "... Three nubile lasses ... on the chessboard of marriage-making that is a full-time activity for the titled class"—*The Stanbroke Girls*.

Hodge, Jane Aiken
"... A willful miss who objects so strongly to being married, sight unseen, to an arrogant lord, friend of her dead brothers, that she runs away from her dreadfully mercenary uncle"—*Runaway Bride*.

Lee, Elsie
"... A spirited beauty.... The problem is ... to find her a husband"—*A Prior Bethrothal*.

MacKeever, Maggie

Roby, Mary Linn

SeBastian, Margaret

Smith, Joan

Stables, Mira

Walsh, Sheila

Saga

The family saga romance has ties to both the historical and period romances, although there are popular examples with contemporary settings. Most of these romances are in several volumes. The saga, or generational history, covers the interrelations of succeeding generations within a family, usually with emphasis on a patriarchal or matriarchal figure. Those series in which the family relationships provide the basic plot elements are firmly in the romance tradition. Those with an embracing historical sweep (notably the series devised by Engel such as "The Kent Family Chronicles" and "Wagons West") have men as the pivotal characters. Women are not ignored in these historical series (for Engel is cannily aware that 70% of the fiction readers are women), but they provide romantic background rather than the dominant romantic story line.

Because the genre proved so popular in the seventies, the saga label appears in publishers' advertising and on paperback covers for single-volume novels barely within the definition. Some novels, such as the Poldark series, achieve saga label through number of volumes and an extensive cast of characters. Others among historical and period romances have a sequel, or sequels, without real similarity to the saga pattern.

Several patterns are dominant in current sagas. In the United States, this type of romance takes the form of: an immigrant family rising to wealth and power over several generations; plantation life in the Deep South with an emphasis on master-slave relations; history from colonial times and the movement westward. In Britain, the pattern might be: landed family history and relations between aristocrats and their servants; a family of any class or period or periods, changing through the generations. By the end of 1981, it is expected that some 25 saga series will be on the stands in paperback.

Several of the series current in the United States are designed and "produced" by Book Creations, Inc., the brainchild of Lyle Kenyon Engel. Engel originates the series idea, makes contracts with the authors, does the editorial work, and arranges for publication with major paperback publishers.

These prototype examples show that one or two dominant characters may ensure an enduring readership for a saga:

De La Roche, Mazo. Jalna series (16 novels, the first in 1927).

Galsworthy, John. *The Forsyte Saga* (3 volumes, 1922, followed by *A Modern Comedy* (3 volumes) and *End of the Chapter* (3 volumes).

Walpole, Hugh. The Herries Chronicle (4 volumes, the first in 1930).

Many generational series or sagas are now appearing. Only time will tell which ones will survive for continued readership. The historical adventure series tends to intermingle with the saga. Two new sagas feature women in historical adventure, with a strong romantic interest, and may forecast a new trend: Women at War series (the second volume in 1982 is set in the American Revolutionary period); and the Making of America series, Part Two: Women Who Won the West series (the sixth volume appeared in 1982). These two series are not included in the listings below. Volumes are noted to date.

Coleman, Lonnie
    Beulah Land series. (Plantation South, 3 volumes).

Cradock, Fanny
    Lorme family. (British, 5 volumes).

Delderfield, R. F.
    Swann family. (British, 3 volumes)
    Craddock family. (British, 2 volumes).

Fast, Howard
    Lavette family. (U.S., 3 volumes).

Gellis, Roberta
    The Roselynde Chronicles. (Engel creation).
    The Heiress series. (French Revolution. Engel creation).
    Royal Dynasty series. (English history. Engel creation).

Gilchrist, Rupert
    Dragonard series. (Caribbean plantation, 5 volumes).

Giles, Janice Holt
    Cooper and Fowler families. (U.S. West, 4 volumes).

Graham, Winston
    Poldark series. (British, 6 volumes).

Harris, Marilyn
    Eden family. (British, 4 volumes).

Hill, Deborah
    Merrick family. (New England, 2 volumes).

Jakes, John
    Kent Family Chronicles (U.S., 8 volumes. Engel creation).

Johnson, Walter Reed
Oakhurst saga. (U.S., 4 volumes. Engel creation; sweet-and-savage).

Jourlet, Marie de
Windhaven series: Bouchard family. (U.S. South and West, 6 volumes; sweet-and-savage and plantation).

Laker, Rosalind
Easthampton trilogy. (England).

L'Amour, Louis
Sackett clan. (England and U.S. West, 14 volumes).

Lavender, William
Hargrave Journal trilogy. (U.S.)

Long, William Stewart
The Australians. (To be 6 volumes. Engel creation).

Macdonald, Malcolm
Stevenson family. (England, 4 volumes).

Nicolayson, Bruce
de Kuyper family. (Colonial U.S., to be 5 volumes).

Nicole, Christopher
Caribbean saga. (5 volumes).
Haggard family. (England, to be 5 volumes).

Porter, Donald Clayton
Colonization of America series. (Engel creation).

Rayner, Claire
Performers series. (England, 7 volumes).

Ross, Dan Fuller
Wagons West series. (2 volumes. Engel creation).

Scott, Michael William
Rakehell Dynasty. (U.S., Engel creation, 3 volumes).

Smith, George
The American Freedom series: Glencannon family. (2 volumes).

Falconhurst series.
Plantation romance series begun by Lance Horner and continued by several authors, Ashley Carter producing the ninth to date.

The following are examples of sagas in single volumes or with sequels:

Briskin, Jacqueline. *Paloverde* (California).

Cleary, John. *The Beaufort Sisters* (Australia).

Coffman, Virginia. *The Gaynor Women. Dinah Faire. Veronique. Marsanne* (The South).

Ellis, Julie. *The Hampton Heritage. The Hampton Women* (The South).

Howatch, Susan. *The Rich Are Different. Sins of the Fathers* (New York).

Johnson, Barbara Ferry. *Delta Blood. Homeward Winds the River. The Heirs of Love* (The South).

McCullough, Colleen. *The Thorn Birds* (Australia).

Melville, Ann. *The Lorimer Line. Alexa.*

Rofheart, Martha. *The Savage Brood.*

Sweet-and-Savage Romance

"Hot Historicals," as the publishers gloatingly label them within the trade, also known as sweet-and-savage romances, have evoked a host of epithets: "erotic histories" (more erotic than history), "rape sagas," "bodice rippers," "hysterical Romance," "tit-and-bum epics," "sand-and-tit epics." They are too "hot" for the genteel reader of historical romances, who, fortunately, can recognize—and avoid—them by their length (400 to 600 pages) and by their titles. (Are the combinations in titles infinite of love, desire, passion, captive, madness, fire, savage, fury, torment?)

Rosemary Rogers launched this subgenre in 1974 with a novel that gave the subgenre its label—*Sweet, Savage Love.* A reviewer succinctly epitomized the subgenre's plot in *Sweet, Savage Love* in one sentence: "The heroine is seduced, raped, prostituted, married, mistressed." Another reviewer as tersely summed up the subgenre's characteristics: "The prose is purple, the plot thin, and the characters thinner" (*The Wolf and the Dove*, by Kathleen E. Woodiwiss). Exotic historical settings are used lavishly, particularly those allowing for pirates, sultans, and harems. A variation of the sweet-and-savage romance is the plantation romance, with basic ingredients of miscegenation, incest, Cain versus Abel, slave uprisings, insanity, and murder. Usually they are set in the post-Civil War South but may be in the West Indies or any locale in which the basic plot ingredients can seeth. Both types are loaded with sex scenes, explicit to the extent of justifying the label "soft porn." Women readers may not want their sexual fantasies to be realistic but do want them to be explicit. (For the male reader there are the sexual fantasies provided by Ian Fleming's James Bond and Mickey Spillane's Mike Hammer.)

The works by the following authors range from the blatantly sexual to the overtly suggestive. There is a trend for the sweet-and-savage characteristics to be subsumed within the saga or historical romance rather than being the dominating aspect.

Blake, Jennifer
  "Melanie, a young bluestocking, slips into a bedchamber of her father's archenemy, who mistakes her for a harlot and rapes her"—*Tender Betrayal.*

Blake, Stephanie

Busbee, Shirlee
  "My idea of the most perfect book I could write would be a sexy, lurid Georgette Heyer story."

Dailey, Janet
  "America's best-selling romance novelist." Fifty-seven novels since 1975, set in each of the 50 states, with contemporary rather than historical

background. (Author of about 50 Harlequins without the "slightly risque love scenes" of the sweet-and-savage romances.) "Until Dailey adds a final unexpected twist, the plot adheres closely to the captive-in-love-with-captor formula...." — *Touch the Wind.*

DuPont, Diana
"Her ship is hijacked and she lands up as a slave in the harem of the Pasha Mohammed Ali of Egypt" — *The Emerald Embrace.*

Esler, Anthony
"... Tamar de la Barca ... has romantic notions of love — until the night she is raped by dark and mysterious Don Diego Aguilar" — *For Love of a Pirate.*

Fairman, Paula
"Neither escapes Stacey's vast sexual appetite" — *The Fury and the Passion.* "... 17-year-old Charity early on is sold into slavery, ravished, rescued, seduced, ravished yet again, all en route to England" — *In Savage Splendour.*

Gallagher, Patricia

Granbeck, Marilyn
"Poor Emilie: somehow men know just by looking that she is a woman of turbulent passions" — *Winds of Desire.*

Grice, Julia

Hagan, Patricia

Hall, Gimone
"In apparent desperation, Miranda takes on several other lovers, including a samurai and the Emperor of Japan" — *Fury's Sun, Passion's Moon.*

Leigh, Susanna
"688 passion-filled pages" — *Glynda.* "... Before long our wandering heroine lands herself in a bordello" — *Winter Fire.*

Leonard, Phyllis G.
"Brutally kidnapped, plucky Lily is forced to barter for her virtue by singing in a disreputable saloon" — *Tarnished Angel.*

McBain, Laurie
"The beautiful orphan Elysia Demarice ran away from her evil aunt and stopped at an inn for the night. She awoke in the morning to find herself in the bed of Alex Trevigne, the handsome Marquis they called 'The Devil.' She didn't know how she had gotten there and he was not about to let her go." "He seemed propelled by demons as he loved into the night and morning — becoming more of her body and soul than she herself...." "... A totally plotless 428-page novel" — *Devil's Desire.*

Matthews, Patricia
"Sarah is sexually abused at every turn — not that she minds. Still, as a lady should be, she's ever faithful in spirit to her true love, the first man who raped her" — *Love's Wildest Promise.*

Ten consecutive best-sellers on *New York Times* paperback list:
Love's Avenging Heart; Love's Dying Dream; Love, Forever More; Love's

Golden Destiny; Love's Magic Moment; Love's Many Faces; Love's Pagan Heart; Love's Raging Tide; Love's Sweet Agony; Love's Wildest Promise.

Michaels, Fern
Pseudonym of two women whose plot plan calls for a nine-page explicit but fantasy sex scene every 35 pages. "Instead of expiring in the Saracen prison where Berengeria had dumped her, Valentina is raped, then sold at auction" — *Valentina.*

Morgan, Michaela
"... A daring, beautiful heroine who seems to be rape-and-abduction prone." "At 1019 pages this must set a record for sweet-savagery" — *Madelaina.*

Peters, Natasha

Radcliffe, Janette
"Predictably, he proceeds to rape Barbara, whom he takes as his concubine until his ship is captured by pirates" — *Stormy Surrender.*

Riefe, Barbara
"Paul is put in irons and Lorna is raped by sinister Captain Dragut" — *So Wicked the Heart.* Sequel to *Tempt Not This Flesh* and followed by *Black Fire.* "Deirdre, who has been captured and brutally raped by Chinese pirates, is sold into prostitution in Peking" — *Fire and Flesh.* Ends trilogy of *This Ravaged Heart* and *Far beyond Desire.*

Rogers, Rosemary
"Most women do have a rape fantasy. But there is a difference between actual rape, which is horrifying, and fantasy. In the rape fantasy, you pick the man and the circumstances. It's not at all scary." Interview with Rosemary Rogers.

"Overpowered by her lover-turned-husband and repeatedly raped by bandits and sex-starved soldiers, she bounces back each time as fresh and beautiful and feisty as ever" — *Dark Fires.* "She writhed, gasping, as his fingers touched her intimately, exploringly, and for a moment, as his body poised over her, she thought he would let her go. Her lips parted ... there was a stabbing shaft of agony between her thighs that seemed to tear all the way into her belly, causing her body to arch up against his with shocked surprise." "Flickering torchlights and wine forced between her lips.... With a feeling of shock she found her thighs nudged apart.... There was a stabbing shaft of agony. Her last thought as she slipped into unconsciousness was, 'And I don't even know his name.' " " 'I'm tired of being raped. Don't I count as a person?' " — *Wicked Loving Lies,* with the last plaintive query being on page 654.

Ross, Marilyn

Savage, Christine
Pseudonym of two men, Texans.

Sherwood, Valerie

Shiplett, June Lund

Steel, Danielle

Wilde, Jennifer

Woodiwiss, Kathleen E.
"I'm insulted when my books are called erotic. I believe I write love stories with a little spice"—Woodiwiss.

"Aislin, a Saxon maid, is raped by Ragnor, one of the Norman conquerors, who also kills her father and degrades her mother"—*The Wolf and the Dove*. "She makes a desperate deal with a condemned man who is to be executed the next day. If he marries her, she will spend the night with him." "Each touch was fire, each word was bliss, each movement in their union a rhapsody of passion that rose and built until it seemed that every instrument in all the world combined to bring the music of their souls into a consuming crescendo that left them still and quiet, warm like the softly glowing after-coals of a universal holocaust"—*Shanna*.

Zide, Donna Comeaux
"... Waylaid by cowboy kidnappers, bound up in the back room of a brothel, force-bed opium and raped"—*Lost Splendour*.

Plantation Romance

Its basic ingredients are interracial sex, incest, Cain versus Abel, slave uprisings, insanity, and murder. *Mandingo*, by Kyle Onstott (1957), set the pattern and is continually used as a comparative reference.

Most of the following examples depend on the series aspect for continuing appeal:

Carter, Ashley
Continuing the Falconhurst series started by Lance Horner. "In the savage and sensual *Mandingo* tradition"—*The Sword of the Golden Stud*.

Cato, Nancy. *Cindera* (Australia).

Coleman, Lonnie
A trilogy *not* in the sweet-and-savage pattern: *Beulah Land; Look Away, Beulah Land; The Legacy of Beulah Land*.

Ellis, Julie

Gentry, Peter
"The novel doesn't discriminate. Black and white, everybody's preposterous"—*Rafe*.

Gilchrist, Rupert. Dragonard series.

Giles, Raymond. Sabrehill series.

Horner, Lance
Golden Stud and continuing series.

Jourlet, Marie de. Windhaven series.

McNeill, George
"... A world of naked sins and secret guilts ... more sensational than *Mandingo*"—*The Plantation*.

Nicole, Christopher. Hilton family series.

Yerby, Frank
The Dahomean and sequel *A Darkness at Ingraham's Crest* (the latter his 29th novel).

TOPICS

Bibliography and Biography

Biographical sketches of the authors currently writing romantic novels for both hardcover and paperback publishers appear in the journals listed in a later section under "Review Journals." Recognizing the great popularity of the romance, many women's magazines have, in recent years, featured articles on best-selling authors of romantic novels. The only biographical volume on these writers, however, is the following:

Falk, Kathryn. *Love's Leading Ladies*. Pinnacle Books, 1982.
The author is the publisher of *Romantic Times* (described in a later section) and an ardent fan of the romance. Collected here are brief sketches of 65 living romance writers, largely American, but the book does include Barbara Cartland and Victoria Holt. The tone is wholly admiring. There is a small photograph of each author accompanied by a quotation of passionate intensity from one of her novels. The sketch, with few exceptions, concludes with one of the author's favorite recipes. There is a bibliography of each author's in-print titles in hardcover and paperback editions.

Twentieth Century Romance Writers. London: Macmillan.
Announced in 1981 but no publication date was given. This should follow the pattern of the other titles in this series (the ones on crime and mystery writers and science fiction writers are described with the books on these genres and the one on writers of westerns is announced for publication). This volume should supply brief biographies, bibliographies, and criticism for several hundred romance writers.

History and Criticism

Romance as a genre has been woefully neglected by historians, bibliographers, and critics. (Literary historians have treated the eighteenth- and nineteenth-century Gothic novel, however, with only tangential significance for the modern genre romance.) What is available is largely in periodicals: newspapers and popular and trade magazines have had a joyous time celebrating the blooming of romance in recent years with articles on best-selling authors, publishers' series, and the phenomenon of romance as a genre. Little of this publicity is critically definitive nor has this ephemera been gathered into a bibliography. The genre has not (as have westerns, detective fiction, science fiction, and fantasy) been systematized into a recognized course of study at the college level, with the resultant paraphernalia of bibliographies, guides, histories, scholarly journals, and the like. There is an indication of increasing interest by academics in this area as more articles on genre romance appear in the *Journal of Popular Culture* and a few papers are presented at the joint annual conventions of the Popular Culture Association and the American Culture Association. (The

1981 convention program evidenced a strong feminist tone in several presentations on other genres — western, detective, science fiction, horror, fantasy — and a few talks on aspects of the romance: "Reading the Romance: Popular Literature and Fantasies of Compensation"; "The Love of Rape: Women as Victim in the Bodice-Ripper"; "True Confessions: Sin, Suffering and Reformation"; "The Feminine Mistake: The Covert Functions of Popular Romance.") These two examples of historical criticism indicate how much remains to be done for this genre:

> Anderson, Rachel. *The Purple Heart Throbs: The Sub-Literature of Love.* London: Hodder, 1974.
> This unique and hard-to-obtain book is discussed at the beginning of this chapter. The authors described are largely British, but many were also read in the United States.

> Mussell, Kay. *Women's Gothic and Romantic Fiction: A Reference Guide.* Greenwood Press, 1981.
> This is the first attempt to systematize the material — bibliography, history, criticism — on the romance genre. The emphasis is on the romance in American culture, although, necessarily, there is much reference to British prototypes. Coverage is from colonial times, with much material on nineteenth-century romance writers. The chapters are critical and bibliographical essays that generally have bibliographies and notes appended. The chapter titles give the scope: "History of Women's Gothic and Romantic Fiction"; "Bibliographies, Reference Works, and Sources for the Study of Major Authors of Gothic and Romantic Fiction"; "Related Genres: Mystery Stories, Governess Stories, Melodrama, and Film Adaptations"; "Literary and Social History Approaches to Gothic and Romantic Fiction"; "Sociological and Psychological Approaches to Gothic and Romantic Fiction: Studies of Reading and Audience"; "Popular Commentary on Gothic and Romantic Fiction: Journalism, Reviews, and How-to Advice." There are two appendices: "Collection and Research Facilities"; "Selected Chronology." (The book does not include any reference to Radcliffe's *Gothic Novels of the Twentieth Century*, annotated in a following section on the Gothic.)

The best survey of the romance in the United States is in Russel Nye's *The Unembarrassed Muse: The Popular Arts in America* (Dial, 1970) in the chapters on "Stories for the People" and "Novels in the Marketplace," covering reading from colonial times.

Gothic — Bibliography

As noted in the annotation, this lone bibliography serves also for other types of romance:

> Radcliffe, Elsa J. *Gothic Novels of the Twentieth Century: An Annotated Bibliography.* Scarecrow Press, 1979.
> This bibliography is omnivorous and eccentrically uncritical in scope, defining the Gothic very broadly to include many novels of detection, mystery, romantic suspense, historical romance, and some simple,

sentimental romances. The compiler also lists works noted "not Gothic" simply because the author is being listed for other works. About half of the 1973 listings are annotated in a very personal and idiosyncratic manner — some are helpful and amusing, particularly when critical, others are of questionable judgment. However, one instance will indicate the caution necessary in using the bibliography. Under Mary Stewart, noting that her works are often published as Gothics but that the compiler does not consider them Gothic, she lists 13 titles, six with annotation, but does *not* annotate the one title that is pure Gothic, *Nine Coaches Waiting.*

Gothic — Criticism

There was an exceedingly large amount of critical writing on the Gothic, a good deal of it in newspapers and magazines, and the following samples given an inkling of the fervent interest the form aroused. There is a single annotation for the group.

Jennings, Gary. "Heathcliff Doesn't Smoke L&M's." *New York Times Book Review*, July 27, 1969, pages 4, 5, 24, 25.

Minudri, Regina. "From Jane to Germaine, with Love." *School Library Journal* (February 1973), pages 82-83.

Mussell, Kay J. "Beautiful and Damned: The Sexual Woman in Gothic Fiction." *Journal of Popular Culture* 9 (Summer 1975), pages 84-89.

Mussell, Kay J. "Gothic Novels." In Inge, M. Thomas, ed. *Handbook of American Popular Culture*. 1978. Vol. 1, pages 151-69.

West, Katherine. *Chapter of Governesses: A Study of the Governess in English Fiction, 1800-1949.* London: Cohen & West, 1949.

Critical works on the Gothic novel are listed in the bibliography to Munsell's essay, including much popular comment in journals. "Heathcliff Doesn't Smoke L&M's" is a delightfully satirical rundown of the characteristics of the Gothic heroine, hero, and villain with devastating quotations. Minudri, a public librarian of wide reading tastes, makes a strong defense for usually maligned heroines: "These Gothic heroines are strong, they are intelligent, they are educated, curious, and, for the most part, they are unable to accept the strictures of a society which push them toward patterns of behavior they find untenable." While the Gothic heroine's goals are marriage and motherhood, fulfilling the traditional feminine roles in domesticity of wife and mother, she is opposed by the Gothic villainess, anatomized in "Beautiful and Damned": "Passionate women who are villains as well as rivals are guilty of such specific crimes as murder, attempted murder, theft, fraud, gambling, and smuggling. The novels usually suggest that the crime is linked to one of the villain's weaknesses as a woman rather than to a more conventional motive like greed. A passionate woman may commit a crime because she succumbs to a male villain rather than influencing him away from evil, because she is jealous of another woman, or because her beauty has made her so self-centered and vain that she fails to recognize her feminine duties." Louisa May Alcott, noting in her journal that she was "tired of providing moral pap for the young," created some marvelously villainous heroines in her anonymously published thrillers that have been recently republished:

Behind a Mask: The Unknown Thrillers of Louisa May Alcott. Edited and with an introduction by Madeleine Stern. Morrow, 1975.

Plots and Counterplots: More Unknown Thrillers by Louisa May Alcott. Edited and with an introduction by Madeleine Stern. Morrow, 1976.

The governess is ubiquitous in the Gothic novel, and her situation in life and fiction is surveyed in *Chapter of Governesses*, with sections on *Jane Eyre* and *East Lynne*.

Review Journals

These journals are for the devoted readership of the genre and are much more than review journals, as the annotations indicate. Their emergence parallels the genre's recent and amazing publishing activity and growth in reading audience.

Barbra Critiques, Ltd. 1980- .
> Barbara Wren, bookseller in Independence, Missouri, writes and publishes this monthly journal of annotations, author biographies, and publishing news. The commentary is lively and includes a section, "I've Read—Don't Bother." She uses a one- to six-star rating code and identifies romances by category: contemporary, Regency, historical, Victorian, Medieval, Edwardian or Elizabethan, contemporary romantic mystery, transcendental, suspense, and Gothic.

Boy Meets Girl: A Weekly Review of Romance Authors, Agents, Publishers, and Fiction. 1981- .
> This is a sharply written and sophisticated weekly of reviews, news on trends in publishing, biographical notes on authors, and cogent criticism of the genre. It is edited by Vivien Lee Jennings of Rainy Day Books, Fairway, Kansas.

Romantic Times. 1981- .
> This bimonthly tabloid contains reviews, annotations, excerpts from new romances, publishing and author news, biographies of romance authors, interviews, and advertisements. The romance reader who is as enthralled as the publisher with every tidbit about romance will have a feast. The publisher and editor, Kathryn Falk, is an active apologist and publicist for romance. *Romantic Times* and Long Island University's Institute for Continuing Education, with Kathryn Falk as a conference director, announced the first Romantic Book Lovers Conference in New York City for April 17, 1982.

Authors' Associations

Romance writers do not feel comfortable within the standard authors' associations and have formed their own groups. While the association in the United States is some 20 years behind its British counterpart, it has gotten off to a very lively and enthusiastic start.

Romance Writers of America
The founding convention was held in Houston, Texas in June 1981 and drew an unexpectedly large attendance of writers and fans. An award, the Golden Heart, was established as the association's prize. The second convention was held in Long Beach, California in June 1982.

Romantic Novelists Association
This British group was founded in 1960. It presents an annual award for the best romance, often having runner-up awards and a historical romance award. Its members are highly articulate apologists for the genre. (Although not given by this association, there is another romance award in England, "Historical Novel Prize in Memory of Georgette Heyer," honoring her not for her Regency romances but for her historical romances in which she took pride.)

Book Clubs

The romance reader is usually an omnivorous reader, wanting a weekly supply of one or more volumes. Many readers buy or borrow as many as they can get their hands on. After the demise of Doubleday Romance Library, the fan had no regular book club but could subscribe directly with some publishers as noted below. Mills and Boon, the British publisher now owned by Harlequin, has used such subscription methods for many years as their books were not carried by bookstores until their present issuance of some in paperback. Many of their subscribers report personal libraries of several hundred Mills and Boon romances.

Doubleday Romance Library
The club was discontinued with volume 40, 1981, but as it was such a good example of a useful club, the description is retained. Among the advertising slogans used were the following: "Welcome to the New World of Romance Where Love Conquers All"; "Love is never far away with the Doubleday Romance Library." Each monthly volume contained three complete novels: usually two with a modern setting, one being foreign, and the third was a period romance, usually Regency. Most were reprints from paperback originals or British publications, often hardbound originals, and were reprinted within one or two years of original publication. Well printed and bound, they were an excellent and inexpensive source of good romances for the public library.

Mills and Boon, Harlequin Books
Both have subscription plans; the subscriber may order all titles or select by type of romance.

Silhouette Book Club
The club sends out monthly the "Silhouette" series published jointly by Pocket Books and Simon & Schuster. "Take your fantasies further than they've ever been through the exciting world of Silhouette Romances" is the advertising slogan.

Publishers

Romance blossoms in the book world.
— From the premier issue, May-June 1979,
Chapter One

Of about 400 new paperback titles each month (1980), almost one-fourth are original romances; adding reprints of hardcover originals to that figure would raise the total to one-third. Most paperback houses feature a romance line with a distinctive series name (readers have brand name loyalty, knowing what type of romance to anticipate). Romances sell well—a very popular author's new title may have an initial printing of 1 million copies; a new author will often sell 100,000 copies; a standard printing for a series line is about 300,000 copies; Harlequin titles average 700,000 to 800,000 copy sales. Two or three romances are usually on the weekly paperback best-seller list. A marketing study by Simon & Schuster prior to launching the Silhouette Romance line found that the annual per capita consumption of romances in the United States was 800 per 1,000 women. (This is paltry as compared to 1,500 in Canada and 1,800 in Holland per 1,000 women.)

Romance novels are known by their covers, hardback or paperback. A book distributor noted: "A Gothic book jacket has a house, a Victorian has a horse and a contemporary Romance has an apple-cheeked smiling couple deeply in love." Usually there is a pair of lovers embracing—if merely hugging, probably a family saga; if kissing, the sex is probably explicit. The illustration for the Gothic novel became a stock joke, but extremely effective, as identification of genre: a dark and stormy landscape or moor complete with sinister cliff, nearby a sombre mansion with one lamp (candle) in a window; in the foreground the fleeing, obviously distressful, heroine in white. (That the picture has become a part of folk culture is witnessed by a full-page advertisement by Xerox Corporation in *Publishers Weekly*, February 7, 1977: a typically Gothic illustration has this message—

> The surf dashing upon the rocky shore sounded a cacophony in the disappearing night.
> A lone gull swooped, a cackling reminder to the angry sea.
> Through the mist that crept along the edge of the cliff, two figures moved eerily toward a climactic confrontation.
> A sliver of moonlight bathed their faces as he reached out and swept her up into his embrace.
> And with the passion born of centuries he whispered, "Did you know that Xerox is a registered trademark of Xerox Corporation and, as a brand name, should be used only to identify its products and services?")

HARDCOVER PUBLISHERS WITH A REGULAR OR STRONG ROMANCE LINE

These publishers issue a variety of types of romances. When other publishers issue an occasional romance, it is usually of the historical novel or historical romance type.

Arbor House

Cassell (British)

Collins (British; also extensive reprinting in hardcover)

Coward-McCann

Delacorte

Dodd, Mead

Doubleday (Starlight Romances series announced in 1980)

Dutton

Eyre Methuen (British)

G. K. Hall (large-print reprints)

Robert Hale (British)

Houghton, Mifflin

Lenox Hill Press ("Discriminating light fiction suitable for all public libraries.")

Macmillan

Mills and Boon (British; see notes under paperback publishers)

Morrow

Putnam

St. Martin's

Walker

PAPERBACK PUBLISHERS

The following notes do not indicate the types of romance each publisher publishes, except for some series. Quotations used, with few exceptions, are from publishers' advertisements or publicity releases.

Ace

The Hall of Fame Historical Novel series was announced in 1979 for books out of print at least 10 years and never before in paperback. Caprice Romances were announced for 1982 publication, a series of contemporary realistic romances for young adults that allow the reader to "discover the pain and wonder of first love."

Avon

"Millions of women avid for Avon's historical Romance." Avon originated the trade paperback format for such best-sellers as *Shanna*.

Ballantine

"This Christmas give yourself a gift of Romance." The series Love & Life was announced to begin in August 1982. The novels will have heroines aged from 28 to 40 and will "deal with all the needs of the 80's woman." The publisher's advertisement says they will be "For the millions of women coping with life, hoping for love."

Bantam Books

This publisher issues a steady stream of novels by Grace Livingston Hill and Barbara Cartland. Another line is "Barbara Cartland's Library of Love" — older romances abridged by Barbara Cartland, including novels by Elinor Glyn, Ethel R. Hull's *The Sheik*, and several by Ethel M. Dell. ("I am proud to admit that I owe it all [success of novels] to Ethel M. Dell's formula of passion and purity, sanctified and made holy by the power of love" — Cartland.) "These books which I loved when I was young still thrill me, for underneath the passion there is tenderness, beneath the violence, gentleness and always an awareness of the Divine. Perhaps their revival will bring to a new generation true values and the ideal love which we all seek in our hearts, our minds and our souls" — Cartland. Announced for 1982 is a new series, Circle of Love, contemporary romances, with six novels issued each month. A series for teenagers, Sweet Dreams Romances began in 1981.

Berkeley

Zodiac Gothic: "Each book in the original series will feature a youthful heroine born under a certain astrological sign which influences both her character and the story action."

Dell

In the Candlelight Romance series, there are six novels issued each month, three Regency romances and three modern romances. No. 575 (1980) in the series is an ethnic romance (the first in U.S. publishing history?), *Entwined Destinies*, by Rosalind Wells: "...Beautiful black woman foreign correspondent ... ultimately achieves romantic fulfillment in the arms of a handsome black executive of an international oil corporation." More are planned for other ethnic groups — American Indian, Chinese-American. (None are planned for Spanish because there are too many Spanish dialects in the United States ["Paperback Talk," August 13, 1980, *New York Times Book Review*.] There is a Spanish-language romance series published in Mexico, "Novelas Rosadas," which includes romances translated from U.S. publications as well as originals, many written under a house author's name. Sex is *never* explicit in this series.)

The Candlelight Ecstasy Romance series was new in 1980, with six novels issued each month. The series is "more sensual and realistic" than the original Candlelight series. The heroines are slightly older (25-35) and confront problems of modern relationships. "They are sensuous, sexy adult novels involving real people."

The publisher's young adult line, Laurel Leaf books, Young Love series, began in 1980 with 72 titles. The titles indicate that they are for young adults (e.g., *My First Love and Other Disasters*).

Fawcett

The Coventry Books series contains "Love stories set in the Regency, Georgian, Victorian and other colorful periods of history." The publisher has a strong Gothic line, including such standby authors as Holt, Eden, Lofts, and Whitney. Books for Young Lovers began in 1981 for teenagers.

Futura (British)

"Authors will be developed rather than single titles," announced this publisher in 1980. There are to be 20 titles a year, with increases to 60 planned.

Harlequin

"Love for sale" is how Harlequin advertises the 12 uniform packages a month it issues. "Contemporary romances with exotic settings" about a virginal young woman in love with a virile older man describes a new series in 1979: "Harlequin Presents." The new series was devised in "acknowledgement of changing sexual mores ... [being] more candid in their treatment of the love relationships" but still "wholesome and upbeat." The "Harlequin Historical" series began in 1978, and the first number was a Regency novel. The "Mystique Books" series began in 1978 and is for the romantic suspense novel, "About people who love dangerously." There are four each month. "Our romances are clean, wholesome fiction with no overt sex or violence, and always with an upbeat, happy ending." Heroines are more virtuous than Barbara Cartland's (if possible?), and there is no explicit sex. (As a fan remarked at a Harlequin fan party: "We have good imaginations.")

In 1981 a new series of more sensuous (for Harlequin) contemporary romances was begun, Superromance. So as not to sully the chaste Harlequin image, these are labeled as from Worldwide Library and distributed by Harlequin.

In 1979 Harlequin sold 168 million copies in 21 languages in 80 countries. (Harlequin romances sell very well in Japan but not in France!) "In the Romance market, Harlequin is number one ... by far." Harlequin reports an 800% increase in sales from 1970 to 1979.

The publisher uses a stable of authors, mostly British, and no men (not sensuous enough in describing dress and other details women love and want to make sex too explicit). Many of the authors have written over 50 novels for Harlequin. The publisher promotes the line, not individual authors, though some do achieve a following. "Our customers know exactly what they're going to get — just as they do when they buy Coca Cola or Ivory Soap." Harlequin bought the British firm, Mills and Boon, in 1972, and the Mills and Boon imprint is still used in Great Britain. Mills and Boon is an old firm with a large line of hardcover romances and is now also publishing in paperback.

Harlequin holds regional luncheons, each for about 250 women, at which an author speaks and prizes are given, attended with a great deal of publicity. The firm does extensive television and magazine advertising, and the following slogans have appeared in both media: "The world's most popular love stories because Harlequin understands how you feel about love." "Who says you can't buy love." "Love is sweeping the country." "Remember when you first fell in love?" "We're having a love affair with over 50 million women." Another form of advertising was the following widely distributed history: *Harlequin's 30th Anniversary: 1949-1979. The First Thirty Years of the World's Best Romance Fiction* (Harlequin Books, 1979). This book noted that by 1979 Harlequin had published over 2,000 titles. Included in the volume are the firm's history and biographical sketches with pictures of Harlequin's authors, with lists of their titles.

These sample happy endings in Harlequin romances will illustrate what readers of Harlequin romances want:

With a murmur she twined her arms around his neck and placed her mouth on his. It her diaphanous costume, her body was as transparent as her feelings and Daniel's hands gently moved her away from him....

She pulled his head to her breast. "I want you, Daniel; so much that I can't find the right words."

"Don't bother with words. There are other ways." Behind them Bella could be heard banging on the door, and he stood up and moved over to it. "I'll show you what I mean later tonight," he said huskily, "and tomorrow night and all the nights after that."

Heart in her eyes, Briony smiled at him. Daniel was hers and life was wonderful.

— Rozelle Lake
If Dreams Come True

"Oh, Alain!" Her tears flowed again. "I don't know what to say."

"Thank Heaven for that," he said, and gently moved his lips against hers.

"Alain, I--."

"No more words," he whispered. "We've a lifetime ahead for explanations. Right now there's only one thing I want to do."

"What's that?" she asked, starry-eyed.

"I'll show you," he replied.

And did.

— Rozelle Lake
Chateau in Provenence

Jove

This publisher began to reissue one of Georgette Heyer's titles every other month beginning in 1980. The "Second Chance at Love" series began in 1981, issuing each month two titles with a modern setting and one with a Regency setting. These are the advertising slogans: "Every woman wants a second chance at love." "For the millions of women devoted to romance, here are dramas that *begin* when the 'happily ever after' ends ... stories of women — single, widowed, divorced — looking to the future, eager for a passionate and enduring new relationship." "Every *Second Chance* novel spotlights an attractive heroine whose first romance has ended, but who finds true love with 'Mr. Right'—stories that every woman can identify with." "Romance readers were 'tired of trembling 18-year-old virgins' and ready for fiction representing more mature, experienced, worldly heroines in 'realistic as well as escapist circumstances.' " The trademark on the cover is a butterfly.

These excerpts from the publisher's tip sheet, guidelines for authors of the series, outline the formula to be followed in each novel.

1) The plot must involve the heroine's second chance at love. She may be a divorcee or a widow. She will find all the happiness she has missed or lost before.

2) The heroine should be from 20 to 29. She is not naive and virginal but a mature woman. Although she has suffered, she is never to be portrayed as depressed or depressive! She must have a vivacious spirit, never be dreary.

3) The hero in the contemporary novel—American or foreign—need not be rich but must be successful. He can possess a complex personality, but serious problems or neuroses—alcoholism, impotence, addictive gambling—must be avoided. Nor should there be any "Gothic" elements—a wife hidden away in a secret wing of the house.

4) The hero and heroine may make love even when unmarried and with plenty of sensuous detail. But the explicit details will be used only in foreplay, and the fadeout will occur before actual intercourse. The setting and circumstances of the lovemaking are also crucial and should contribute to a slow buildup of sexual tension. In the Regency novel the sex can stop before intercourse, since the lack of birth control devices creates an element not present in the contemporary romance.

5) The hero or heroine can be a parent, but the plot is not to be built around children nor should children create complications.

6) The length should be 65-70,000 words.

7) The story is to be told in the third person and from the heroine's point of view.

MacFadden
"Fall in love tonight with MacFadden paperback romances."

Mills and Boon
This major British publisher specializing in romance was purchased by Harlequin in 1972. The firm publishes in hardback and, recently, in paperback. One of the firm's editors stated that "the success of the romantic novel has always depended upon the ability of authors and publishers to judge exactly what kind of wish fulfilment a large section of the female population require in their reading matter at any particular time." There are several series: the "Masquerade" historical romance series, two each month ("Five out of ten women read romances. Four out of ten read historical romances."); doctor-nurse series, two each month; "Classics" series, about 14 each month.

New American Library
One of this publisher's established lines is the Signet Regency Romance series. The Signet Double Romance series presents "Two new novels of romance and passion that readers will find irresistible," the advertisement states. New in 1981 was the Mid-City Hospital series of nurse romances. Announced for 1982 was the Rapture series, described as "very sensual, with definitely adult situations." Projected for 1983 are two series: Adventures in Love, a series of contemporary romances, and September Romance, a series on love in the golden years.

Pinnacle
This company publishes the Contemporary Romance series, two each month, and the Aston Hall Romance series. "Reprinted from the original British editions."

Playboy Paperbacks

This firm regularly publishes romantic-suspense and historical romance novels (strongly sweet-and-savage). (Playboy has a line labeled in its catalogue "Erotic Fiction"—as Pocket Books has similarly labeled some titles "Erotica"—but these are not romances within the definition of the genre, and cannot even be classified as sweet-and-savage. They are soft-core pornography. This raises a ticklish question—in "Paperback Talk," *New York Times Book Review* of October 12, 1980, Ann Douglas, a Columbia University professor, is quoted as saying that Harlequin's "insipid tales of virginal innocence" are soft-core pornography, "stories that candidly elaborate the physiological and psychological conditions of girls in love." She quoted what she said is a "typical passage" that describes the hero's "razor-sharp features" as he "presses" the heroine to his "contours," which are "bruisingly hard." This ticklish question of definition is noted here merely to bring it to light: discussion is beyond the scope of this guide.)

Pocket Books

This firm publishes several series. The Cotillion Regency Romances began in 1980, with one title being issued each month. Richard Gallen Books began in 1981, with four titles each month, two being contemporary and two historical romances. Silhouette Romances began in 1980 with six original contemporary romances issued each month. The series is published jointly with Simon & Schuster. Here are several advertising slogans: "When it comes to Romance, Experience is the Best Teacher." "Romance the way it used to be." "The beautiful ending makes you feel so good." "They sooth away the tensions of the day." The firm will develop a "stable" of authors similar to Harlequin's. Before publication was begun on the Silhouette Romances, the firm made a marketing survey and publicized the following findings:

65% of the market were women under 40 and college graduates; 50% were women employed in a wide range of occupations; they are "traditional women," horrified by excesses of contemporary literature and yearning for the wholesome romances of the forties and fifties. What did these women want? "The heroine should not be too much younger than the hero—five to ten years age difference was preferable; and the 18 to 35 age group enjoyed the 'travelogue' aspect of the romance almost as much as the love story and wanted detailed information on locales. All women in the focus group [18-35] preferred—even insisted—that the hero be bold and confident, the heroine virginal and the story's ending happy."

The publisher's format guidelines for authors imposes the pattern for the series:

1) The heroine should be young and high-spirited; clothes and physical appearance are to be described in detail.

2) The hero should be older than the heroine and be masterful and virile. His clothes and physical appearance are important.

3) Among the additional characters may be the other woman, the other man, the housekeeper, and others.

4) The plot is *not* that of a Gothic nor a novel of suspense nor adventure — the action explores the relationship between lovers. The narrative should be sequential and straightforward.

5) The setting is always contemporary, preferably exotic or lush, and may romanticize a familiar setting.

6) The style of writing should be colloquial and contemporary, with natural dialogue.

7) The length is about 180 pages.

The success of Silhouette romances has led to new variations of the series being announced for 1982, one being Silhouette Rendezvous. Silhouette Special editions is another, being longer (256 pages as compared to 180 in the usual romance), and is a contemporary sophisticated romance, with a heroine who may be over 26 years old. Upon querying Silhouette's readers, the publisher found that 86% appreciated greater sensuality than the usual romance provides. So the third new series will be Silhouette Desire for "women who want a more sensual and provocative romance." On the front cover will be the slogan "You'll be swept away," and on the back cover this caution: "Because Silhouette Desires emphasize sensual detail they may not be for everyone. But if you want to experience firsthand all the excitement, passion and pure joy of falling in love, Silhouette Desire is for you." There is also a series for teenagers: First Love.

Scholastic Book Service

The Wildfire Romance series for teenagers began in 1980. The following is the publisher's description: "The heroines are 17-year-old girls who live in a typical American town or small city with a pair of strong parents whom they respect and secretly admire. They dress in the jeans and plaids and speak the vernacular of the 80's, but are faced with youth's eternal problems: how to interest a boy who interests them, how to be sure they are really in love, what to do if they really are. The story always ends happily, with no closer physical contact between the young lovers than an old-fashioned kiss." This remark comes from a fan letter quoted in an advertisement: "I would buy one *Wildfire* a week if I could." The publisher maintains a stable of authors. The Wishing Star series began in 1981. This is the publisher's description: "Young girls coping satisfactorily with such contemporary situations as dividing one's time between divorced parents." A third series, Windswept, was announced for 1982.

Warner Books

This firm has the Library of Regency Romance series.

5 Science Fiction

He writes science fiction, you write speculative fiction, I am exploring the interface between the technological and the human. And no one at all writes "SF," though millions will admit, roguishly, to reading it. But it is a useful label, resented by those who resent labels, and doesn't carry the immediate misleading reference to science, to whose methods the methods of SF are utterly antithetical, since science is a procedure for verification. "Speculative fiction," apart from being unbearably pompous, suggests that its practitioners deal in ideas, a notion popular also with blurb-writers ("inventive" is a favorite word); but ideas are just what SF has a desperate dearth of, partly because it consumes them rapidly and partly because, to speak delicately, some of its practitioners have a little difficulty in that region.
   —Eric Korn
   (*TLS*, July 8, 1977)

The last man on earth sat in a room. There was a knock on the door.
   —Anonymous

"I love you sons of bitches. You're the only ones with guts enough to *really* care about the future, who *really* notice what machines do to us, what wars do to us, what cities do to us, what tremendous misunderstandings, mistakes, accidents and catastrophes do to us. You're the only ones zany enough to agonize over time and distances without limit, over mysteries that will never die, over the fact that we are right now determining whether the space voyage for the next billion years or so is going to be Heaven or Hell."
   —Kurt Vonnegut, Jr.
   God Bless You, Mr. Rosewater

The science fiction writer is a journalist in a hurry; he reports on what happened tomorrow.
   —George Steiner

The reader trying to comprehend and understand science fiction is faced with two obstacles: the lack of an encompassing definition for all aspects and types of science fiction and the over-exuberance of its fandom who give the impression that the major aspect of science fiction is simply expressed as *Star Wars*. Theodore Sturgeon laments: "Never before in literary history has a field been judged so exclusively by its bad examples."

Science fiction *is* speculative — speculative about the potential uses of science and speculative about the potential future of mankind on this world and within the universe. The two themes may combine within the same novel, usually with one being subordinate. Although authors in the field tend to specialize in an aspect or aspects of science fiction, most do wander through the universe of science fiction themes. Unlike other genres, the best examples of the work and ideas of science fiction authors are often found in the short story.

That it is short on characterization and long on gimmicks and ideas is a frequent criticism of science fiction. (Space opera is said to have only adventure and neither characterization nor ideas.) Much science fiction is thesis fiction, bearing a statement about science fact, human nature, man in relation to nature or the universe, man in conflict with the universe, man speculating on his future in the universe. Greater emphasis, therefore, is often placed on situations or solutions than on the creatures (not necessarily human) who are the protagonists.

The critical works pose science fiction as the most philosophical, poetical, intellectual, and religious of the genre fictions. It is concerned with the mystery of the universe, man's place in it, and man's ultimate destiny: the continuation of humankind in its basic nature and humanity. Science fiction expresses faith in human ingenuity, human intelligence, and the human spirit. Technology is considered in terms of service to mankind and the natural world. The biological sciences are considered as they might heighten or increase the capacity and quality of the human mind. Religion is viewed as a means of salvation. The end is to augment the quality of life. Science fiction has been labeled a fiction of questions: What if....? If only....? If this goes on....?

The following analysis of science fiction themes shows their diversity, each defining an aspect of the genre.

THEMES AND TYPES

Hard Science

The term scientific "extrapolation" is often used concerning stories of hard science — not necessarily the prediction of what will come through scientific experimentation and increased knowledge but an imaginative projection of possibility if not probability. (The folklore of science fiction abounds in instances, of rare validity, of scientific discoveries first predicted in a science fiction tale.) The pride of authors in this field *is* that their scientific information is authentic: what they do with it may not, as yet, be known to science.

Here are some of the hard sciences played with in science fiction:

Mathematics (the fourth dimension, spatial or in time)

Cybernetics (the mind of the machine, artificial intelligence)

Meteorology (They *do* something about the weather.)

Archaeology (carbon-14 dating)

Exobiology ("The study of life-forms beyond the earth — has been defined as a science without a subject. Despite this, its nonexistent material has fascinated mankind for at least 2000 years." [From *Time Probe: The Sciences in Science Fiction*, edited by Arthur C. Clarke. Delacorte, 1966].)

Physics (gravity, relativity — faster than light, atoms and neutrons, antimatter)

Medicine (extraterrestrial medicine, brain surgery, plague)

Astronomy (space flight, black holes)

Physiology (effect of change of atmosphere on human body in space travel)

Chemistry (drugs)

Biology (mutations, genetic future, immortality)

Other topics: computers, cosmology, cryonics, cyborgs, rockets, technology, and inventions.

Many examples of the use of hard science will be found in the short story as well as the novel, and the following list is only a brief sampling of authors:

Anderson, Poul. *Brain Wave.*

Asimov, Isaac

Campbell, John W.

Clement, Hal. *Mission of Gravity.*

Heinlein, Robert A. "... And He Built a Crooked House"

Herbert, Frank

Niven, Larry

Simak, Clifford D.

Wells, H. G.

Space Opera

These novels may be called westerns in space suits, naive space adventure stories of extravagant and fantastic dimensions, usually involving galactic empires and their space battles. The serious science fiction author and fan complain that space opera gives science fiction a bad name, though a few examples of the form are good straightforward adventure stories, and a few are realistic space adventure. Some are written with humor or as comedy or parody. (See also the section Galactic Empires.) The following list could almost be extended to infinity!

Aldiss, Brian. *The Eighty-Minute Hour: A Space Opera.*

Blish, James. *Earthman Come Home.*

Brunner, John. *The Super Barbarians.*

Burroughs, Edgar Rice. Barsoom (Mars) series.

Campbell, John W., Jr. *The Black Star Passes.*

Delany, Samuel R. *Nova.*

Dickson, Gordon R. Dorsai series. *Naked to the Stars.*

Hamilton, Edmond. *Outside the Universe. Doomstar.*

Harrison, Harry. *Bill, the Galactic Hero* (parody); *Planet Story*, illustrated by Jim Burns (parody).

Harrison, M. John. *The Centauri Device* (parody).

Heinlein, Robert A. *Starship Troopers.*

Laumer, Keith. *Galactic Odyssey.*

Leinster, Murray. *Checkpoint Lambda.*

Moorcock, Michael. *The Sundered Worlds* (alternate title: *The Blood Red Game*).

Smith, Edward E. "Doc." *The Skylark of Space.*

van Vogt, A. E. *The Voyage of the Space Beagle.*

Wallace, Ian. *Croyd* and sequel *Dr. Orpheus.*

Williamson, Jack. *The Legion of Space.*

New Wave

Human nature realistically treated, however exotic the context, takes precedence over hard science and gadgetry, still liberally used, in these novels deriving from the soft sciences (psychology, sociology, religion, and the like). Sex, drugs, oriental religions, art, morality, ecology, overpopulation, politics — the topics encompassed within the subgenre seemingly have no limit. The amorphousness of definition for new wave as a distinctive type of science fiction simply indicates that new wave aspects were always present in the works of some science fiction writers. There was, however, a movement toward liberalizing the scope for themes acceptable for science fiction and expanding the imaginative vision for writers and readers. So much current science fiction, apart from the strictly adventure types, is imbued with new wave aspects that the new wave label is now little used. The following authors were influential in making new wave ideas standard in science fiction:

Ballard, J. G.

Delany, Samuel R.

Ellison, Harlan

Farmer, Philip José

Malzberg, Barry N.

Moorcock, Michael

Russ, Joanna

Sladek, John

Spinrad, Norman

Sturgeon, Theodore

Tiptree, James, Jr.

Wolfe, Gene

Zelazny, Roger

Science Fantasy

This term is not susceptible of simple definition. While science fiction basically subscribes to the laws of nature as we know them, science fantasy invents new laws, new nature, a new cosmology. There was close relationship between science fiction and fantasy in the early development of the genre (*The Magazine of Fantasy and Science Fiction, Fantastic Science Fiction, Science Fantasy*—these magazine titles indicate the merging), and the writers of science fiction may intermingle science fiction and fantasy, or write both. (In this guide there is an arbitrary separation of some types of works into the later chapters on fantasy and on horror, while alternate and parallel worlds, time travel, and other fantasy themes are included here under science fiction.) These few authors will illustrate an approach to science fiction now used by many authors:

Brown, Fredric

Bradbury, Ray

Sheckley, Robert

Smith, Cordwainer

Alien Beings

The possible and ingenious forms taken by alien beings are seemingly limitless: the authors' imaginations run wild. They may be monsters (perhaps plant-like or reptilian), or humanoid (a freak of Darwinian evolution, perhaps), or godlike, or even disembodied intelligences (as in Fred Hoyle's *The Black Cloud*). They may be invaders of earth or encountered by man on other planets. The relationships of man and alien, friendly or antagonistic, offer the writers ingenious possibilities. Space opera and fantasy have a field day in the creation of alien beings, especially BEM or Bug-Eyed Monsters, whose portrayal on the magazine cover *made* science fiction art an abiding joy. Monsters of another type appear in the chapter on horror. Color paintings of the aliens found in the works of several novelists (e.g., Larry Niven's "Thrints," van Vogt's "Ixtl," Jack Chalker's "Czill," James Blish's "Lithians") are found in Wayne Douglas Barlowe's and Ian Summers' *Barlowe's Guide to Extra-Terrestrials* (Workman, 1979). The following is only a brief sampling, and many examples are found in the short story. (Several anthologies on alien beings are listed among the "Theme Anthologies" in a later section.)

Aldiss, Brian. *The Dark Light Years.*

Asimov, Isaac. *The Gods Themselves.*

Brunner, John. *The Atlantic Abomination.*

Clarke, Arthur C. *Imperial Earth.*

Clement, Hal. *Mission of Gravity. Needle.*

de Camp, L. Sprague. *Rogue Queen.*

Dick, Philip K. *The Game-Players of Titan. Galactic Pot-Healer. Our Friends from Folix-B.*

Disch, Thomas M. *The Genocides. Mankind under the Leash.*

Farmer, Philip José. *The Lovers.*

Gunn, James E. *The Listeners.*

Haldeman, Joe. *The Forever War.*

Heinlein, Robert A. *The Puppet Masters.*

Hoyle, Fred. *The Black Cloud.*

LeGuin, Ursula K. *The Left Hand of Darkness.*

Lem, Stanislaw. *Solaris.*

Niven, Larry, and Jerry Pournelle. *The Mote in God's Eye.*

Silverberg, Robert. *Voyage of the Space Beagle. Invaders from Earth.*

Stapledon, Olaf. *Star Maker.*

Wells, H. G. *The War of the Worlds.*

Alternate and Parallel Worlds

History as it might have been: What if there had been a significant change in a historical event; what, then, would have been the pattern of history? This theoretical analysis of historical cause and effect — what would the present be and why — is often conjoined to the parallel world theme: parallel earths and parallel universes existing simultaneously with our earth, conceived, perhaps, along a spatial fourth dimension. (In the world of fantasy, the character is transported from either parallel universe into the other.) This theme has intrigued many science fiction authors in addition to those listed here, as well as authors of the mainstream novel (e.g., Vladimir Nabakov listed here).

Amis, Kingsley. *The Alteration.*

Anderson, Poul. *Guardians of Time.*

Asimov, Isaac. *The End of Eternity.*

Bayley, Barrington J. *The Fall of Chronopolis.*

Brown, Fredric. *What Mad Universe.*

Brunner, John. *Times without Number.*

Davidson, Avram. *Master of the Maze.*

de Camp, L. Sprague. *Lest Darkness Fall.*

Dick, Philip K. *The Man in the High Castle. Now Wait for Last Year. Flow My Tears, the Policeman Said. Eye in the Sky.*

Eklund, Gordon. *All Times Possible. Serving in Time.*

Farmer, Philip José. *The Gate of Time. Sail On, Sail On.*

Harrison, Harry. *Tunnel through the Deeps.*

Laumer, Keith. *Worlds of the Imperium.*

Leiber, Fritz. *Destiny Times Three.*

Moorcock, Michael. *The Wrecks of Time.*

Nabokov, Vladimir. *Ada.*

Roberts, Keith. *Pavane.*

Shaw, Bob. *The Two-Timers.*

Scheckley, Robert. *Mindswap.*

Williamson, Jack. *Legion of Time.*

Antiscience Science Fiction

A niggling suspicion that one does *not* trust the vision of the scientists does arise seriously (in Bradbury) and as parody (in Brown). More pervasive throughout many science fiction novels is the theme of anti-intellectualism—not just distrust of a world designed by scientists but a distrust of intellectuals, whether humanist or scientist. There is frequent reference to the "Frankenstein effect": the fear that technology will, if it has not already, become a monster that will destroy mankind. (See also the sections: Apocalypse; Dystopias/Utopias.) The influence of new wave science fiction writers made this a pervasive theme. The two listed here are considered prototype authors:

Bradbury, Ray. *The Martian Chronicles. Fahrenheit 451.*

Brown, Fredric. *What Mad Universe.*

Apocalypse

Survival after almost total destruction of earth is a common theme: the nature of the disaster, its effect on the nature of man, and the shape of society thereafter. The disaster may be natural (e.g., plague, or planet colliding with earth) or man-caused (e.g., nuclear war). This theme pervades the works of many science fiction writers besides those listed here:

Aldiss, Brian W. *Barefoot in the Head. Greybeard.*

Ballard, J. G. *The Drowned World. The Burning World. The Crystal World.*

Balmer, Edwin, and Philip Wylie. *When Worlds Collide.*

Brunner, John. *The Sheep Look Up.*

Christopher, John. *The Death of Grass.*

Crichton, Michael. *The Andromeda Strain.*

Hoyle, Fred, and Geoffrey Hoyle. *The Inferno.*

Lessing, Doris. *Memoirs of a Survivor.*

Miller, Walter M., Jr. *A Canticle for Leibowitz.*

Stewart, George R. *Earth Abides.*

Tucker, Wilson. *The Long Loud Silence.*

Vonnegut, Kurt, Jr. *Cat's Cradle.*

Wyndham, John. *The Day of the Triffids.*

Yarbro, Chelsea Quinn. *Time of the Fourth Horseman.*

Dystopia/Utopia

Opposed to the ideal society, utopia, is the dystopia, a horrid society, frequently the subject of science fiction. Dystopia comes into existence through many causes. Frequently it derives from the failure or corruption of rule by a scientific elite. Technology and human nature prove incompatible; psychology is used to manipulate, not improve, man's nature; biological tinkering evolves monsters, and so on. The pessimism of dystopian science fiction is political and sociological as well as antiscience and antitechnology. Dystopian novels are hortatory and polemical: heed them and see the alternate utopia or better future. (There is, however, little positive utopian vision beyond a return to a simpler, more idyllic society or a religious salvation. See Messianic/Religious.) As this theme has a long literary history, it has been the topic of novels not usually considered as science fiction. Among the following authors are several whose writings are outside the realm of this genre (Bellamy, Huxley, Orwell and Skinner):

Asimov, Isaac. *Pebble in the Sky. The Caves of Steel.* Foundation Trilogy.

Bellamy, Edward. *Looking Backward: 2000-1887.*

Bradbury, Ray. *Fahrenheit 451.*

Brunner, John. *Shockwave Rider.*

Burroughs, William S. *Nova Express.*

Gunn, James E. *The Joy Makers.*

Harrison, Harry. *Make Room! Make Room!*

Heinlein, Robert A. *Starship Troopers.*

Hoyle, Fred. *Ossian's Ride.*

Huxley, Aldous. *Brave New World.*

Leiber, Fritz. *Gather, Darkness!*

Orwell, George. *Nineteen Eighty-Four.*

Pohl, Frederik, and Cyril Kornbluth. *The Space Merchants.*

Skinner, B. F. *Walden Two.*

Vonnegut, Kurt, Jr. *Player Piano.*

Messianic/Religious

Disillusionment sullied the euphoric promise for the future offered by science and technology. Human needs and emotions somehow remained unsatisfied in the millennium of technology. A saviour, messiah, or superman brings redemption and salvation. Questions of theology and metaphysics regarding the expanding universe imagined by science fiction have uneasily juxtaposed science and faith and introduced speculation on future religions. The authors below base their books on religions currently in practice, or else they invent their own theology.

Blish, James. *A Case of Conscience.*

Clarke, Arthur C. *Rendezvous with Rama. Childhood's End.*

Dick, Philip K. *Galactic Pot-Healer.*

Farmer, Philip José. *The Lovers.*

Gunn, James E. *This Fortress World.*

Heinlein, Robert A. *Stranger in a Strange Land.*

Henderson, Zenna. *The People: No Different Flesh. Pilgrimage.*

Herbert, Frank. *Dune. Dune Messiah. Children of Dune. The God Makers.*

Lewis, C. S. *Out of the Silent Planet. That Hideous Strength.*

Miller, Walter M., Jr. *A Canticle for Leibowitz.*

Moorcock, Michael. *Behold the Man!*

Simak, Clifford D. *Time and Again.*

Vonnegut, Kurt, Jr. *The Sirens of Titan. Cat's Cradle.*

Zelazny, Roger. *Land of Light. Isle of the Dead.*

Ecology

Three themes emerge in novels on man and his natural environment: the manipulation and control of the environment; corruption of the environment by man and the destruction of some or all forms of life on earth; alien environments with distinctive characteristics and flora and fauna. Catastrophe is often linked to overpopulation and pollution as well as to planned changes in environmental patterns. Obviously, the following authors only suggest the discouraging kinds of ecological problems facing the world:

Anthony, Piers. *Omnivore.*

Ballard, J. G. *The Wind from Nowhere. The Crystal World.*

Blish, James, and Norman L. Night. *A Torrent of Faces.*

Boyd, John. *The Pollinators of Eden.*

Brunner, John. *Stand on Zanzibar. The Sheep Looked Up.*

Clement, Hal. *Cycle of Fire. Close to Critical.*

Disch, Thomas M. *334.*

Harrison, Harry. *Make Room! Make Room!*

Niven, Larry, and Jerry Pournelle. *The Mote in God's Eye.*

Silverberg, Robert. *The World Inside.*

Thomas, Theodore L., and Kate Wilhelm. *The Year of the Cloud.*

Wylie, Philip. *Los Angeles: A.D. 2017.*

Yarbro, Chelsea Quinn. *Time of the Fourth Horseman.*

Fourth Dimension

Time may be considered as a fourth dimension: time travel. The fourth dimension in space is basic to the idea of parallel worlds. Both of these concepts have been toyed with in science fiction and fantasy, sometimes with a gloss of mathematical justification but often dependent on a fanciful imagination. The following authors illustrate the mathematical and fantastical:

Abbott, Edwin. *Flatland.*

Ballard, J. G. *The Disaster Area.*

Heinlein, Robert A. "... And He Built a Crooked House."

Wells, H. G. *The Time Machine.*

Galactic Empires

While galactic empires are the setting for space opera adventures, they are also the subject of serious views of communities and worlds of humans and aliens in a variety of political and sociological relationships. Although adventure enters into the following books, these authors are more interested in sociological and political comment:

Asimov, Isaac. Foundation series.

Brunner, John. *Endless Shadow.*

Heinlein, Robert A. *A Citizen of the Galaxy.*

LeGuin, Ursula K. *The Left Hand of Darkness.*

Lessing, Doris. *Shikasta. The Marriages Between Zones Three, Four, and Five. The Sirian Experiments.*

Niven, Larry, and Jerry Pournelle. *The Mote in God's Eye.*

Simak, Clifford D. *Way Station.*

Stapledon, Olaf. *Star Maker.*

Vance, Jack, and James E. Gunn. *Star Bridge.*

van Vogt, A. E. *The Weapon Shops of Isher. The Weapon Makers.*

Immortality

Whether science can ultimately confer immortality upon mankind is considered in science fiction, but whether such immortality would be a blessing or a curse is the real question. There are immortal beings in science fiction stories. (One such immortal in *Venus on the Half-Shell*, by Kilgore Trout, says bluntly, "Immortality is a pain in the ass." For more on this book, see the section on Parody and Poetry.) The following books treat the theme seriously:

Aldiss, Brian W. *Moment of Eclipse.*

Gunn, James E. *The Immortals.*

Heinlein, Robert A. *Time Enough for Love.*

Shaw, Bob. *One Million Tomorrows.*

Silverberg, Robert. *Born with the Dead.*

Vance, Jack. *To Live Forever.*

van Vogt, A. E. *The Weapon Makers.*

Zelazny, Roger. *This Immortal.*

Extrasensory Perception

The powers of precognition, telepathy, clairvoyance, telekinesis, and teleportation displayed by characters in science fiction make current research in parapsychology seem naive. Science fiction invented the term "psionics" (psychic electronics) to describe these powers of the mind. Such powers are often inherent in the superman theme and are manifest among alien beings. The variations on this theme have fascinated many science fiction authors besides the following ones:

Bester, Alfred. *The Stars My Destination. The Demolished Man.*

Blish, James. *Jack of Eagles.*

Brunner, John. *The Whole Man.*

Clement, Hal. *Needle.*

Dickson, Gordon R. *Dorsai!.*

Harrison, Harry. *Death Word.*

Henderson, Zenna. *Pilgrimage.*

Herbert, Frank. *Dune.*

LeGuin, Ursula K. *The Lathe of Heaven.*

McCaffrey, Anne. *To Ride Pegasus.*

Pohl, Frederik. *Drunkard's Walk.*

Roberts, Keith. *The Inner Wheel.*

Russ, Joanna. *And Chaos Died.*

Silverberg, Robert. *Dying Inside.*

Simak, Clifford D. *Time Is the Simplest Thing.*

Sturgeon, Theodore. *The Dreaming Jewels. More Than Human.*

van Vogt, A. E. *Slan.*

Zelazny, Roger. *The Dream Master.*

Lost Worlds

These are the matter of romantic science fiction, now largely displaced as a subject by the interplanetary universe. There are large elements of fantasy and adventure in the many examples still popular, with their prehistoric animals, strange races of men, and background in archaeology and anthropology. These examples are among the prototypes:

Burroughs, Edgar Rice. *At the Earth's Core.*

Doyle, Sir Arthur Conan. *The Lost World.*

Haggard, H. Rider. *She. King Solomon's Mines.*

Verne, Jules. *Journey to the Centre of the Earth.*

Robots, Androids, Cyborgs

The robot is a machine, usually in human form but purely mechanical. An android is an artificial man, organic in composition. A cyborg is a man altered with artificial parts to perform certain functions or modified to exist in outer space. The computer is essential to all forms. Pervading all these stories is the often tricky problem of interrelationship of man and machine. One true bit of science fiction folklore exists for the robot, Asimov's three laws of robotics: 1) A robot may not injure a human being or, through inaction, allow a human being to come to harm; 2) A robot must obey the orders given by human beings, except where such orders would conflict with the first law; 3) A Robot must protect its own existence as long as such protection does not conflict with the first or second law. The robots in the following books are more sophisticated than those now available and give intriguing hints of a possible future:

Asimov, Isaac. *I, Robot. Caves of Steel.*

Bayley, Barrington J. *The Garments of Caean.*

Čapek, Karel. *R.U.R.* [play]

Compton, D. G. *The Unsleeping Eye.*

Dick, Philip K. *Do Androids Dream of Electric Sheep? We Can Build You.*

Harrison, Harry. *War with the Robots.*

Kuttner, Henry. *Robots Have No Tails.*

Laumer, Keith. *A Plague of Demons.*

Leiber, Fritz. *The Silver Eggheads.*

Lem, Stanislaw. *The Cyberiad.*

McCaffrey, Anne. *The Ship Who Sang.*

Pohl, Frederik. *Man Plus.*

Shelley, Mary. *Frankenstein.*

Silverberg, Robert. *Tower of Glass.*

Simak, Clifford D. *City. Time and Again. A Choice of Gods.*

van Vogt, A. E. *Mission to the Stars.*

Williamson, Jack. "With Folded Hands...." "... And Searching Mind."

Social Criticism

The sociological bases of human society are an insistent theme in science fiction, notably in the projection of utopias and dystopias. The science fiction authors also study the phenomena of social change to anticipate direction and project consequences. The following authors may be forecasting possibility, however strange the new society may seem:

Aldiss, Brian W. *The Dark Light Years.*

Anderson, Poul. *War of the Wing-Men.*

Asimov, Isaac. *The Gods Themselves.*

Brunner, John. *Stand on Zanzibar.*

de Camp, L. Sprague. *Rogue Queen.*

Delany, Samuel R. *Triton.*

Farmer, Philip José. *The Lovers.*

Gunn, James E. *The Joy Makers.*

LeGuin, Ursula K. *The Left Hand of Darkness.*

Panshin, Alexei. *Rite of Passage.*

Pohl, Frederik, and Cyril M. Kornbluth. *The Space Merchants.*

Roberts, Keith. *Pavane.*

Simak, Clifford D. *City.*

Wells, H. G. *The First Men in the Moon.*

Wylie, Philip. *The Disappearance.*

Space Travel

Although space flight has actually been achieved, its reality only adds to the obsession of science fiction with spaceships, starships, interstellar travel, and galactic empires. Flight in space is still *the* romantic theme dominating science fiction. Not to be caught short when colonizing follows exploration, science fiction has a guide ready (covering eight extrasolar planets earth has colonized): Wolfe, L. Stephen, and Roy L. Wysack. *Handbook for Space Pioneers: A Manual of the Galactic Association (Earth Branch).* Grosset, 1978.

The theme as used by the following authors ranges from space travel as science to space travel as fantasy:

Anderson, Poul. *Tau Zero.*

Balchin, Nigel. *King of Infinite Space.*

Brown, Fredric. *The Lights in the Sky Are Stars.*

Clarke, Arthur C. *2001: A Space Odyssey. Prelude to Space. Rendezvous with Rama.*

Geston, Mark. *Lords of the Starship.*

Heinlein, Robert A. *Citizen of the Galaxy.*

Herbert, Frank. *Destination: Void.*

Malzberg, Barry N. *The Falling Astronauts.*

Pohl, Frederik. *Gateway.*

Simak, Clifford D. *Shakespeare's Planet.*

Stableford, Brian. *Man in a Cage.*

van Vogt, A. E. *Rogue Ship.*

Verne, Jules. *From the Earth to the Moon.*

Superman

The superman in science fiction is *not* the comic-strip figure. Whether an evolutionary projection of man, an alien, or an immortal god, the superman is endowed with capacities of extraordinary, supersensory or supernatural mental power and may or may not also be of superman physical powers. The relationship of man with superman is uneasy, and many of the stories show mutual antagonism or that supermen are a danger to mankind. The superman as messiah is also used. As in the following examples, this theme usually causes the books to be disturbingly philosophical:

Anderson, Poul. *Brain Wave.*

Bester, Alfred. *The Computer Connection.*

Clarke, Arthur C. *Childhood's End.*

Henderson, Zenna. *Pilgrimage. The People: No Different Flesh.*

Stapledon, Olaf. *Odd John.*

Sturgeon, Theodore. *More Than Human.*

van Vogt, A. E. *Slan.*

Watson, Ian. *Alien Embassy.*

Weinbaum, Stanley G. *The New Adam.*

Williamson, Jack. *Darker Than You Think.*

Time Travel, Time Warp

Travel into either past or future is a dream in all literature and not restricted to science fiction. Whether limited to the body or mind, the experience is both desirable and frightening. Science fiction uses great ingenuity in the methods of travel and equal imagination in depicting the experiences of the travelers. This is a favorite ploy in space opera and fantasy. Playing with time has intrigued many science fiction and fantasy writers, and the following list merely suggests the number of books on the theme. Many examples may also be found in children's books.

Aldiss, Brian A. *Cryptozoic! Frankenstein Unbound.*

Anderson, Poul. *Tau Zero. The Corridors of Time.*

Asimov, Isaac. *Pebble in the Sky. The End of Eternity.*

Ballard, J. G. *The Crystal World.*

Blish, James. *Midsummer Century.*

Brunner, John. *The Productions of Time. Quicksand. Timescape.*

Dick, Philip K. *Counter-Clock World.*

Dickson, Gordon R. *Time Storm.*

Graves, Robert. *Seven Days in Crete* (U.S. title: *Watch the North Wind Rise*)

Haldeman, Joe. *The Forever War.*

Harrison, Harry. *The Technicolor Time Machine.*

Heinlein, Robert A. *Farnham's Freehold.*

Hoyle, Fred. *October the First Is Too Late.*

Laumer, Keith. *The Great Time Machine Hoax.*

MacDonald, John D. *The Girl, the Gold Watch and Everything.*

Niven, Larry. *A World Out of Time. World of Ptavvs.*

Norton, Andre. Witch World series.

Pohl, Frederik. *The Age of the Pussyfoot.*

Shaw, Bob. *Who Goes There?*

Silverberg, Robert. *The Masks of Time. The Time Hoppers.*

Taine, John. *The Time Stream.*

Wells, H. G. *The Time Machine. When the Sleeper Wakes.*

Wright, S. Fowler. *The World Below.*

Women, Love, Sex

These three themes were late bloomers in science fiction and are often still of secondary or minor interest. They assumed importance with the new wave and the emergence of the soft sciences, particularly psychology and sociology, as the concern of many science fiction authors. A shift in emphasis from the dominant thesis toward the story of human relations, however bizarre the context, increased the scope for the love story and/or sexual relationships and, incidentally, often gave some much needed depth to characterizations. That more women are writing science fiction undoubtedly hastened this change. (Sex often introduces some welcome humor: "On Saturn the sexes are three" begins a limerick by B. T. H. Xerxes, found in Tom Boardman's anthology, *An ABC of Science Fiction*, Avon, 1966.) The books below are quite specifically on the topics of women, love, and sex, but the reader may find many recent science fiction novels in which these topics are more fully treated than in earlier examples of the genre.

Aldiss, Brian. *The Primal Urge. Barefoot in the Head.*

Anderson, Poul. *Virgin Planet.*

Ballard, J. G. *Crash.*

Delany, Samuel R. *Dhalgren.*

Farmer, Philip José. *Flesh. The Lovers. The Image of the Beast. Strange Relations. A Feast Unknown.*

Heinlein, Robert A. *Time Enough for Love.*

LeGuin, Ursula K. *The Left Hand of Darkness. The Dispossessed.*

Pohl, Frederik, and Cyril Kornbluth. *Search the Sky.*

Russ, Joanna. *The Female Man. We Who Are about To....*

Spinrad, Norman. *Bug Jack Barron.*

Sturgeon, Theodore. *Venus Plus X.*

Wilson, Richard. *The Girls from Planet 5.*

Wyndham, John. "Consider Her Ways."

Computers, Automation

The computer is capable of an amazing number of ingenious functions under human programming, but the science fiction authors see the computer as a thinking machine. So well does it think and plan and even reproduce itself in some stories that it makes man unnecessary: a future in which the machines hum contentedly and man is obsolete. Whether man and computer will live in cooperative harmony or in a master-slave relationship provides a controversial theme for science fiction authors. The worry that the machine — computer, robot — may end up running human society is one of the recurring doubts in science fiction: whether science, in all its aspects, is a blessing or curse for mankind. The idea of a completely automated society is analyzed in a similar manner. The books listed below present some aspects, both intriguing and disturbing, of man's coexistence with the computer:

Blish, James. *Midsummer Century.*

Brunner, John. *The Shockwave Rider.*

Compton, D. G. *The Steel Crocodile.*

Dick, Philip K. *Vulcan's Hammer.*

Frayn, Michael. *The Tin Men.*

Heinlein, Robert A. *The Moon Is a Harsh Mistress.*

Herbert, Frank. *Destination: Void.*

Johannesson, Olaf. *The Tale of the Big Computer.*

Lafferty, R. A. *Arrive at Easterwine.*

Pohl, Frederik. *Man Plus.*

Detectives in Space

A neat combining of two genres produces galactic policemen and private eyes — human, alien, and mechanical. For a good historical survey, see the chapter "Crime: From Sherlock to Spaceships" in Sam Moskowitz's *Strange Horizons* (Scribner's, 1976). Anthologies collect some of the short stories, and readers may be interested in the following:

Asimov, Isaac, Martin Harry Greenberg, and Charles G. Waugh, eds. *The 13 Crimes of Science Fiction.* Doubleday, 1979.

Each of the stories is labeled: Hard-Boiled Detective; Psychic Detective; Spy Story; Analytical Detective; Whodunit; Why-Done-It; Inverted; Locked Room; Cipher; Police Procedural; Trial; Punishment.

De Ford, Miriam Allen, ed. *Space, Time & Crime*. Paperback Library, 1964.

Santesson, Hans Stefan, ed. *Crime Prevention in the 30th Century*. Walker, 1969.

As in the standard detective story, there is the use of a series detective in several of the examples listed below:

Abbott, Keith. *Rhino Ritz*.

Asimov, Isaac. *The Caves of Steel. The Naked Sun*.
  Features detective Lige Baley and robot R. Daneel Olivaw.

Bear, David. *Keeping Time*.
  "Last of the private eyes" in the twenty-first century.

Bester, Alfred. *The Demolished Man*.

Clement, Hal. *Needle*.

Garrett, Randall. *Too Many Magicians*.

Goulart, Ron. *Dr. Scofflaw*.

Haiblum, Isidore. *Nightmare Express. Outerworld*.

Killough, Lee. *Deadly Silents. The Doppelgänger Gambit*.

Lem, Stanislaw. *Tales of Pirx the Pilot*.
  "Technological detective stories."

Spruill, Steven G. *The Psychopath Plague*.
  Detective team: Human and alien.

Wallace, Ian. *The Purloined Prince. Deathstar Voyage. The Sign of the Mute Medusa*.
  Claudine St. Eyre, detective.

Parody and Poetry

Despite the serious tenor of most science fiction, there is a persistent stream of comedy and parody. Parody is the delight of the sophisticated reader who will come across instances naturally. The novice should *not* start with parody, so here are only a couple of samples of this subgenre:

Adams, Douglas. *The Hitchhiker's Guide to the Galaxy*. Harmony Books, 1979.

Trout, Kilgore. *Venus on the Half-Shell*. Dell, 1975.
  The author is Philip José Farmer. Kilgore Trout is a character invented by Kurt Vonnegut. Trout is a writer of science fiction and his works are discussed, with much delightful quotation, in Vonnegut's *God Bless You, Mr. Rosewater*. (Among the many organizations and fan groups involved in science fiction is to be found the "Friends of Kilgore Trout.")

Lucie-Smith, Edward, ed. *Holding Your Eight Hands: An Anthology of Science Fiction Verse*. Doubleday, 1969.
By science fiction authors and others.

Theme Anthologies

There are a great number of anthologies of science fiction because the short story is so copious and popular in the genre. The short story seems ideally suited to the genre's speculative treatment of ideas. These anthologies provide an intriguing introduction to the imaginative variety of attitudes on most of the themes explored and to the authors in the genre. The theme is noted in the list below, unless the title is self-explanatory. A useful guide is *Index to Stories in Thematic Anthologies for Science Fiction*. Edited by Marshall B. Tymn, Martin H. Greenberg, L. W. Currey, Joseph D. Olander. With an introduction by James Gunn (G. K. Hall, 1978).

Aldiss, Brian, ed. *Galactic Empires*. St. Martin's, 1977. 2v.

Anderson, Susan Janice, and Vonda N. McIntyre, eds. *Aurora: Beyond Equality*. Fawcett, 1976. (Women).

Asimov, Isaac, ed. *Tomorrow's Children*. Doubleday, 1966.

Asimov, Isaac, et al., eds. *The Seven Deadly Sins of Science Fiction*. Crest, 1980.

Bryant, Edward, ed. *Among the Dead, and Other Events Leading Up to the Apocalypse*. Macmillan, 1973.

Carr, Terry, ed. *The Fellowship of the Stars*. Simon & Schuster, 1975. (Alien beings).

Carr, Terry, ed. *Dream's Edge: Science Fiction Stories about the Future of the Planet Earth*. Sierra Club, 1980.

Clarke, Arthur C., ed. *Time Probe: The Science of Science Fiction*. Delacorte, 1966.

Conklin, Groff, ed. *Invaders of Earth*. Grosset, 1962. (Alien beings).

Conklin, Groff, ed. *Science Fiction Thinking Machines*. Vanguard, 1954.

Dann, Jack, ed. *Wandering Stars: An Anthology of Jewish Fantasy and Science Fiction*. Harper, 1974. (Religion).

Derleth, August, ed. *Beachheads in Space*. Pellagrini, 1952. (War).

Disch, Thomas M., ed. *Bad Moon Rising*. Harper, 1973. (Politics).

Disch, Thomas M., ed. *The Ruins of Earth: An Anthology of Stories of the Immediate Future*. Putnam, 1971. (Ecological disaster).

Dozois, Gardner, ed. *A Day in the Life: A Science Fiction Anthology*. Harper. (Future life).

Elder, Joseph, ed. *Eros in Orbit: A Collection of All New Science Fiction Stories about Sex*. Trident, 1973.

Elwood, Roger, ed. *And Walk Now Gently through the Fire and Other Science Fiction Stories*. Chilton, 1972. (Biology and religion).

Elwood, Roger, ed. *Chronicles of a Comer and Other Religious Science Fiction Stories*. John Knox, 1974.

Elwood, Roger, ed. *Future City*. Trident, 1973.

Elwood, Roger, ed. *Invasion of the Robots*. Paperback Library, 1965.

Elwood, Roger, ed. *Saving Worlds*. Doubleday, 1973. (Ecology).

Elwood, Roger, ed. *Signs and Wonders*. Revell, 1972. (Religion).

Fermen, Edward L., and Barry N. Malzberg, eds. *Graven Images*. Nelson, 1977.

FitzGerald, Gregory, ed. *Neutron Stars*. Fawcett, 1977. (Decay of our supernovaed culture).

Gerrold, David, ed. *Ascents of Wonder*. Popular Library, 1977.

Goldin, Stephen, ed. *The Alien Condition*. Ballantine, 1973. (Alien beings).

Ghidelia, Vic, ed. *The Devil's Generation*. Lancer, 1973. (Child's mind).

Ghidelia, Vic, ed. *The Oddballs*. Manor, 1973.

Greenberg, Martin Harry, and Patricia S. Warrick, eds. *Political Science Fiction: An Introductory Reader*. Prentice-Hall, 1974.

Greenberg, Martin Harry, and Joseph D. Olander, eds. *Tomorrow, Inc.: Science Fiction Stories about Big Business*. Taplinger, 1976.

Haldeman, Joe, ed. *Cosmic Laughter: Science Fiction for the Fun of It*. Holt, 1974.

Haldeman, Joe, ed. *Study War No More: A Selection of Alternatives*. St. Martin's, 1977.

Harrison, Harry, ed. *The Year 2000*. Doubleday, 1970.

Hill, Douglas, ed. *The Shape of Sex to Come*. London: Pan, 1978.

McNelly, Willis E., and Leon S. Stover, eds. *Above the Human Landscape: A Social Science Fiction Anthology*. Goodyear, 1972.
    Imaginative and unusual illustrations.

Margulies, Leo, and Oscar J. Friend, eds. *From Off This World*. Merlin, 1949. (Alien beings).

Mason, Carol, Martin H. Greenberg, and Patricia Warrick, eds. *Anthropology through Science Fiction*. St. Martin's, 1974.

Milstead, John, ed. *Sociology through Science Fiction*. St. Martin's, 1975.

Mohs, Mayo, ed. *Other Worlds, Other Gods*. Doubleday, 1971. (Religion).

Monteleone, Thomas F., ed. *The Arts and Beyond: Visions of Man's Aesthetic Future*. Doubleday, 1977.

Moskowitz, Sam, ed. *The Coming of the Robots*. Collier, 1963.

Moskowitz, Sam, ed. *When Women Rule*. Walker, 1972.

Mowshowitz, Abbe, ed. *Inside Information: Computers in Fiction*. Addison-Wesley, 1977.
    Includes librarian-author Hal Draper's "Ms Fnd in a Lbry." Required reading for all librarians.

Ofshe, Richard, ed. *The Sociology of the Possible.* Prentice-Hall, 1970.

Pohl, Frederik, and Carol Pohl, eds. *Jupiter.* Ballantine, 1973.

Pronzini, Bill, and Barry N. Malzberg, eds. *Bug-Eyed Monsters.* Harvest/ HBJ, 1980.

Salmonson, Jessica Amanda, ed. *Amazons.* DAW, 1979.

Sargent, Pamela, ed. *Bio-Futures: Science Fiction Stories about Biological Metamorphosis.* Vintage, 1976.

Sargent, Pamela, ed. *Women of Wonder: Science Fiction Stories by Women about Women.* Vintage, 1975.

Sargent, Pamela, ed. *More Women of Wonder.* Vintage, 1976.

Sauer, Bob, ed. *Voyages: Scenarios for a Ship Called Earth.* Ballantine, 1971.

Scortia, Thomas, ed. *Strange Bedfellows: Sex and Science Fiction.* Random, 1973.

Scortia, Thomas, and George Zebrowski, eds. *Human Machines: An Anthology of Stories about Cyborgs.* Vintage, 1975.

Silverberg, Robert, ed. *Deep Space.* Nelson, 1973. (Space travel).

Silverberg, Robert, ed. *Galactic Dreams: Science Fiction as Visionary Literature.* Random, 1977.

Silverberg, Robert, ed. *The Infinite Web.* Dial, 1977. (Ecology).

Silverberg, Robert, ed. *Mind to Mind.* Dell, 1974. (Telepathy).

Silverberg, Robert, ed. *The Science Fiction Bestiary.* Dell, 1974.

Silverberg, Robert, ed. *Trips in Time.* Nelson, 1977.

Stone, Idella, ed. *14 Great Tales of ESP.* Fawcett, 1969.

Stover, Leon E., and Harry Harrison, eds. *Apeman, Spaceman.* Doubleday, 1968. (Anthropology).

Van Tassel, D., ed. *Computers, Computers, Computers: In Fiction and in Verse.* Elsevier, 1977.

Warrick, Patricia, Martin Henry Greenberg, and Joseph Glander, eds. *Science Fiction: Contemporary Mythology.* The SFWA-SFRA Anthology. Harper, 1978.
Ten sections, each with an introductory essay and a critical bibliography: technology and progress; journeys into the unknown; dimensions of time and space; alien; machine and robot; androids, cyborgs; the city; utopias and dystopias; apocalypse.

Wollheim, Donald, ed. *The End of the World.* Ace, 1956.

Wright, Stephen, ed. *Different: An Anthology of Homosexual Short Stories.* Bantam, 1974.

Another access to reading by theme may be found through the "Checklist of Themes" in *The Science Fiction Encyclopedia,* edited by Peter Nicholls. (See Encyclopedias for fuller description.) For each theme, the encyclopedia article provides definition, history, and criticism of the treatment of the theme in general literature as well as in science fiction, including the key works both in short story and novel. Most of the themes analyzed here are listed, and the following is a short selection to indicate the diverse approaches available to the reader: black holes, clones, communications, cosmology, cryonics, discovery and invention, genetic engineering, mathematics, metaphysics, mutants, politics, psychology, reincarnation, terraforming, time paradoxes, war, weather control.

The Visual Encyclopedia of Science Fiction, edited by Brian Ash (see Encyclopedias), is arranged under themes and has a similar access to both novels and short stories. There are 19 major themes, with further subdivision under each theme, e.g., under "Warfare and Weaponry," a division on "War with the Aliens." The major themes are: spacecraft and star drives; exploration and colonies; biologies and environments; warfare and weaponry; galactic empires; future and alternative histories; utopias and nightmares; cataclysms and dooms; lost and parallel worlds; time and nth dimensions; technologies and artefacts; cities and cultures; robots and androids; computers and cybernetics; mutants and symbiotes; telepathy, psionics and ESP; sex and taboos; religion and myths; inner space.

TOPICS

"Best" Authors and Their Best

A list of "best" authors and their best works is impossible to compile except on an eccentric basis. Included here are most of the winners of Hugo and Nebula awards, and the award-winning titles are listed. Many of these authors are listed as examples in the earlier "theme" section, as are authors not listed here. Not included are classic authors (Edgar Rice Burroughs, Jules Verne, H. G. Wells, and others) and many no longer writing whose works may still be available in paperback. Most of the authors listed are currently writing or appear regularly on lists of the "best." (This author is indebted to my students for critical assistance in deciding the authors who must be read for a comprehensive introduction to science fiction.) Many more titles could be listed for most of these authors. The ones listed are those most often cited. A few authors are listed without title, indicating that critics consider important the influence of the author's work as a whole.

Aldiss, Brian. *The Long Afternoon of Earth. Greybeard. The Dark Light Years. Barefoot in the Head.*

Anderson, Poul. *Brain Wave. Tau Zero. The Star Fox. Three Hearts and Three Lions.*

Anthony, Piers. *Chthon. Omnivore.*

Asimov, Isaac. *The Gods Themselves.* The Foundation Trilogy. *Opus 100.*
The last title is 99 works tied together with autobiographical notes.

Ballard, J. G. *The Wind from Nowhere. The Crystal World. Vermilion Sands.*

Bass, T. J. *Half Past Human.*

Bester, Alfred. *The Demolished Man. The Stars My Destination.*

Blish, James. *Cities in Flight. A Case of Conscience.*

Bloch, Robert

Boucher, Anthony

Bradbury, Ray. *I Sing the Body Electric. The Martian Chronicles. The October Country. The Illustrated Man.*

Brown, Fredric. *Martians Go Home.*

Brunner, John. *Squares of the City. Stand on Zanzibar.*

Budrys, A. J. *Rogue Moon. Who?*

Bulchev, Kirill. *Half a Life and Other Stories.*

Burgess, Anthony. *A Clockwork Orange. The Wanting Seed.*

Burroughs, William S. *Nova Express.*

Clarke, Arthur C. *Rendezvous with Rama. Childhood's End.*

Clement, Hal. *Close to Critical. Needle. Mission of Gravity.*

Compton, D. G. *Synthajoy.*

Davidson, Avram. *Or All the Seas with Oysters.*

Delany, Samuel R. *Nova. Babel 17. Dhalgren. The Einstein Intersection.*

Del Rey, Lester. *Nerves.*

Dick, Philip K. *The Man Who Japed. The Man in the High Castle.*

Dickson, Gordon R. *Soldier Ask Not Why. Dorsai!.*

Disch, Thomas M. *334.*

Ellison, Harlan. *I Have No Mouth and I Must Scream. The Beast Who Shouted Love at the Heart of the World. Ellison Wonderland.*

Farmer, Philip José. *To Your Scattered Bodies Go.*

Finney, Jack. *The Body Snatchers.*

Galouye, Daniel F. *Dark Universe.*

Haldeman, Joe. *The Forever War.*

Harrison, Harry. *Bill, the Galactic Hero. Make Room! Make Room!*

Heinlein, Robert A. *Time for the Stars. Double Star. Glory Road. Starship Troopers. Stranger in a Strange Land. The Moon Is a Harsh Mistress.*

Herbert, Frank. *Oregon in the Sea. Dune.*

Keyes, Daniel. *Flowers for Algernon.*

Knight, Damon. *Hell's Pavement.*

Kornbluth, Cyril. *The Syndic.*

Kuttner, Henry. *Mutant. The Dark World. Earth's Last Citadel. Fury.*

Lafferty, R. A. *The Reefs of Earth. Past Master.*

Latham, Philip

LeGuin, Ursula K. *The Left Hand of Darkness. The Dispossessed.*

Leiber, Fritz. *The Wanderer. A Spectre Is Haunting Texas.*

Leinster, Murray

Lem, Stanislaw. *Mortal Engines. Solaris.*

McCaffrey, Anne. *Dragonflight. Restorer. The Ship Who Sang.*

McIntyre, Vonda N. *Dreamsnake.*

Malzberg, Barry N. *Beyond Apollo.*

Matheson, Richard. *I Am Legend. The Shrinking Man.*

Miller, Walter M., Jr. *A Canticle for Leibowitz.*

Moorcock, Michael. *Behold the Man. The Cornelius Chronicles.*

Niven, Larry. *A Gift from Earth. Neutron Star. Ringworld.*

Pangborn, Edgar. *A Mirror for Observers.*

Panshin, Alexei. *Rite of Passage.* Anthony Villiers series.

Pohl, Frederik. *Man Plus. Gateway.*

Reynolds, Mack

Roberts, Keith. *Pavane.*

Russ, Joanna. *And Chaos Died.*

Shute, Nevil. *On the Beach.*

Silverberg, Robert. *A Time of Changes. The Masks of Time.*

Simak, Clifford D. *Way Station. City. Here Gather the Stars.*

Sladek, John. *Mechasm.*

Smith, Cordwainer R. *You Will Never Be the Same. Space Lords.*

Smith, George O. *Highways in Hiding.*

Spinrad, Norman. *The Iron Dream.*

Stapledon, Olaf. *The Star Maker. Last and First Men. Odd John.*

Strugatsky, Arkady, and Boris Strugatsky. *Prisoners of Power. Roadside Picnic. Monday Begins on Saturday.*

Sturgeon, Theodore. *More Than Human. The Dreaming Jewels.*

Taine, John

Tenn, William. *Of Men and Monsters.*

Tiptree, James, Jr.

Vance, Jack. *The Dying Earth. Eyes of the Overworld.*

van Vogt, A. E. *The World of Null-A. Voyage of the Space Beagle.*

Vonnegut, Kurt, Jr. *Sirens of Titan. Slaughterhouse Five. Cat's Cradle.*

Wallace, Ian. *Deathstar Voyage.*

Weinbaum, Stanley G. *The Black Flame.*

Wilhelm, Kate. *Let the Fire Fall. Where Late the Sweet Birds Sang.*

Williamson, Jack. *The Humanoids.*

Wyndham, John. *The Midwich Cuckoos. Day of the Triffids. Rebirth.*

Zelazny, Roger. *Lord of Light. Isle of the Dead. And Call Me Conrad.*

Anthologies

The best way to become acquainted with the characteristics of authors in the genre, particularly to see the work of new authors, is through anthologies. Both the theme anthologies and the critical and historical collections may have stories from all periods and often suffer from repetition of much-anthologized pieces. The short story is a very popular form in both science fiction and fantasy. While the following listing of anthologies is long, it is by no means exhaustive:

Allen, Dick, and Lori Allen, eds. *Looking Ahead: The Vision of Science Fiction.* Harcourt, 1976.

Allen, Dick, and Lori Allen, eds. *Science Fiction: The Future.* Harcourt, 1971.
Both aforementioned anthologies are textbooks with notes and bibliography.

Asimov, Isaac, ed. *Where Do We Go from Here?* Doubleday, 1971.

Ashley, Michael, ed. *The History of the Science Fiction Magazines, 1926-1945.* Regnery, 1974-75. 2v.
Historical introduction and anthology.

Boucher, Anthony, and J. Francis McComas, eds. *The Best from Fantasy and Science Fiction.* Little, Brown, 1952.

Boucher, Anthony, ed. *A Treasury of Great Science Fiction.* Doubleday, 1959. 2v.

Bova, Ben, ed. *Forward in Time: A Science Fiction Story Collection.* Walker, 1973.

Bradbury, Ray, ed. *Timeless Stories for Today and Tomorrow.* Bantam, 1952.

Brodkin, Sylvia A., and Elizabeth J. Pearson, comps. *Science Fiction.* Lothrop, 1973.
Unusual and imaginative illustrations.

Brown, Fredric, ed. *Science Fiction Carnival: Fun in Science Fiction.* Bantam, 1957.

Clareson, Thomas D., ed. *A Spectrum of Worlds.* Doubleday, 1972.

Conklin, Groff, ed. *The Best of Science Fiction.* Crown, 1946.

Edwards, Malcolm, ed. *Constellations: Stories of the Future.* London: Gollancz, 1980.

Ellison, Harlan, ed. *Dangerous Visions.* Doubleday, 1967.

Ellison, Harlan, ed. *Again, Dangerous Visions.* Doubleday, 1972.

Ferman, Edward L., and Barry N. Malzberg, eds. *Final Stage: The Ultimate Anthology.* Charterhouse, 1974.

Harrison, Harry, and Brian W. Aldiss, eds. *The Astounding-Analog Reader.* Doubleday, 1972.

Harrison, Harry, ed. *The Light Fantastic: Science Fiction Classics from the Mainstream.* Scribner's, 1974.

Healy, Raymond J., and J. Francis McComas, eds. *Adventures in Time and Space.* Random, 1946.
    Modern Library Edition: *Famous Science Fiction Stories.*

Healy, Raymond J., ed. *New Tales of Time and Space.* Holt, 1951.

Jakubowski, Maxim, ed. *Travelling towards Epsilon: An Anthology of French Science Fiction.* New English Library, 1976.

Knight, Damon, ed. *100 Years of Science Fiction.* Simon & Schuster, 1968.

Knight, Damon, ed. *A Science Fiction Argosy.* Simon & Schuster, 1972.

Knight, Damon, ed. *Science Fiction of the Thirties.* Avon, 1977.

LeGuin, Ursula K., and Virginia Kidd, eds. *Edges.* Pocket Books, 1980.

Lupoff, Richard, ed. *What If.* Pocket Books, 1981- (to be 4v.).

Merril, Judith, ed. *Science Fiction: The Best of the Best.* Delacorte, 1967.

Moskowitz, Sam, ed. *Masterpieces of Science Fiction.* World, 1966.

Moskowitz, Sam, ed. *Modern Masterpieces of Science Fiction.* World, 1965.

The Playboy Book of Science Fiction and Fantasy. Playboy Press, 1966.

Pohl, Frederik, Martin Harry Greenberg, and Joseph Olander, eds. *The Great Science Fiction Series.* Harper, 1980.
    Twenty-one stories, each introduced by the author. Series following a character or theme are among the most popular types of science fiction.

Rottensteiner, Franz, ed. *Views from Another Shore: European Science Fiction.* Seabury, 1973.

The Science Fiction Hall of Fame. Doubleday, 1970-73. 3v.
    Selections chosen by the Science Fiction Writers of America as the best in the genre.

Silverberg, Robert, ed. *The Arbor House Treasury of Great Science Fiction Short Novels.* Arbor House, 1980.

Silverberg, Robert, ed. *Earth Is the Strangest Planet.* Nelson, 1977.

Silverberg, Robert, ed. *The Mirror of Infinity: A Critic's Anthology of Science Fiction.* Harper, 1970.

Spinrad, Norman, ed. *Modern Science Fiction.* Anchor, 1974.
    The 21 stories—grouped as "The Golden Age," The Postwar Awakening, and The Full Flowering—are preceded by an introduction, and 10 briefer critical essays are interspersed among the stories. An author in the genre and a critic who says baldly "Please understand, this first-generation science fiction was godawful stuff," commands one's respect. The anthology and the criticism are highly recommended as an introduction to the genre.

Williams-Ellis, Amabel, and Michael Pearson, eds. *Strange Universe.* London: Blackie, 1974.

Several works among the annual and numbered series anthologies present only original short stories; the others reprint from the magazines for the genre. A few listed here have ceased publication, but their cumulated numbers form an important anthology. "Best" is not to be taken literally — merely a selection from the year's output.

Andromeda. 1976 -.

The Astounding Analog Reader, 1972-1973. 2v.

The Best from Fantasy and Science Fiction. (22nd series, 1977).

The Best from Galaxy, 1972-1974. 2v.

The Best SF 1-7, edited by Edmund Crispin, 1955-1977.

The Best Science Fiction of the Year. 1967- .

Chrysalis. (#8, 1980).

The Hugo Winners. 1962- (v.3, 1977).

Infinity, #1-5, 1970-1972.

Isaac Asimov Presents the Great SF Stories. (#4, 1980).

Nebula Award Stories. 1965- (#9, 1974).

New Dimensions. 1971- (#7, 1977).

New Writing in Science Fiction. 1964- .

Nova. (#3, 1973).

Orbit, 1965- (#20, 1978).

Quark. #1-4, 1970-1971.

Spectrum. #1-5, 1962-1967.

Star Science Fiction Stories, edited by Frederik Pohl. #1-6, 1953-1959.

Terra SF: The Year's Best European SF. 1981- .

Universe. 1971- (#10, 1980).

The Year's Best Science Fiction, edited by Judith Merril. #1-12, 1956-1968.

Bibliography

Most of these books include authors who write both science fiction and fantasy. Good bio-bibliographical listings are to be found in Nicholls (see Encyclopedias). The annotations indicate that some of the following books include considerable historical and critical material as well as bibliography:

Ash, Brian. *Who's Who in Science Fiction*. Taplinger, 1976.
Brief bio-bibliographical listings with critical evaluations of characteristics as a science fiction writer. Prefaced with a "Chronological Guide: 100 Leading Writers and Editors in Their Main Periods of Production," from 1800 to the 1970s.

Barron, Neil, ed. *Anatomy of Wonder: A Critical Guide to Science Fiction*. Second edition. Bowker, 1981.

The 1975 edition has been much expanded. Critically annotated author listings are grouped by period or type with introductory essays: "The Emergence of Science Fiction: The Beginnings to the 1920s," by Thomas Clareson; "Science Fiction between the Wars: 1918-1938," by Brian Stablefield; "The Modern Period: 1938-1980," by Joe De Bolt and John R. Pfeiffer; "Children's Science Fiction," by Francis J. Molson; "Foreign Language Science Fiction," by several authors, covering German, French, Russian, Italian, Japanese and Chinese. "Research Aids" includes chapters on indexes, bibliographies, history and criticism, author studies, film and television, illustration, classroom aids, magazines, library collections, and a core collection checklist.

Bleiler, Everett Franklin. *The Checklist of Fantastic Literature; A Bibliography of Fantasy, Weird and Science Fiction Books Published in the English Language.* Shasta, 1948.

Clarke, Ignatius Frederick, comp. *The Tale of the Future from the Beginning to the Present Day: An Annotated Bibliography.* 2nd edition. London, Library Association, 1972.

Curry, L. W. *Science Fiction and Fantasy Authors: A Bibliography of First Printings of Their Fiction and Selected Non-Fiction.* G. K. Hall, 1980.
215 authors.

A Reader's Guide to Science Fiction. By Baird Searles, Martin Last, Beth Meacham, and Michael Franklin. With a foreword by Samuel R. Delany. Avon, 1979.
The authors run the Science Fiction Shop, New York City. Lists 200 authors with biocritical annotation. Has a guide to major science fiction series. Useful listing of a suggested basic library of 50 volumes.

Smith, Curtis C., ed. *Twentieth-Century Science Fiction Writers.* London: Macmillan, 1981.
This is the second volume in the publisher's series of bibliographies for genre fiction authors. (The first, on crime and mystery writers, is listed in chapter 3. Two others are announced on romance and Gothic writers and on writers of westerns.) This volume contains bibliographies of 532 British and American writers. An appendix lists 35 foreign language writers and five major fantasy writers. For each author there is brief biographical identification, a signed critical essay, and the bibliography, including non-science fiction works separately grouped. A personal statement was solicited by the editor and is present for some authors. There is an extensive prefatory reading list and a bibliography of studies of individual authors.

Encyclopedias

These encyclopedias contain considerable bibliographical, historical, and critical material:

Ash, Brian, ed. *The Visual Encyclopedia of Science Fiction.* London: Coppleston; New York: Harmony Books, 1977.

Arranged in 19 "Thematics," each section written by a science fiction author known for works in the theme, e.g., Isaac Asimov on robots and androids. Each theme is further subdivided by topics. In addition to works internally discussed, each section has a bibliography. Prefaced by a chronology (1805-1976) of important events and publications. Sections on fandom, science fiction art, cinema and television, magazines, anthologies, and the like. Lavishly illustrated in color and black-and-white.

Nicholls, Peter, ed. *The Science Fiction Encyclopedia.* Dolphin Books, Doubleday, 1979.
Alphabetical arrangement of themes, biography, and other topics, with many cross-references. Historical and critical with extensive bibliographical material. Biographical listings for many little-known authors. Many of the articles are extended critical essays. Black-and-white illustrations.

Tuck, Donald Henry. *The Encyclopedia of Science Fiction and Fantasy through 1968.* Advent, 1974- .
To be complete in three volumes. First two are bio-bibliographical and international in scope.

History

Science fiction history may start in classical literature or in the nineteenth century: the author's definition of the genre determines his scope. Many of these books are critical to the point of being controversial. They are written by authors of the genre and by fans, both lay and academic. In addition to the following books, the reader will find considerable historical material in the encyclopedias listed above and in the critical works in the next section.

Aldiss, Brian W. *Billion Year Spree: The True History of Science Fiction.* Doubleday, 1973.
Begins with Mary Shelley's *Frankenstein.* Bibliography of works consulted.

Appel, Benjamin. *The Fantastic Mirror: Science Fiction across the Ages.* Pantheon, 1969.
From early man's wonder stories and fantastic voyages to the present, with the twentieth century dismissed briefly in the last two chapters. More lyrical than factual.

Del Rey, Lester. *The World of Science Fiction, 1926-1976: The History of a Sub-Culture.* Garland, 1979.
In terms of the magazines that published genre.

Gerber, Richard. *Utopian Fantasy: A Study of English Utopian Fiction since the End of the Nineteenth Century.* 2nd edition. McGraw-Hill, 1973.
Unchanged from 1955 edition except that "Appendix: An Annotated List of English Utopian Fantasies...." now covers 1901-1971.

Gove, Philip Babcock. *The Imaginary Voyage in Prose Fiction; A History of Its Criticism and a Guide for Its Study, with an Annotated List of 215 Imaginary Voyages from 1700 to 1800.* Columbia University Press, 1941.

Green, Roger Lancelyn. *Into Other Worlds: Space-Flight in Fiction from Lucian to Lewis*. Abelard-Schumann, 1958.

Gunn, James. *Alternate Worlds: The Illustrated History of Science Fiction*. Prentice-Hall, 1975.

Kyle, David. *A Pictorial History of Science Fiction*. London: Hamlyn, 1976.
Both of the above books cover from Greek times to the present, lavishly illustrated in color and black-and-white.

Nicholson, Marjorie Hope. *Voyages to the Moon*. Macmillan, 1948.
Fictional voyages through the eighteenth century, with an "Epilogue" on the nineteenth and twentieth centuries. Delightful text and illustrations.

Rottensteiner, Franz. *The Science Fiction Book: An Illustrated History*. London: Thames and Hudson, 1975.
Topically organized (e.g., "Why there is no sex in science fiction") and imaginatively illustrated in color and black-and-white. Important for the survey of science fiction in European countries: Soviet Union, France, Japan, Italy, Spain, Rumania, Germany. Appended chronology: c.160 (Lucian) to 1974.

Scholes, Robert, and Eric S. Rabkin. *Science Fiction: History, Science, Vision*. Oxford, 1977.
The first one-third of the book is history, the later parts are criticism.

Criticism

The quantity of critical exposition on science fiction is daunting. The quality varies from the fandom popular to the academic obscurant, with, fortunately, some lively and imaginative discussion in between by both authors of the genre and fans in the academic world. The following is merely a sampling to show the wealth of commentary available:

Aldiss, Brian W., ed. *Hell's Cartographers: Some Personal Histories of Science Fiction Writers*. London: Weidenfeld, 1975.
Essays by Robert Silverberg, Alfred Bester, Harry Harrison, Damon Knight, Frederik Pohl, Brian Aldiss.

Allen, L. David. *Science Fiction: An Introduction*. Cliff Notes, 1973.

Allen, L. David. *The Ballantine Teachers' Guide to Science Fiction: A Practical Creative Approach to Science Fiction in the Classroom*. Ballantine, 1975.
The teaching of science fiction, junior high school through college, is flourishing. The two guides define the genre and, together, present criticism of an anthology and 23 major works of fiction.

Amis, Kingsley. *New Maps of Hell: A Survey of Science Fiction*. Harcourt, 1960.
Distinguishes science fiction as social criticism from science fiction as adventure.

Ash, Brian. *Faces of the Future: The Lessons of Science Fiction*. Taplinger, 1975.

Berger, Harold L. *Science Fiction and the New Dark Ages.* Popular Press, 1976.
> The threat of science, catastrophe, and dystopias as forecast in science fiction.

Bretnor, Reginald, ed. *Science Fiction Today and Tomorrow: A Discussive Symposium.* Harper, 1974.
> Fifteen essays by authors in the genre defining and criticizing the genre.

Carter, Paul A. *The Creation of Tomorrow: Fifty Years of Magazine Science Fiction.* Columbia University Press, 1977.

Clareson, Thomas D., ed. *Many Futures, Many Worlds: Theme and Form in Science Fiction.* Kent State University Press, 1977.

Clareson, Thomas D., ed. *SF: The Other Side of Realism.* Popular Press, 1971.

Clareson, Thomas D., ed. *Voices for the Future: Essays on Major Science Fiction Writers.* Volume 1. Popular Press, 1976.
> All three collections above contain essays on diverse topics by genre authors and academic fans.

Delany, Samuel R. *The Jewel-Hinged Jaw: Notes on the Language of Science Fiction.* Dragon Press, 1977.

Knight, Damon, ed. *Turning Point: Essays in the Art of Science Fiction.* Harper, 1977.
> Twenty-three essays by authors in the genre.

Lundwell, Sam J. *Science Fiction: What It's All About.* Ace, 1971.
> Translated from the Swedish.

Moskowitz, Sam. *Strange Horizons: The Spectrum of Science Fiction.* Scribner's, 1976.
> Chapters on: Religion, Anti-Semitism, Civil Rights, Women's Liberation, Birth Control, Psychiatry, Crime, Teen-Agers, War, Unexplained Phenomena, Art.

Nicholls, Peter, ed. *Science Fiction at Large: A Collection of Essays by Various Hands about the Interface between Science Fiction and Reality.* London: Gollancz, 1976.
> Eleven lectures presented at an institute held in London.

Parrinder, Patrick. *Science Fiction: Its Criticism and Teaching.* London: Methuen, 1980.
> This British textbook is a work of critical definition, introducing and analyzing the genre.

Riley, Dick, ed. *Critical Encounters: Writers and Themes in Science Fiction.* Ungar, 1978.
> Nine essays.

Rose, Mark, ed. *Science Fiction: A Collection of Critical Essays.* Prentice-Hall, 1976.
> Eleven essays defining the genre.

Scholes, Robert. *Structural Tabulation: An Essay on Fiction of the Future.* University of Notre Dame Press, 1975. (Ward-Phillips Lectures in English Language and Literature, Vol. 7).

Suvin, Darko. *Metamorphoses of Science Fiction: On the Poetics and History of a Literary Genre*. Yale University Press, 1979.

Tymn, Marshall B. "Science Fiction." In Inge, M. Thomas, ed. *Handbook of American Popular Culture*. 1978. Vol. 1, pages 251-73.

Williamson, Jack, ed. *Teaching Science Fiction: Education for Tomorrow*. London: Chiswick Press, 1980.
Anthology of essays by science fiction authors and teachers at several school levels.

Wolfe, Gary K. *The Known and the Unknown: The Iconography of Science Fiction*. Kent State University Press, 1979.
The themes of science fiction and the images relating to them.

Wollheim, Donald A. *The Universe Makers: Science Fiction Today*. Harper, 1971.
Idiosyncratic, imaginative, and amusing: by a science fiction editor and a fervent fan.

Manuals

The following are meant to instruct writers in their craft but are also illuminating for the reader in understanding the genre:

Bretnor, Reginald, ed. *The Craft of Science Fiction: A Symposium on Writing Science Fiction and Science Fantasy*. Harper, 1976.
Essays by 15 preeminent authors of the genre.

Grant, C. L., ed. *Writing and Selling Science Fiction*, by the Science Fiction Writers of America. Writer's Digest, 1976.
Ten essays by members of SFWA.

Intersections: The Elements of Fiction in Science Fiction. By Thomas L. Wymer, Alice Calderonello, Lowell P. Leland, Sara Jayne Steen, and R. Michael Evers. Popular Press, 1978.
Chapters on: Plot, Character, Setting, Point of view, Language, Tone, Theme and value, Symbol and myth.

Science Fiction Art

One of the most entrancing aspects of science fiction and fantasy is its art illustration. The pulp and current science fiction and fantasy magazines are notable for their covers, and many of the titles now being issued in hardback and paperback are illustrated. Perhaps the best examples of this art may be found in the illustrated encyclopedias and histories previously listed. The following listing does not include the several publications collecting science fiction and fantasy illustrations by individual artists:

Aldiss, Brian, comp. *Science Fiction Art*. Crown, 1975.

Frewin, Anthony. *One Hundred Years of Science Fiction Illustration, 1840-1940*. Pyramid Books, 1975.

Holdstock, Robert, and Malcolm Edwards. *Alien Landscapes*. Mayflower, 1979.

Ten worlds, illustrated by 10 artists, inspired by the works of science fiction writers: Rama (Arthur C. Clarke); Pern (Anne McCaffrey); Okie Cities (James Blish); Mesklin (Hal Clement); Eros (Harry Harrison); Arrakis (Frank Herbert); Ringworld (Larry Niven); Trantor (Isaac Asimov); Hothouse (Brian Aldiss); End of the World (H. G. Wells).

Planet Story, by Harry Harrison and Jim Burns. A&W Visual Library, 1979.

A superb example of melded illustration and story. Harrison wrote the outrageous space opera parody and Burns did the marvelous full-color illustrations. A large-format book, equally divided between text and full-page and double-spread illustrations.

Film

There is a publishing side-industry derived from *Star Wars* and *Star Trek*, attesting to fandom's engrossment with the movies. (The neatest comment on these is in the parody short film feature "Hardware Wars.") This should not obscure the continued presence of the many and often serious science fiction and fantasy films that have a devoted following. These films reflect the current interest in science fiction themes:

Baxter, John. *Science Fiction in the Cinema*. Barnes, 1970.

Brosnan, John. *Present Tense: The Cinema of Science Fiction*. St. Martin's, 1979.

Clarens, Carlos. *An Illustrated History of the Horror Film*. Putnam, 1967.

Johnson, William, ed. *Focus on the Science Fiction Film*. Prentice-Hall, 1972.

Lee, Walt, comp. *Reference Guide to Fantastic Films: Science Fiction, Fantasy, and Horror*. Chelsea-Lee, 1972-74. 3v.

Willis, Donald C. *Horror and Science Fiction Films: A Checklist*. Scarecrow Press, 1972.

Magazines

Of the hundreds of science fiction and fantasy magazines started since the twenties, few have survived. The multitude of original paperback anthologies possibly contributed to their demise. However, a few are still successful and an important showcase for new authors. Most contain reviews and critical and science explication articles. For a full history of the magazines, see the encyclopedias listed previously. The magazines listed below usually include fantasy; they also provide reviews and often columns or articles on science:

Amazing Stories. 1926- .

Analog. (*Astounding Science Fiction*). 1930- .

Argosy Science Fiction. 1977- .

Galaxy. 1950- .

Galileo. 1977- .

Isaac Asimov's Science Fiction Magazine. 1977- .

Magazine of Fantasy and Science Fiction. 1949- .

Critical Journals

There are a multitude of fanzines of varying quality — and uncertain continuance — containing news, articles, and reviews. Three have endured to achieve more general interest and circulation:

Riverside Quarterly. 1964- .

Science Fiction Review. 1978- .

Starship: The Magazine about SF (formerly *Algol*). 1963- .

Two journals resulting from the increasing interest of academics in science fiction are strong in articles on history and criticism:

Extrapolation: Journal of the MLA Seminar on Science Fiction. 1959- . Modern Language Association, U.S.

Foundation: The Review of Science Fiction. 1972- . British.

The International Science Fiction Yearbook 1979

The contents of this book are truly international in coverage. The first issue had 29 sections, including Book Publishing; Magazines; Organizations; Fanzines; Anthologies; Criticism, Commentary, Bibliography; Libraries; Book Clubs; Book Sellers; Conferences & Workshops; Conventions; Awards; Artists; Films; TV. There is critical and imaginative presentation of information, e.g., in Section 29, Fringe Interests, there are essays on pseudoscience, artificial intelligence, and space research. Included are black-and-white art illustrations and cartoons.

Reviews

Most of the magazines and the fanzines of science fiction contain reviews. (Two specialized review journals did not survive: *Delap's Fantasy and Science Fiction Review* and *Science Fiction Review Monthly*.) Available for the general reader is the occasional column by Gerald Jonas in the *New York Times Book Review*, which is tops for interesting and critical reviews. For librarians, there is a column in *Library Journal* (first appearance, January 15, 1979) and the reviews in *Booklist* and *Virginia Kirkus*, between them offering fairly complete coverage of hardbound and paperback issues.

Associations and Conventions

Science Fiction Writers of America

The association was founded in 1965. It sponsors the annual "Nebula" awards for several categories of science fiction writing. It has as a motto: The Future Isn't What It Used to Be.

Fans and writers form many associations and hold innumerable conventions, usually combining science fiction and fantasy and often adding horror and the supernatural. *The International Science Fiction Yearbook 1979* provides a long list of both types. "Con" is usually part of the conference name. Here are two of the most general "cons":

> World Science Fiction Convention. "Worldcon." The first, 1939; the thirty-seventh was held in Brighton, England, 1979.
>
> World Science Fiction Writers' Conference. The first, 1976; the second was held in 1978.

(William Marshall writes a series of detective novels featuring Detective Chief Inspector Harry Feiffer and the police of the Yellowthread Street station in Hong Kong. In *Sci Fi: A Yellowthread Street Mystery* [London: Hamish Hamilton, 1981], the city has been taken over by the All-Asia Science Fiction and Horror Movie Congress: the streets and jails are full of fans in costume and The Spaceman is on a murder spree.)

Awards

The following are the major awards for science fiction:

Hugo; awarded at World Science Fiction Conventions

Nebula; awarded by The Science Fiction Writers of America

Locus; resulting from a poll by fanzine *Locus*.

Lists of award-winning titles are found in several of the bibliographies, histories, and encyclopedias listed previously.

Science Fiction Book Clubs

There are two major clubs, one in the United States and one in Britain. The British club reprints or distributes the publisher's hardcover edition. The U.S. club, owned by Doubleday, publishes hardcover club editions of both hardcover and paperback originals and also original omnibus editions. The clubs issue an extensive number of titles and are an important source for libraries of hardcover editions. For other book clubs in the United States, England, and Europe, see *The International Science Fiction Yearbook 1979*.

The Science of Science Fiction

Whether the authors consider themselves writers of science fiction or of speculative fiction, they are concerned with both the hard and soft sciences. So, too, are the serious readers of the genre. The encyclopedias, histories, and books of criticism give cursory-through-thorough background on these sciences, and the genre magazines run columns or articles on the state of science. The following selective listing under themes suggests the variety of material, including pseudoscience, of interest to the science fiction fan:

Alien Beings

Bergier, Jacques. *Extraterrestrial Visitations from Prehistoric Times to the Present*. Regnery, 1973.

Bracewell, Ronald N. *The Galactic Club: Intelligent Life in Outer Space*. Scribner's, 1975.

Cohane, John Philip. *Paradox: The Case for the Extraterrestrial Origin of Man*. Crown, 1977.

Keyhoe, Donald E. *Aliens from Space: The Real Story of Unidentified Flying Objects*. Doubleday, 1973.

Von Daniken, Erich. *The Gold of the Gods*. Putnam, 1973.

Black Holes

Kaufmann, William J. *Black Holes and Warped Space Time*. Freeman, 1979.

Sullivan, Walter. *Black Holes: The Edge of Space, the End of Time*. Doubleday, 1979.

Astronomy

Macvey, John. *Where Will We Go When the Sun Dies*. Stein, 1981.

Medicine

Hoyle, Fred, and N. C. Wickramasinghi. *Diseases from Space*. London: Dent, 1980.

UFOs

Bowen, Charles, ed. *Encounter Cases from Flying Saucer Review*. NAL, 1980.

Story, Ronald D., and J. Richard Greenwell, eds. *The Encyclopedia of UFOs*. Doubleday, 1980.

Space Travel

Calder, Nigel. *Spaceships of the Mind*. Viking, 1978.

Macvey, John W. *Interstellar Travel: Past, Present and Future*. Stein, 1977.

Nicholson, Iain. *The Road to the Stars*. Morrow, 1978.

Von Braun, Wernher, and Frederick Ira Ordway. *New Worlds: Discoveries from Our Solar System*. Doubleday, 1979.

Apocalypse

Gribbin, John. *The Death of the Sun*. Delacorte, 1980.

Galactic Wars

Macvey, John W. *Space Weapons, Space War*. Stein, 1979.

Space Colonies

Barry, Adrian. *The Next Ten Thousand Years*. Saturday Review Press, 1974.

Brand, Stewart, ed. *Space Colonies.* Penguin, 1977.

Heppenheimer, T. A. *Colonies in Space.* Warner, 1977.

O'Neill, Gerald K. *The High Frontier.* Bantam, 1977.

Publishers

Isaac Asimov, at the SFWA annual banquet in 1973, said science fiction is "the only thriving form of fiction in America today." The international list of publishers in *The International Science Fiction Yearbook 1979* is extensive. Most science fiction publication appears to be in paperback, both original works and reprints, but hardbound publication seems to be increasing. Anthologies appear widely in both forms. Critical works that used to be largely in hardcover are now appearing regularly in both formats. Illustrated novels of both science fiction and fantasy are published in both formats but, notably, in greater numbers in originals in paperback; some, unillustrated in the original hardback, are illustrated in the paperback reprint.

The following U.S. paperback publishers issue science fiction and fantasy, most issuing both originals and reprints. Special series and aspects are noted.

A&W
Mainly illustrated works.

Ace
Mainly reprints.

Avon
"Science Fiction Rediscovery Series" of reprints.

Ballantine

Bantam

Berkley
Berkley/Putnam Fiction is the hardcover line.

DAW
Specializes in science fiction and fantasy, issues six novels per month.

Dell

Del Rey Books
Ballantine's Science Fiction imprint for both hardcover (since 1978) and paperback, six titles per month. "Gold Seal" series announced 1981 for trade paperbacks of classic science fiction and fantasy.

Dover
Excellent quality trade paperbacks for both science fiction and fantasy, specializes in reprinting the classics.

Fawcett

Jove

Manor

New American Library (Signet)

Pinnacle

Playboy

Pocket Books
"Timescape: Science Fiction & Fantasy" series in conjunction with Simon & Schuster, announced 1981, 6 hardcover and 60 paperbacks per year.

Popular Library

Vintage

Warner

Zebra
Mainly fantasy.

U.S. HARDCOVER PUBLISHERS

Bobbs-Merrill

Crown

Del Rey Books (see under paperbacks)

Dial
Quantum Science Fiction series.

Doubleday
Also owns Science Fiction Book Club.

Harcourt

Harper

Knopf

Morrow

Putnam (see Berkley paperbacks)

Random House

St. Martin's

Simon & Schuster (see also Pocket Books under paperbacks)

Taplinger

Walker
Many reprints.

Viking

BRITISH PAPERBACK PUBLISHERS

Corgi; Coronet; Fontana; Futura; Granada; Magnum; New English Library (hardcover also); Paladin; Pan; Penguin; Sphere.

BRITISH HARDCOVER PUBLISHERS

Cape; Dobson; Faber & Faber; Gollancz (probably the major publisher); Robert Hale; Hutchinson; Millington; Sidgwick; Weidenfeld.

U.S. HARDCOVER REPRINT PUBLISHERS

Reprint anthologies and critical works as well as novels. Output is not limited to the series quoted.

Arno
"Lost Race & Adult Fantasy Fiction" series.

Garland
"Garland Library of Science Fiction," 45 titles.

G. K. Hall
Gregg Press reprints; Gregg Fantastic series.

6 Fantasy

A fiction evoking wonder and containing a substantial and irreducible element of supernatural or impossible worlds, beings or objects with which the reader or the characters within the story become on at least partly familiar terms.
　　　　— C. N. Manlove
　　　　Modern Fantasy

A Fantasy work [is] ... one which at some point (or *in toto*) reaches the edge of the probable and then steps over.
　　　　— Naomi Lewis

Fantasy deals with the supernatural, while science fiction takes what is known and projects it further. But they overlap.
　　　　— Madeleine L'Engle

"So knights are mythical!" said the younger and less experienced dragons. "We always thought so."
　　　　— J. R. R. Tolkien
　　　　Farmer Giles of Ham

Modern fantasy is inextricably entangled with science fiction because of its publishing history: most of the pulp magazines and anthologies feature both. Also, many of the authors write in both fields or use elements of both in one or the other forms. A very simple distinction can be made: science fiction deals with the possible (though not necessarily probable) because it is based on scientific (hard or soft) knowledge, however tenuously at times; fantasy deals with the impossible, being based on magic or the supernatural. To put it another way, science fiction follows and obeys the laws of nature in the universe as we know it, however fantastic some of its devices may seem; fantasy strictly follows a set of laws formulated by each author for an imaginary world, rules which need have no congruence with the laws of nature as we know them but which must conform to their own logic. What fantasy and science fiction share is a preoccupation with "other" worlds — science fiction in a universe still full of mystery but potentially to be understood; fantasy in a universe boundlessly extended through the author's imagination.

There is a distinction made between high and low fantasy. Low fantasy is set in the world we know governed by nature's laws. Nonrational happenings occur but are not explained, rationally or irrationally — by natural law they just shouldn't happen! Magic and supernatural beings are not present. High fantasy is set in imaginary, secondary worlds, their "natural" order or laws set by supernatural beings (gods, fairies); magical powers abound amongst wizards and magicians, and a fantasy flora and fauna provide dragons, unicorns, or whatever. Dark fantasy is used to describe the horror, ghost, and supernatural tales of the next chapter.

This analysis could go on ingeniously to the amazement of any reader with firm convictions about the similar or dissimilar natures of science fiction and fantasy. Argument is rendered futile by the characteristics of the works themselves. The authors may rationalize the fantastic elements of the story, doing without the devices of magic or sorcery, so that the irrational may seem possible. This book evades distinguishing the two fields by definition, and arbitrarily (through this author's fantastic logic) places certain categories within the science fiction themes: Science Fantasy, Alternate/Parallel Worlds, Extrasensory Perception, Time Travel. In addition, of course, many of the novels cited under science fiction contain elements of fantasy. The reader must consider the chapters on science fiction and fantasy as being symbiotic.

Weird fantasy, centering on horror, the occult, and supernatural creatures, makes an appearance in science fiction and in the categories of fantasy discussed in this chapter. Again, weird fantasy is considered arbitrarily in the next chapter on horror and the supernatural.

To further confuse the definition of fantasy is the reader's prior association of fantasy with literature for children. The world of faery, myth, and an unnatural bestiary (e.g., dragons, unicorns) is the accepted realm of childhood's imaginings. That adults continue to love fairy tales, folklore, mythology, and odd little people and monsters is attested by the popularity of adult fantasy. (Many adults also continue to enjoy fantasy written for children.) We stubbornly believe in and welcome magic whatever our chronological age.

THEMES AND TYPES

Sword-and-Sorcery

The world of adventure in which magic works, in which heroes and heroines wage epic combat with forces of evil, is the matter of fantasy's currently most popular type of publication — the heroic fantasy or fantastic romance. These tales feature sorcerers and magicians, large elements of the supernatural, much romance, and often a quest of daunting hazards. Some use magic only sparingly, concentrate on adventure, and are often noted as being in the tradition of Edgar Rice Burroughs' Barsoom series. Usual backgrounds are galactic or akin to medieval European kingdoms. Multiple-volume series are common. Many of the authors appear also on the science fiction lists.

The following are several anthologies containing only sword-and-sorcery stories:

Asprin, Robert, ed. *Thieves' World*. Ace, 1979.

Carter, Lin, ed. *Flashing Swords*. Dell. (Continuing series).

Carter, Lin, ed. *Realms of Wizardry*. Doubleday, 1976.

de Camp, L. Sprague, ed. *Warlocks and Warriors*. Putnam, 1970.

Page, Gerald W., and Hank Reinhardt, eds. *Heroic Fantasy.* DAW, 1979.

Parry, Michel, ed. *Savage Heroes: Tales of Magical Fantasy.* Taplinger, 1980.

Salmonson, Jessica Amanda, ed. *Amazons: High Adventure in Heroic Fantasy.* DAW, 1979.

As is obvious in the following list, the sword-and-sorcery authors frequently use a series hero or heroine:

Akers, Alan Burt. Davy Prescott series.
  Burroughs tradition.

Anderson, Poul. *Three Hearts and Three Lions. Midsummer Tempest.*

Anthony, Piers. *A Spell for Chameleon. The Source of Magic. Castle Roogna.*

Brackett, Leigh. Stark series.

Bradley, Marion Zimmer. Darkover series.

Burroughs, Edgar Rice. Barsoom series.

Carter, Lin. Thongor of Lemuria series.

Cherryl, C. J. *Gate of Ivrel. Well of Shiuan.*

de Camp, L. Sprague. Pusedian series. Novaria series.

Gaskell, Jane. Atlan series.

Heinlein, Robert A. *Glory Road.*
  His only sword and sorcery novel.

Howard, Robert E. Conan the Barbarian series. King Kull series. Bran Mak Morn series. Solomon Kane series.
  Conan series continued by Poul Anderson, L. Sprague de Camp, Lin Carter, Bjorn Nyberg.

Jakes, John. Brak the Barbarian trilogy.

Kuttner, Henry. Elak of Atlantis series.

Lancour, Gene. Dirshan the God-Killer series.

Lee, Tanith. *The Birthgrave.*
  Swordswoman.

Leiber, Fritz. Fafhrd and the Grey Mouser series.

Lord, Jeffrey. Richard Blade series.

McKillip, Patricia. Riddle-Master of Hed trilogy.
  For children but read by adults.

Moorcock, Michael. Elric series. Corum series. Hawkmoon series.

Moore, C. L. Jirel of Joiry series.

Norman, John. Gor series.

Pratt, Fletcher. *The Well of the Unicorn.*

Norton, Andre. Witch World series.

Russ, Joanna. Alyx series.
Swordswoman.

Van Lustbader, Eric. Sunset Warrior trilogy.

Zelazny, Roger. *Nine Princes in Amber. The Guns of Avalon. Sign of the Unicorn.*
A distinctive style of sword-and-sorcery places the adventure in the world of saga, myth, and legend (Eddic, Welsh, etc.) or the kingdoms of medieval times. Some of the authors listed use a recognizable country while others invent a fantasy land.

Alexander, Lloyd. Chronicles of Prydain series.

Cabell, James Branch. Poictesme series.

Chant, Joy. *Red Moon and Black Mountain. The Grey Mane of Morning.*

Cullen, Seamus. *Astra and Flondrix.*
Although all sword and sorcery is full of romance, few share this one's erotic label.

Donaldson, Stephen R. *The Chronicles of Thomas, the Unbeliever.*
Trilogy, followed by *The Second Chronicles of Thomas, the Unbeliever.*

Eddison, E. R. *The Worm Ouroboros. Fish Dinner in Memison. Mistress of Mistresses.*

Kurtz, Katherine. The Chronicles of the Deryni series.

LeGuin, Ursula K. Orsinian series.

McCaffrey, Anne. Dragonworld series.

Moorcock, Michael. *Gloriana.*

Walton, Evangeline. Mabinogion series.

Many sword-and-sorcery tales derive from the Arthurian story and feature the magician Merlin. Examples include:

Berger, Thomas. *Arthur Rex.*

Bradshaw, Gillian. *Hawk of May.*

Kane, Gil, and John Jakes. *Excalibur!*

Monaco, Richard. *Parsival. The Grail War.*

Munn, H. Warner. *King of the World's Edge. Merlin's Godson. Merlin's Ring.*

Norton, Andre. *Merlin's Mirror.*

Stewart, Mary. *The Crystal Cave. The Hollow Hills. The Last Enchantment.*

White, T. H. *The Once and Future King.*
Collective title for *The Sword in the Stone. The Witch in the Wood. The Ill-Made Knight. The Book of Merlyn* concludes the series.

Three Classic Authors

The popularity and influence of these three writers are pervasive. It is interesting that the works by Lewis and Tolkien appeal equally to children and adults.

Lewis, C. S. *Out of the Silent Planet. Perelandra. That Hideous Strength.*
Interplanetary romances, conflict of good and evil with strongly religious tone. Elements of Arthurian legend, using magician Merlin.

Narnia series.
For children, witches, and magic; religious message. Also enjoyed by adults.

Ford, Paul. *Companion to Narnia.* Harper, 1980.

Schakel, Peter J. *Reading with the Heart: The Way into Narnia.* Eerdmans, 1980.

Peake, Mervyn. Gormenghast trilogy: *Titus Groan, Gormenghast, Titus Alone.*

Tolkien, J. R. R. *Lord of the Rings* trilogy. *The Silmarillion.*
The Middle Earth of the elves, complete with language and laws. A heroic quest, conflict of good and evil. Strong influence on writers of sword-and-sorcery.

Beard, Henry N., and Douglas C. Kenney. *Bored of the Rings: A Parody of J. R. R. Tolkien's The Lord of the Rings.* NAL, 1969.
Product of the *Harvard Lampoon.*

Day, David. *A Tolkien Bestiary.* Random, 1979.

Foster, Robert. *The Complete Guide to Middle-Earth: From The Hobbit to The Silmarillion.* Del Rey, 1978.

Helms, Randal. *Tolkien's World.* Houghton, 1974.

Kocher, Paul Harold. *Master of Middle Earth: The Fiction of J. R. R. Tolkien.* Houghton, 1972.

Tyler, J. E. A. *The New Tolkien Companion.* St. Martin's, 1980.

World of Faery

The little people—elves, goblins, fairies—enter into many fantasy works for children. There are some notable adult treatments. Lord Dunsany and MacDonald have been influential on modern writers of fantasy. As these examples show, adults often retain a love of the fairy world:

Dunsany, Lord. *The King of Elfland's Daughter* (1924).

MacDonald, George. *Fantastes: A Faerie Romance for Men and Women* (1858).
A nineteenth-century author of children's books.

Warner, Sylvia Townsend. *Kingdom of Elfin* (1977).
Sophisticated series of stories, first published in *The New Yorker.*

Mythology and Legend

All fantasy is full of myth and legend. The following is a sampling of those in which myth and legend dominate:

Beagle, Peter. *The Last Unicorn.*

Crichton, Michael. *Eaters of the Dead.*
Beowulf legend.

de Camp, L. Sprague, and Fletcher Pratt. *The Compleat Enchanter: The Magical Misadventures of Harold Shea.*

Finney, Charles. *The Circus of Dr. Lao.*

LeGuin, Ursula K. Earthsea trilogy.

McKillip, Patricia A. *The Forgotten Beasts of Eld.*

Swann, Thomas Burnett. *The Forest of Forever.*

Literary and Fictional Characters Live!

The characters of fiction and other forms of literature take on historical reality in a fantasy world rich in literary allusion. Some of their creators join their characters. The following books make the reader draw on whatever allusions a lifetime's reading has provided:

Anderson, Poul. *A Midsummer Tempest.*

Davidson, Avram. *The Phoenix and the Mirror.*
Virgil as a wizard.

de Camp, L. Sprague, and Fletcher Pratt. *The Compleat Enchanter: The Magical Misadventures of Harold Shea.*

Farmer, Philip José. Riverworld series: *The Fabulous Riverboat. To Your Scattered Bodies Go. The Dark Design. The Magic Labyrinth.*
The authors join with the characters.

Myers, John Myers. *Silverlock.*
An ignored and woefully neglected classic. The picaresque hero's adventures are in the worlds of great Western literature. The reader's delightful challenge is to identify stories, characters, and allusions.

Human Comedy

Fantasy written strictly for adults is merely a variation of "mainstream" fiction. Most of the titles previously listed are considered adult fantasy—many are enjoyed equally by children and adults. The following samples are *not* childlike:

Ballard, J. G. *The Unlimited Dream Company.*

Beagle, Peter. *A Fine and Private Place.*

Cabell, James Branch. *Poictesme* series.
This series includes the once banned (incomprehensibly by present standards) *Jurgen*. While loosely grouped as sword-and-sorcery, this series is ironically adult.

Finney, Charles. *The Circus of Dr. Lao*.
Contains one of this writer's favorite passages in modern literature:

> "I am a calm, intelligent girl," Miss Agnes reassured herself. "I am a calm, intelligent girl, and I have not seen Pan on Main Street. Nevertheless, I will go to the circus and make sure."

Hales, E. E. Y. *Chariot of Fire*.

TOPICS

Anthologies

There is often a combining of fantasy and ghost or horror stories in the anthologies. Several of the following anthologies have considerable critical material as well as stories:

Boyer, Robert H., and Kenneth Zahorski, eds. *The Fantastic Imagination: An Anthology of High Fantasy*. Avon, 1977-78. 2v.

Boyer, Robert H., ed. *Dark Imaginings: A Collection of Gothic Fantasy*. Delta Book/Dell, 1978.
The second anthology is in two parts, high and low fantasy. High fantasy exists in an imaginary (secondary world) in which the magical powers of gods, wizards, or enchantresses have power. Low fantasy "is set in the recognizable history and geography of the primary world," lacking magic, but having "inhuman beings that intrude upon the rational order." Both deal with the impossible.

Carter, Terry, ed. *Kingdoms of Sorcery*. Doubleday, 1976.

Carter, Terry, ed. *Realms of Wizardry*. Doubleday, 1976.
Carter edits several annuals: *The Year's Best Fantasy Stories* (6th, 1980); *The Year's Finest Fantasy* (2nd, 1979); *Fantasy Annual* (3rd, 1981).

Carter, Terry, and Martin Harry Greenberg, eds. *A Treasury of Modern Fantasy*. Avon, 1981.

Mobley, Jane, ed. *Phantasmagoria: Tales of Fantasy and the Supernatural*. Anchor, 1977.
Two sections: "The Wondrous Fair: Magical Fantasy"; "The Passing Strange: Supernatural Fiction."

Neugroschel, Joachim, comp. & ed. *Yenne Velt: The Great Works of Jewish Fantasy and Occult*. Stonehill, 1976; Pocket Books, 1978.

Rabkin, Eric S., ed. *Fantastic Worlds: Myths, Tales, and Stories*. Oxford University Press, 1979.
This is a critical analysis of fantasy as well as an anthology, for the essay commentary is extensive. The scope is eclectic, covering fantasy as a literature in both mainstream and genre examples. Divisions are: Myth;

Folktale; Fairy Tale; Fantasy; Horror Fiction; Ghost Stories; Heroic Fantasy; Science Fiction; Modern Fantasy. There is an annotated bibliography.

Schiff, Robert David, ed. *Whispers: An Anthology of Fantasy and Horror.* Doubleday, 1977- .
The second series appeared in 1979. Stories from the magazine *Whispers.*

The World Fantasy Awards. Doubleday, 1977- .
The second volume, 1980.

Bibliography, Biography, Guides

Many of the works listed under science fiction contain material on fantasy. The following works illustrate that fantasy as a genre relates both to children's and adults' interests:

Ashley, Mike. *Who's Who in Horror and Fantasy Fiction.* Elm Tree Books, 1977.
Annotations and critical bio-bibliography for 400 authors. Additional sections: "Chronology," c.2000 B.C.-1977; "An Index to key stories and books"; "Selected weird fiction anthologies," annotated; "Weird and horror fiction magazines," annotated; "Awards," August Derleth Fantasy Award and World Fantasy Award.

Rovin, Jeff. *The Fantasy Almanac.* Dutton, 1979.
Alphabetical definitions of authors, characters, mythological and supernatural beings and beasts, places, and the like in mythology, folklore, fairy tale, literature, comic strip, motion picture, and television. Illustrated.

Tymn, Marshall B., Kenneth J. Zahorski, and Robert H. Boyer. *Fantasy Literature: A Core Collection and Reference Guide.* Bowker, 1979.
The core collection, more than 240 works, is an alphabetical and critically annotated selection of adult fantasy, although much of the material is suitable for all ages. There is an extensive introductory essay. The listings of "Fantasy Scholarship," periodicals, societies, and organizations are briefly annotated.

Waggoner, Diana. *The Hills of Fantasy: A Guide to Fantasy.* Atheneum, 1978.
An eclectic selection of 996 titles, critically annotated, of interest to adults. There is an extensive and critical introductory essay. An appendix, "Subgenres of Fantasy," lists titles (numbered as in the annotated list) by type: magic, mythic fantasy, faerie, ghost fantasy, horror fantasy, sentimental fantasy, magic time travel, travels from one universe to another, science fantasy, fairy-story fantasy, toy tales, animal fantasy, worlds of enchantment, new histories, new universes.

Gazetteers and Atlases

These two delightful books will enchant all fans of fantasy and many of science fiction, for they describe and map the lands that readers' imaginations have made real.

Manguel, Alberto, and Gianni Guadalupi. *The Dictionary of Imaginary Places*. Illustrated by Graham Greenfield. Maps and Charts by James Cook. Macmillan, 1980.

Clearly this is a labor of love. Imaginary places (countries, castles, islands, whatever) from all types of literature and films are described in straight-faced gazetteer style, complete with information on the inhabitants, flora and fauna, and social customs. The source work is cited. There are 150 maps and 100 illustrations. The scope is international and, of course, encompasses much more than genre fiction. There is an index of authors and titles. This is not simply a reference book but may be read with delight for its own sake: "Should a traveller lose his way in Wonderland, information can be obtained from a knowledgeable caterpillar smoking a hookah.... Several places in Wonderland are worth a visit: the White Rabbit's dainty cottage; the Duchess' house with its spicy though somewhat neglected kitchen; and the Mad Hatter's outdoor tearoom, open all hours." This writer notes, with regret, the absence of Commonwealth (John Myers Myers, *Silverlock*) and Abalone, Arizona (Charles G. Finney, *The Circus of Dr. Lao*). The authors invite additional citations for a supplement or revised edition.

Post, J. B., comp. *An Atlas of Fantasy*. Revised edition. Ballantine, 1979.

This is much improved in map reproduction from the first edition (Mirage Press, 1973), with some changes. The following is a selection from the contents; many are for works cited in this guide. The listing is in order of sequence in the atlas.

Baum, L. Frank. "Oz and Environs."

Burroughs, Edgar Rice. "The Worlds of ...:" Barsoom [Mars]; Pal-Ul-Don (Tarzan series); Land of the Ant Men (Tarzan series); Onthar and Thenar (Tarzan series); The Lost Empire (Tarzan series); Amtor (Venus series); Pellucidar (Hollow Earth-Pellucidar series); The Moon (*The Moon Maid*); Poloda and Umos (*Beyond the Furthest Star*); Caspak and Caprona (*The Land That Time Forgot*); Wild Island.

Cabell, James Branch. "Poictesme."

Howard, Robert E. "Hyperborian Age." (Conan series).

Tolkien, J. R. R. "The Worlds of ...:" Middle Earth (*Lord of the Rings*); Gondor and Modor (*Lord of the Rings*); Thror's Map (*The Hobbit*); Wilderland (*The Hobbit*); Beleriand (*The Silmarillion*).

Eddison, E. R. "The Three Kingdoms and Ouroboros Country": Ouroboros Country (*The Worm Ouroboros*); The Three Kingdoms (*Mistress of Mistresses*); The Campaign in North Rerek and the Meszrian Border (*Mistress of Mistresses*).

Sleigh, Bernard. "Fairyland." (*Ancient Mappe of Fairyland*).

Lewis, C. S. "Narnia."

Myers, John Myers. "Commonwealth." (*Silverlock*).

Hamilton, Edmond. "The Worlds of Captain Future," (*Captain Future*, a pulp magazine, 13 maps).

Brackett, Leigh. "Leigh Brackett's Mars."

Smith, Clark Ashton. "Hyperborea." (*Hyperborea*); Zothique (*Hyperborea*).

Norton, Andre. "The Witch World."

LeGuin, Ursula. "Earthsea." (*A Wizard of Earthsea*).

Zelazny, Roger. "Dilfar and Environs." (*Warlocks and Warriors*).

Moorcock, Michael. "The Young Kingdoms." (Elric series).

Vance, Jack. *"The Dying Earth."*

Leiber, Fritz. "Lankhmar in the Land of Nehwon." (Fafhrd and the Grey Mouser series).

Alexander, Lloyd. "Prydain." [three maps].

Carter, Lin. "Lemuria."

Bradbury, Ray. "Mars." ("The Million Year Picnic.")

Campbell, J. Ramsey. "The Severn Valley at Brichester." (*The Inhabitant of the Lake*).

Herbert, Frank. *"Dune."*

Kuttner, Henry. "Atlantis." (Elek series).

Jakes, John. "Tyros." (Brak series).

Dain, Alex. "Kanthos, Sulmannon, and Anzor." (*Banc of Kanthos*).

Kurtz, Katherine. "Gwynadd and Its Neighbors." (Dernyi series).

McCaffrey, Anne. "Pern." (The Dragonriders of Pern series).

Fraser, George MacDonald. "The Duchy of Strackanz." (*Royal Flash*).

Lovecraft, H. P. "The Worlds of H. P. Lovecraft:" Dreamworld; Arkham.

Adams, Richard. "The Beklan Empire." (*Shardik*)

Brackett, Leigh. "The Worlds of Eric John Stark." (*The Ginger Star. The Hounds of Skaith. The Reavers of Skaith*).

Brooks, Terry. "The Four Lands." (*The Sword of Shannara*).

Donaldson, Stephen R. "The Land." (*The Chronicles of Thomas Covenant the Believer*).

History and Criticism

In addition to the following works, material on fantasy will be found among some of the works on science fiction:

Carter, Lin. *Imaginary Worlds: The Art of Fantasy.* Ballantine, 1973.
On sword-and-sorcery.

de Camp, L. Sprague. *Literary Swordsmen and Sorcerers: The Makers of Heroic Fantasy.* Arkham House, 1976.
The key authors discussed are William Morris, Lord Dunsany, H. P. Lovecraft, E. R. Eddison, Robert E. Howard, Fletcher Pratt, Clark Ashton Smith, J. R. R. Tolkien, and T. H. White.

Hillegas, Mark R., ed. *Shadows of Imagination: The Fantasies of C. S. Lewis, J. R. R. Tolkien, and Charles Williams.* Southern Illinois University Press, 1969.
Twelve essays.

Irwin, W. R. *The Game of the Impossible: A Rhetoric of Fantasy.* University of Illinois Press, 1976.

LeGuin, Ursula K. *The Language of the Night: Essays on Fantasy and Science Fiction.* Putnam, 1979.

Manlove, C. N. *Modern Fantasy: Five Studies.* Cambridge University Press, 1975.
The authors discussed are Charles Kingsley, George MacDonald, C. S. Lewis, J. R. R. Tolkien, and Mervyn Peake.

Rabkin, Eric S. *The Fantastic in Literature.* Princeton University Press, 1976.

Rottensteiner, Franz. *The Fantasy Book: An Illustrated History from Dracula to Tolkien.* Collier Books, 1978.
There are 202 illustrations, 40 in color, from books of fantasy, the pulps, and motion pictures. A good part relates to the following chapter on ghosts and horror. There is a section on "The International Contribution." The bibliography is excellent, with many foreign citations.

Background

There is a wealth of literature on the denizens of fantasyland. The following listing is simply to suggest the variety available:

Arrowsmith, Nancy, with George Moorse. *A Field Guide to the Little People.* Farrar, 1971.

Beer, Rudiger Robert. *Unicorn: Myth and Reality.* Mason/Charter, 1977.

Briggs, Katherine. *An Encyclopedia of Fairies: Hobgoblins, Brownies, Bogies, and Other Supernatural Creatures.* Pantheon, 1976.

Briggs, Katherine. *The Faeries in Tradition and Literature.* London: Routledge, 1967.

Dickinson, Peter. *The Flight of Dragons.* Harper, 1979.

Huygen, Wil. *Gnomes.* Illustrated by Rien Poortvliet. Abrams, 1977.

Associations and Conventions

The following listings are specifically for fantasy, but many of the science fiction associations and conventions also involve fantasy:

American Tolkien Society

British Fantasy Society
Founded 1971. Publication: *Dark Horizons,* 1971- .

The Fantasy Association
  Founded 1973. Publication: *Fantasies.*

The International Wizard of Oz Club
  Founded 1957.

Fantasy Faire Science Fiction Convention
  Eleventh, 1981, Los Angeles.

World Fantasy Convention
  First, 1975.

Other specialized groups and fanzines are listed in Tymn's *Fantasy Literature* and in *The International Science Fiction Yearbook 1979.*

Awards

In addition to the fantasy awards, special recognition for fantasy is often found among the science fiction awards.

August Derleth Fantasy Award
  The British Fantasy Society, 1972- .

Grand Master of Fantasy Award: "Gandalf"
  World Science Fiction Convention, 1974- . Also called the Tolkien Award; named for Tolkien character.

World Fantasy Award: "Howard"
  World Fantasy Convention, 1975- . Award named for Howard Phillips Lovecraft and Robert E. Howard.

Other awards are cited in *The International Science Fiction Yearbook 1979.*

Publishers

See listing under Science Fiction.

7 Horror

When my companion in the railway carriage abruptly asked me whether I believed in ghosts, I replied "Well--er--no."

"Neither do I," he giggled, and vanished.

— Anonymous

... Ghost stories celebrate the inexplicable.

— J. I. M. Stewart

T. S. Eliot once insisted, surely quite wrongly, that it was only possible to appreciate ghost stories if you believed in ghosts. In fact, people who enjoy fantasies of horror do so whether or not, with their conscious, rational selves, they are believers in werewolves, spooks or vampires.

— A. N. Wilson

All argument is against it; but all belief is for it.

— Dr. Johnson on ghosts

The house creaks; the cat stares fixedly at something about three feet tall which you cannot quite see, there behind the armchair. Is there, perhaps, a webfooted person in the basement.

— Ursula LeGuin (on Lovecraft)

... We do not judge whether a horror film or a ghost story is "good" by the same standards by which we judge a real work of literature. All that matters here is whether we have been frightened.

— A. N. Wilson

Terror of the unknown haunts us all. Some readers avoid the horror genre; others delight in being frightened. The emotional and spiritual response to reading horror stories—true fright in the reader—must be evoked for the tale to be successful. This reaction may be labeled an affective fallacy in academic jargon but is, nevertheless, a truly visceral reaction. The appeal of horror is not to the intellect, however staunchly the reader thinks he can distinguish between reality and fantasy.

The matter of horror stories derives from the supernatural and the occult: ghosts, ghouls, apparitions, poltergeists, witches and warlocks; vampires and werewolves; monsters and mummies; demonology and black magic; voodoo and witch doctors; nightmares and hallucinations; reincarnation and mind or soul stealing; extrasensory perception as in precognition, telepathy, telekinesis. In a more embracing sense, we fear the inimical, dark forces of nature that are beyond both our comprehension and control. (There *is* something arising from that primordial slime when the moon is full!)

The label weird fantasy is common. The magazine *Weird Tales*, 1923-1954, supplied stories for many anthologies. (There are three anthologies of this magazine's stories: two edited by Robert Weinberg, *Weird Tales 50*, 1974, and *The Weird Tale Story*, 1977; *Weird Tales*, edited by Peter Haining, 1976). Horror tales have always appeared and still appear in the science fiction and fantasy magazines, and anthologies and authors often write all three types of genres. The Bug-Eyed Monster popular in science fiction loses some quality of horror by not being of this world.

Horror fiction has a literary source in the Gothic novel of the eighteenth and nineteenth centuries that reveled in the supernatural while adding a gloss of romance. The twentieth-century Gothic novel is determinedly romantic while using scary occult and supernatural plot devices. The mystery-suspense and detective subgenres also use elements of horror as does the disaster subgenre.

The mingling of genres through the use of horror's more obvious themes leads to inconsistent labeling of novels by publishers and reviewers and to confusion on the part of the reader as to which genre the book belongs. Faced with a novel called "medical-horror," the reader of doctor-nurse romances is unlikely to be tempted, but other instances are not as obvious. There is also the labeling of novels of psychological suspense, admittedly filled with terror, as horror stories, though they lack elements of the occult or supernatural.

As in all the genres, there is imitation, especially in original paperbacks, of a successful novel: the endless variations of *Rosemary's Baby*, vampires, haunted houses, demonic possession, evil children, monstrous animals, and so on. The following listings are very selective, illustrating a variety of horror themes rather than myriad authors. Some of the titles cited are collections of short stories, many authors writing almost entirely in this form. As in fantasy, a number of the authors are not those usually categorized as genre authors.

THEMES AND TYPES

Ghost Stories

The ghost story is quite often in the short story form, and several of the following listings are for collected stories by an author:

Aickman, Robert. *Cold Hand in Mine. Intrusions. Painted Devils. Powers of Darkness. Sub Rosa.*

Ashe, Rosalind. *Moths.*

Bierce, Ambrose

Blackwood, Algernon. *Tales of the Mysterious and the Macabre. Tales of the Uncanny and Supernatural.*

Collins, Wilkie. *Tales of Terror and the Supernatural.*

Dickens, Charles

Fraser, Anthea. *Whistler's Lane.*

James, Henry. *The Turn of the Screw.*

James, M. R. *Ghost Stories of an Antiquary.*

Le Fanu, J. S. *Best Ghost Stories of....*

Lofts, Norah. *Gad's Hall.*

Straub, Peter. *Ghost Story.*
"... Nightmares, apparitions, werewolves, blood-letting viragos and hosts of the undead."

Wakefield, H. Russell. *The Best Ghost Stories of....*
The author required a ghost story should "bring upon you the odd, insinuating little sensation that a number of small creatures are simultaneously camping on your scalp and sprinkling ice-water down your back-bone."

Demonic Possession and Exorcism

This listing is very selective, as there have been seemingly countless recent books on these themes, particularly in original paperback editions.

Blatty, William. *The Exorcist.*

Coyne, John. *The Piercing. The Searing.*

Household, Geoffrey. *The Sending.*

Levin, Ira. *Rosemary's Baby.*

Ross, Clarissa. *Satan Whispers.*

Thompson, Gene. *Lupe.*

Satanism, Demonology, and Black Magic

There is considerable historical and theological publication on these topics, too extensive and specialized for listing here. These examples illustrate the variety of current fictional approaches to the topics:

Bester, Alfred. *Golem 100.*

Collier, John. *Of Demons and Darkness.*

King, Stephen. *The Stand.*

Stewart, Fred Mustard. *The Mephisto Waltz.*

Wheatley, Dennis. *The Devil Rides Out. The Satanist. Strange Conflict. To the Devil a Daughter.*

Witches and Warlocks

Witches often appear in the historical romance, but as secondary characters. In these examples the witch and the warlock are persons of reality in the present as well as the past and may be practitioners of either white or black witchcraft:

Buchan, John. *Witch Wood.*

Copper, Basil. *Not after Nightfall.*

Hamilton, Jessica. *Elizabeth.*

Harris, Marilyn. *The Conjurers.*

Levin, Ira. *Rosemary's Baby.*

Warner, Sylvia Townsend. *Lolly Willowes.*
  A genteel classic. Witchcraft without horror; a witch's coven in an English village in this century.

Reincarnation and Possession

These themes sometimes are used in thrillers of psychological suspense, and reincarnation sometimes in the historical romance. In neither of these subgenres is the purpose the unmitigated horror found in the following examples:

DeFelitta, Frank. *Audrey Rose.*

Ehrlich, Max. *The Reincarnation of Peter Proud.*

Vampires

Although there has been a recent trend toward making the vampire legend humorous, the following examples are largely horrifying:

Daniels, Lee. *The Black Castle. The Silver Skull.*

Lee, Tanith. *Sabella; Or, The Blood Stone.*

Linssen, John. *Tabitha fffoulkes: A Love Story about a Reformed Vampire and His Favorite Lady.*

Raven, Simon. *Doctors Wear Scarlet.*

Rice, Anne. *Interview with a Vampire.*

Saberhagen, Fred. *The Dracula Tapes.*

Stoker, Bram. *Dracula.*
  First published in 1897, the novel, like its hero, has never died and has produced blood-thirsty progeny in novel, stage play, and motion picture. The Count Dracula Society, founded in 1962, publishes *The Count Dracula Quarterly*, and presents annual awards for films, literature, and television, the Mrs. Ann Radcliffe Awards. *The Illustrated Dracula* (Drake, 1975) contains stills from the 1931 Bela Lugosi film. *The Dracula Book*, by Donald F. Glut (Scarecrow, 1975) is illustrated from films and comic strips.

Strieber, Whitley. *The Hunger.*

Tremayne, Peter. *Bloodright*: A Memoir of Mircea, Son of Vlad Tepes, Prince of Wallachia, Also Known as Dracula ... Born on This Earth in the Year of Christ 1431, Who Died in 1476 but Remained Undead.... *The Revenge of Dracula.*

Yarbro, Chelsea Quinn. *Hotel Transylvania. The Palace. Blood Games.*

Werewolves

Werewolves abound in folklore, but these examples show the modern use of the theme:

Strieber, Whitley. *The Wolfen.*

Tessier, Thomas. *The Nightwalker.*

Monsters

Monstrous creations by a freakish nature—taking unnatural form from any of the elements of water, earth, air, or plant or animal—abound in horror fiction. Here are two examples of man-made monsters or automata whose history goes back to the legendary golem created by Jewish cabalistic rites:

Shelley, Mary. *Frankenstein; Or, The Modern Prometheus.*
First published in 1818. May be considered as part of science fiction, e.g., androids, mad scientist. Many imitations and film versions.

Stevenson, Robert Louis. *The Strange Case of Dr. Jekyll and Mr. Hyde.*
First published in 1886. The drug and psychological aspects are influential for science fiction also.

Paranormal Powers

The use of such powers is to be found in science fiction and fantasy but usually not for the horrifying purposes found in the following examples:

King, Stephen. *The Shining. The Dead Zone.*

Stewart, Ramona. *The Nightmare Candidate. Sixth Sense.*

The Occult and Supernatural

Here are stories of the unseen and malevolent, the macabre and ghostly: poltergeists; girls transformed by night into bats, cats, monkeys, snakes; souls being stolen or sold to the Devil; minds being read or invaded. The possibilities for inexplicable acts are limited only by the author's dark imagination. Many of the horror stories currently being published center on psychological horror and the terrors often do have an explicable cause, however deranged the mind from which the horror emanates. For the much-imitated Lovecraft school of horror, see the notes on Lovecraft below. The older writers on these themes wrote often in the short-story form, and many of the listings below are collections of their stories. Recently there have been many full-length novels by authors who also write in the short story form.

Aiken, Joan. *The Windcreep Weepers. The Green Flash.*

Andrews, V. C. *Flowers in the Attic. Petals in the Wind.*

Barham, Richard Harris. *The Ingoldsby Legends.*
First published 1857.

Bloch, Robert. *Cold Chills. Out of the Mouths of Graves. Psycho.*

Bowen, Elizabeth. *The Cat Jumps and Other Stories.*

Bradbury, Ray. *The October Country.*

Campbell, Ramsey

Collier, John

Copper, Basil. *And Afterward, the Dark. Here Be Daemons: Tales of Horror and the Uneasy. Voices of Doom: Tales of Terror and the Uncanny. Necropolis.*

Dahl, Roald

Derleth, August

Doyle, Sir Arthur Conan. *The Best Supernatural Tales of....*

Du Maurier, Daphne. *Echoes from the Macabre: Selected Stories.*

Dunsany, Lord

Hallahan, William H. *Keeper of the Children.*

Harvey, W. F.

Herbert, James. *The Dark. The Spear.*

Hinckemeyer, Michael T. *The Harbinger.*
"Tales that go straight through you like rats' fangs."

Kipling, Rudyard. *Phantoms and Fantasies.*

Kuttner, Henry

Leiber, Fritz. *Our Lady of Darkness. Conjure Wife.*

Lovecraft, H. P. *At the Mountains of Madness. The Dulwich Horror. The Lurking Fear. The Shuttered Room. The Tomb.*
"All my tales are based on the fundamental premise that common human laws and emotions have no validity or significance in the cosmos-at-large." Lovecraft created an entire mythology, the Cthulhu Mythos, and defined it as "the fundamental lore or legend that this world was inhabited at one time by another race who, in practicing black magic, lost their foothold and were expelled, yet live on outside, ever ready to take possession of this earth again." The publisher Arkham House is named for Lovecraft's fantasy land (for map see Post's *An Atlas of Fantasy*).

Schreffler, Philip A. *The H. P. Lovecraft Companion.* Greenwood, 1977.
Summaries of stories and an "Encyclopedia of Characters and Monsters" of the Cthulhu Mythos.

Berglund, Edward P., ed. *The Disciples of Cthulhu.* DAW, 1976.
An anthology of stories by followers of Lovecraft. The editor says the Cthulhu Mythos, "a malign pantheon, including the octopoid Cthulhu, lurk practically everywhere, and that any mortal mixing with them is going to end up dead, mad or worse."

Machen, Arthur

Merritt, Abraham

Poe, Edgar Allan

Raucher, Herman. *Maynard's House.*

Saki

Sherman, Nick. *The Surrogate.*

Straub, Peter. *Julia. If You Could See Me Now.*

Walter, Elizabeth. *Dead Woman and Other Haunting Experiences. In the Mist and Other Uncanny Encounters. The Sin-Eater and Other Scientific Impossibilities.*

Wells, H. G.

TOPICS

Anthologies

The large number of horror anthologies indicates both the popularity of such collections and the significant incidence of the short story in the genre. There are several inveterate anthologists; the listings here are but a selection from their volumes. Other horror stories will be found in anthologies listed for science fiction and fantasy, and authors from those fields appear in the anthologies below. The anthologies have not been grouped by theme as only a few are completely single-minded in scope.

Alfred Hitchcock's Supernatural Tales of Terror and Suspense. Random, 1974.

Beck, Robert E., ed. *Literature of the Supernatural.* Lothrop, 1974.
The illustrations from museum collections add imaginatively to the stories.

Campbell, Ramsey, ed. *New Tales of the Cthulhu Mythos.* Arkham, 1980.
In the manner of Lovecraft: see his entry for definition of the Cthulhu Mythos.

Campbell, Ramsey, ed. *Superhorror.* St. Martin's, 1977.

Carr, Terry, ed. *The Ides of Tomorrow: Original Science Fiction Tales of Horror.* Little, Brown, 1976.

Curran, Roger, ed. *The Weird Gathering and Other Tales.* Fawcett Crest, 1979.
Mostly about women.

Daniels, Lee, ed. *Dying of Fright: Masterpieces of the Macabre.* Illustrated by Lee Brown Coye. Scribner's, 1976.
An exemplary anthology. Provides prefatory essay for each author and eerie illustrations. Authors: Washington Irving; Edgar Allan Poe; Nathaniel Hawthorne; J. Sheridan Le Fanu; F. Marion Crawford; M. R. James; Ambrose Bierce; Algernon Blackwood; William Hope Hodgson; W. F. Harvey; Lord Dunsany; H. P. Lovecraft; Frank Belknap Long; Henry Kuttner; John Collier; Anthony Boucher; Robert Bloch; Ray Bradbury; Carter Dickson; Fritz Leiber; Richard Matheson; Joseph Payne Brennan.

Disch, Thomas M., and Charles Naylor, eds. *Strangers: A Collection of Curious Tales*. Scribner's, 1977.

Elwood, Roger, ed. *The Berserkers*. Trident, 1974.

Elwood, Roger, ed. *Monster Tales: Vampires, Werewolves and Things*. Rand, 1974.

Fellowell, Duncan, ed. *Drug Tales*. St. Martin's, 1980.
  Alcohol, cigarettes, pills, elixirs.

Grant, Charles L., ed. *Nightmares*. Playboy Press, 1979.

Grant, Charles L., ed. *Shadows I-III*. Doubleday, 1978-1980. 3v.

Green, Roger Lancelyn, ed. *Thirteen Uncanny Tales*. With color frontispiece and line drawings in the text by Ray Ogden. London: Dent, 1970.

Haining, Peter, ed. *Deadly Nightshade*. Taplinger, 1978.

Haining, Peter, ed. *Everyman's Book of Classic Horror Stories*. London: Dent, 1976.

Haining, Peter, ed. *The Fantastic Pulps*. St. Martin's, 1975.

Haining, Peter, ed. *The Third Book of Unknown Tales of Horror*. London: Sidgwick, 1980.

Haining, Peter, ed. *The Witchcraft Reader*. Doubleday, 1970.

Lamb, Hugh, ed. *Cold Fear: New Tales of Terror*. Taplinger, 1978.

Lamb, Hugh, ed. *Return from the Grave*. Taplinger, 1977.

Lamb, Hugh, ed. *Terror by Gaslight*. Taplinger, 1976.

Lamb, Hugh, ed. *The Thrill of Horror*. Taplinger, 1975.

Lamb, Hugh, ed. *Victorian Nightmares*. Taplinger, 1977.

Lamb, Hugh, ed. *A Wave of Fear: A Classic Horror Anthology*. Taplinger, 1974.

McCauley, Kirby, ed. *Dark Forces: New Stories of Suspense and Supernatural Horror*. Viking, 1980.

McCauley, Kirby, ed. *Frights: New Stories of Suspense and Supernatural Terror*. St. Martin's, 1976.

Manley, Seon, and Gogo Lewis, eds. *Ladies of Fantasy: Two Centuries of Sinister Stories by the Gentle Sex*. Lothrop, 1975.

Manley, Seon, and Gogo Lewis, eds. *Sisters of Sorcery: Two Centuries of Witchcraft Stories by the Gentle Sex*. Lothrop, 1976.

Parry, Michel, ed. *Beware of the Cat: Stories of Feline Fantasy and Horror*. Taplinger, 1973.

Parry, Michel, ed. *Great Black Magic Stories*. Taplinger, 1977.

Parry, Michel, ed. *The Hounds of Hell: Stories of Canine Horror and Fantasy*. Taplinger, 1974.

Parry, Michel, ed. *The Roots of Evil: Weird Stories of Supernatural Plants*. Taplinger, 1976.

Parry, Michel, ed. *The Supernatural Solution: Chilling Tales of Spooks and Sleuths.* Taplinger, 1976.

The Playboy Book of Horror and the Supernatural. Playboy Press, 1967.

Pronzini, Bill, ed. *Mummy!: A Chrestomathy of Cryptology.* Arbor House, 1980.

Pronzini, Bill, ed. *Voodoo!: A Chrestomathy of Necromancy.* Arbor House, 1980.

Pronzini, Bill, ed. *Werewolf!* Arbor House, 1979.

Protter, Eric, ed. *A Harvest of Horrors: Classic Tales of the Macabre.* Vanguard, 1980.

Protter, Eric, ed. *Monster Festival.* Illustrated by Edward Gorey. Vanguard, 1965.

Sayers, Dorothy L., ed. *Great Short Stories of Detection, Mystery and Horror.* Series One to Three. London: Gollancz, 1929-34.

Shepard, Leslie, ed. *The Dracula Book of Great Vampire Stories.* Citadel, 1974.

The Times Anthology of Ghost Stories. London: Cape, 1975.

Wolf, Leonard, ed. *Wolf's Complete Book of Terror.* Potter, 1979.

The Year's Best Horror Stories. DAW, Series 8, 1980.

Bibliography

There is a considerable literature and bibliography on the documentation of ghostly and psychic phenomena, but the bibliography on fiction is very dispersed. The work by Tymn, cited here, is a welcome response to a crying need.

Barzun, Jacques, and Wendell Hertig Taylor. "Ghost Stories, Studies and Reports of the Supernatural, Psychical Research, and E.S.P." In *A Catalogue of Crime.* Harper, 1971. pages 699-722.

Tymn, Marshall B. *Horror Literature: A Core Collection and Reference Guide.* Bowker, 1981.
> An engrossing guide. Part I, Fiction, contains five essays, each with extensive annotated bibliography: "The Gothic Romance: 1762-1820," by Frederick S. Frank; "The Residual Gothic Impulse: 1824-1873," by Benjamin Franklin Fisher IV; "Psychological, Antiquarian, and Cosmic Horror: 1872-1919," by Jack Sullivan; "The Modern Masters: 1920-1980," by Gary William Crawford; "The Horror Pulps: 1933-1940," by Robert Weinberg. Part II: "Supernatural Verse in English," by Steve Eng. Part III, Reference Sources, is by Mike Ashley, with chapters on "Biography, Autobiography, and Bibliography"; "Criticism, Indexes, and General Reference"; "Periodicals"; "Societies and Organizations"; "Awards"; "Research Collections." There is a "Core Collection Checklist," and "Directory of Publishers."

History and Criticism

The definitive history and criticism of the horror genre are yet to be written. Until they are, the following books may be used for background on various aspects of the genre:

Briggs, Julia. *Night Visitors: The Rise and Fall of the English Ghost Story*. London: Faber, 1977.

Daniels, Lee. *Living in Fear: A History of Horror in the Mass Media*. Scribner's, 1975.

Haining, Peter. *Terror: A History of Horror Illustrations from the Pulp Magazines*. London: Souvenir Press, 1976.

Jones, Robert Kenneth. *The Shudder Pulps: A History of the Weird Menace Magazines of the 1930's*. Fox Collector's Editions, 1975; NAL, 1978.

Lovecraft, Howard Phillips. *Supernatural Horror in Literature*. With a new introduction by E. F. Bleiler. Dover, 1973.
Essential reading as definition, history, and criticism. "The one test of the truly weird is simply this — whether or not there be excited in the reader a profound sense of dread, and of contact with unknown spheres and powers; a subtle attitude of awed listening, as if for the beating of black wings or the scratching of outside shapes and entities on the known universe's utmost rim."

Punter, David. *The Literature of Terror: A History of Gothic Fictions from 1765 to the Present Day*. London: Longman, 1980.

Sullivan, Jack. *Elegant Nightmares: The English Ghost Story from Le Fanu to Blackwood*. Ohio University Press, 1978.

Film

While horror films have been a staple product of the film industry since its beginnings, they have proved to be one of the most prevalent genres in films of recent years as the following histories testify:

Clarens, Carlos. *An Illustrated History of the Horror Film*. Putnam, 1967.

Everson, William K. *Classics of the Horror Film*. LSP Books, 1975.

Pirie, David. *A Heritage of Horror: The English Gothic Cinema, 1946-1972*. Avon, 1974.

Prewer, S. S. *Caligari's Children: The Film as a Tale of Terror*. Oxford University Press, 1980.

Publishers

The publishers listed for science fiction usually publish horror fiction. Note should be made of Arkham House, founded in 1939 to preserve the writings of

H. P. Lovecraft and now publishing horror, fantasy and science fiction. Dover Books, the reprinter of Lovecraft's *Supernatural Horror in Literature*, has a strong line of trade quality paperback reprints of classics, listed in its catalogue as the "Dover Library of Ghost Stories."

Index:
Genre Authors

This index facilitates locating authors within the several categories and subgenres in each large genre chapter. Some genre authors write in several genres or subgenres and are therefore linked only by the index. Authors are indexed as listed in the text, so some may appear more than once under pseudonyms.

Index:
Secondary Materials

This is an author and title index to books, journals, and critical citations in the text in all chapters and to those listed under "Topics" in each genre chapter. Anthologies are listed under both editor and title.